NURTURE in TIME
and ETERNITY

NURTURE in TIME and ETERNITY

Robert Cummings Neville

CASCADE *Books* • Eugene, Oregon

NURTURE IN TIME AND ETERNITY

Copyright © 2016 Robert Cummings Neville. All rights reserved. Except for brief quotations in critical publications or reviews, no part of this book may be reproduced in any manner without prior written permission from the publisher. Write: Permissions, Wipf and Stock Publishers, 199 W. 8th Ave., Suite 3, Eugene, OR 97401.

Cascade Books
An Imprint of Wipf and Stock Publishers
199 W. 8th Ave., Suite 3
Eugene, OR 97401

www.wipfandstock.com

PAPERBACK ISBN 13: 978-1-4982-8621-3
HARDCOVER ISBN 13: 978-1-4982-8623-7
EBOOK ISBN: 978-1-4982-8622-0

Cataloguing-in-Publication data:

Names: Neville, Robert C.

Title: Nurture in time and eternity / Robert Cummings Neville.

Description: Eugene, OR: Cascade Books, 2016.

Identifiers: ISBN 978-1-4982-8621-3 (paperback) | ISBN 978-1-4982-8623-7 (hardcover) | ISBN 978-1-4982-8622-0 (ebook)

Subjects: LCSH: Sermons—American—21st century. | Methodist Church—Sermons. | Boston University—Marsh Chapel.

Classification: BV4254.2 N49 2016 (print) | BV4254.2 (ebook)

Manufactured in the U.S.A.   06/28/16

All Scripture quotations unless noted otherwise are taken from the New Revised Standard Version of the Bible, copyright, 1989, Division of Christian Education of the National Council of the Churches of Christ in the United States of America. Used by permission. All rights reserved.

For Robert Allen Hill
Friend, Preacher, Pastor

Contents

Preface | ix

1. The Deepest Contradiction | 1
   Romans 7:11–25a; Matthew 11:11–19, 21–30

2. Heaven in Earth | 7
   Genesis 29:11–28; Romans 8:21–39; Matthew 13:31–33, 41–52

3. Wrestle till the Break of Day | 13
   Genesis 32:21–31; Romans 9:1–5; Matthew 14:11–21

4. Who Was Jesus? | 20
   Genesis 45:1–5; Romans 11:1–2a, 21–32; Matthew 15:(11–20) 21–28

5. A Living Sacrifice | 27
   Exodus 1:1—2:10; Romans 12:1–8; Matthew 16:11–20

6. Investment | 34
   Exodus 12:1–14; Romans 13:1–14; Matthew 18:11–20

7. Tolerance and Forgiveness | 39
   Exodus 14:11–31; Romans 14:1–12; Matthew 18:21–35

8. The Arbitrariness of Grace | 45
   Exodus 16:1–15; Philippians 1:21–30; Matthew 20:1–16

9. Face-to-Face with God | 49
   Exodus 33:11–23; 1 Thessalonians 1:1–10; Matthew 22:11–22; Luke 1:41–55

10. The Great Commandment | 55
    Deuteronomy 34:1–12; 1 Thessalonians 2:1–8; Matthew 22:31–46

11. Hypocrisy and Humility | 60
    Joshua 3:1–17; 1 Thessalonians 2:1–13; Matthew 23:1–12

12. Wakefulness and Different Talents | 65
    Judges 4:1–7; 1 Thessalonians 5:1–11; Matthew 25:11–30

13 The Day of the Lord | 70
    Isaiah 40:1–11; 2 Peter 3:1–15a; Mark 1:1–8

14 God with Us | 76
    2 Samuel 7:1–11, 16; Romans 16:21–27; Luke 1:21–38, 41–55

15 The Word Became Flesh | 81
    Isaiah 52:1–10; Hebrews 1:1–4 (1–12); John 1:1–14

16 A Time for Everything | 87
    Ecclesiastes 3:1–13; Revelation 21:1–6a; Matthew 25:31–46

17 God Calls | 93
    1 Samuel 3:1–10; First Corinthians 6:11–20; John 1:41–51

18 Call to Ministry | 99
    Jonah 3:1–5, 10; 1 Corinthians 7:21–31; Mark 1:11–20

19 Authority Now and in the Old Times | 105
    Deuteronomy 18:11–20; 1 Corinthians 8:1–13; Mark 1:21–28

20 Healing, Praying, Preaching | 111
    Isaiah 40:21–31; 1 Corinthians 9:11–23; Mark 1:21–39

21 Witness | 116
    2 Kings 5:1–14; 1 Corinthians 9:21–27; Mark 1:1–45

22 Transformation to See God | 122
    2 Kings 2:1–12; 2 Corinthians 4:1–6; Mark 9:1–9

23 Hypocrisy and Piety | 128
    Joel 2:1–2, 11–17; 2 Corinthians 5:20b—6:10; Matthew 6:1–6, 11–21

24 Baptism | 131
    Genesis 9:1–17; 1 Peter 3:11–22; Mark 1:1–15

25 Money | 136
    Exodus 20:1–17; 1 Corinthians 1:11–25; John 2:11–22

26 Sickness | 141
    Numbers 21:1–9; Ephesians 2:1–16; John 3:11–21

27 Religions | 147
    Jeremiah 31:31–34; Hebrews 5:1–10; John 12:21–23

28 Politics | 151
    Isaiah 50:1–9a; Philippians 2:1–11; Mark 11:1–11

29 Into Your Hands I Commit My Spirit | 156

30 Fear | 158
    Mark 16:1–8

31 Do Not Hold Me | 163
   Acts 10:31–43; 1 Corinthians 15:1–11; John 20:1–18

32 Touch and Light | 168
   Acts 4:31–35; 1 John 1:1–2:2; John 20:11–31

33 Beginnings and Endings,
   Wisdom and Choice | 174
   Deuteronomy 30:19; Ecclesiastes 7:1–14; James 3:13

34 Homily for Simon Parker's Funeral | 177
   Psalm 110:1; First Corinthians 15:21–58

35 The New Commandment: Love One Another | 182
   Acts 10:41–48; First John 5:1–6; John 15:1–17

36 Jesus Leaving | 188
   Acts 1:1–11: Ephesians 1:11–23; Luke 24:41–53

37 Spirit Coming | 194
   Acts 2:1–21; Romans 8:21–27; John 15:21–27; 16:4b–15

38 To Be Born Again | 199
   Isaiah 6:1–8; Romans 8:11–17; John 3:1–17

39 To Grow | 205
   1 Samuel 15:31—16:13; 2 Corinthians 5:1–10 (11–13), 11–17; Mark 4:21–34

40 To Face Life | 211
   1 Samuel 17:31–49; 2 Corinthians 6:1–13; Mark 4:31–41

Preface

Homiletics in America for the last two generations can fairly be said to have been dominated by George Buttrick and David Buttrick, father and son. George was the preacher at Harvard, and his sermons, many of which I heard when he visited Yale where I was a student during his time, reflected a Christian mind relating to the deepest intellectual and existential problems of his day. David is recently retired from Vanderbilt where he taught homiletics for many years and authored the most distinguished textbook of his generation. The point of that book was to teach the techniques of communicating through the sermon form. Communication and performance were the hallmarks of preaching in his generation, with deep concerns for connecting with different ages and social classes of hearers, including the unchurched who had few if any Christian symbolic references. Sensitivity to different styles of preaching, too, became an important preoccupation as the distinctive qualities of African American homiletics entered the larger mainstream, through the influence of preachers such as Martin Luther King Jr. and Jesse Jackson. What dropped out of the central consciousness of the communication/performance/style generation of American homiletics, however, was deep intellectual concern for inquiry into the Word of God in the context of the most complex rational and existential concerns of the time. Not that the preachers of that generation could not do that—many of them, like David Buttrick, were extraordinarily intelligent and engaged: they chose not to do that because the most complex truths do not communicate, entertain, or express stylistic solidarity with the audience they sought. They might be right about that audience.

The loss of the frontline intellectual orientation of preaching was grave, however, because it excused congregations from having to learn to think complexly about religious matters, suggesting that being entertained and motivated is enough. This fed Christian anti-intellectualism. Moreover,

Preface

this loss often fostered contempt for the shallowness of Christian thinking among those who do think responsibly. All throughout Christian history the sermon has been the genre for the most important theology, not theology for theologians, nor biblical study for scholars, nor religious social science for secular journalism, but theology that combined all these ways of thought for the sake of the mind of the church. Chrysostom preached as a theologian forming the mind of the church. So did Augustine, Bernard of Clairvaux, Meister Eckhart, Jacob Boehme, Martin Luther, John Calvin, Jonathan Edwards, Charles and John Wesley, Friedrich Schleiermacher, Phillips Brooks, and Paul Tillich. We remember these thinkers as theologians and churchmen. But they were preachers first, and their sermons sacrificed nothing for the sake of communication, entertainment, or stylistic solidarity. Rather, their sermons drew out their audience to master high levels of interpretation, to find excitement in ideas, and to define their spiritual solidarity with the mind of the church, not some more parochial constituency. I once read aloud a forty-five-minute sermon by Charles Wesley to an introductory theology class of master-of-divinity students, and they were enraptured the whole time, despite its archaic language, politically offensive pronouns, and length beyond any sound bite or memorable image. Even if not for Americans who want to be entertained by what can be communicated in a style in which their group already thinks, a need remains to recover the sermon as a form of public theology for the mind of the church.

The pulpit of a university church is the ideal place for such preaching. I was graced by the opportunity to preach at Marsh Chapel for three years, and the sermons in this volume come from that final year, 2005–2006. People in the Marsh Chapel congregation expect its preachers never to talk down to them and always to strive to identify and address the most difficult religious issues that trouble their hearts. The services are broadcast over WBUR and the Internet, and have attracted a large audience of people who say they either cannot or will not attend services elsewhere with preaching less respectful of their intellect and questions.

The university context is not the only place to find people hungering for theological preaching, however. In every community people exist on the margins of congregations who feel that the social and entertainment aspects of the Christian life are not enough. Many avenues other than congregational life present opportunities for service, education, fellowship, and entertaining recreation, unlike earlier times when the church was the only show in town. Moreover, many congregations are socially unstable because

Preface

of the culture wars that divide Christians. The reason to be a Christian now has to be because Christianity offers a truer word, deeper insight, more honest analysis, and a more rigorous discernment of spirits than alternative forms of life. Or at least Christianity has to match the spiritual engagement of alternative forms of life, including other religions.

As a theologian, I am an academic theologian, not a confessional one. The public to which an academic theologian is accountable is anyone, in any religion or in none, who is interested in the theological topic at hand. But academic theology ought also to be useful, creative of nurture in time and eternity, for specific religious groups. Here I preach theologically for Christians and those interested in Christianity. I bear in on the depths of the Christian symbols, rarely those of other religions or secular humanism or scientism.

In many congregations good reasons exist not to preach theologically, and instead to heighten through excellent communication and performance what people already think they believe. These reasons are reinforced by the ethos of democracy, which at its lower end is spiritual consumerism. People do vote with their feet. But the voting trends are mixed. Many people do not return to congregations whose worship and preaching they find boring. Nevertheless, many others do not return because they find the worship and preaching entertaining but shallow, not touching the depth and complexity of the issues that trouble our times and their hearts. So sermons that aim at theological complexity and depth are good to have around in every community, even if not preached from the pulpit. The university is not the only place where people agonize about what truly should be said concerning the Christian Word for our watch.

The sermons in this collection, ordered according to the academic year of university life, reflect the theme of Christian nurture. The complex character of Christian nurture consists in the fact that we are brought closer to God in the divine eternity while we engage more particularly the personal, communal, and social issues of our particular time. Nurture has two dimensions, eternity and time, whose connections are sometimes puzzling and complicated. But we cannot do without both, tied together.

The church sometimes has tried to separate them. The eternal dimension of spiritual nurture leads us upward toward our Creator, beyond space and time, whose immensity is our original home and in whose glory lies our final bliss. The ancient "heresy" of gnosticism showed how pursuit of this dimension wrongly can lead us away from the world into which we

Preface

are created to live. Gnosticism deals with the troubles of the world by recommending that we leave it below for some higher realm. But then God's creation is for naught.

The temporal dimension of spiritual nurture is committed to bringing God's love, justice, and mercy into the affairs of our personal, social, and political lives, amending ourselves, our communities, and our civilization to the extent our efforts and God's grace make possible. Liberal social gospel Christianity sometimes forgets the eternal dimension and reduces spiritual nurture to personal transformation and ethics alone. But you do not need Christianity for ethics or personal transformation, and the created glory of the world, resting in the divine eternity, slips from spiritual efficacy. Both the eternal and temporal dimensions require each other for us to live truly in the face of the ultimacy of divine creation.

How easy it is to get this wrong! A popular mistake today in this regard is the revival of classical dispensationalist theology, according to which the eternal Creator God is reduced to roles within history, fighting evil of cosmic proportions and finding consummation in apocalyptic battles. Often this theology is mixed in our time with jingoistic patriotism to identify political enemies with the forces of evil, so that people think that political armed struggle has apocalyptic religious meaning. This theology distorts the ultimacy of transcendence by representing God as a warrior for righteousness defined by the contest with evil within the world. It also distorts the loveliness of all creation, even the sinners and evil people who are equally children of God and for whom Christ died: if anyone is irrevocably lost, God is not God, only a sorcerer's apprentice. Instead of truly engaging the complex issues of our time, including moral and political ambiguities, this theology reducing God to narrative roles substitutes a dramatized simplification of the world for the complex created reality and fails to grasp God's eternal transcendence with much imagination.

The sermons here probe both the eternal and temporal dimensions of Christian nurture while dealing with the many topics at hand. What it means to live in eternity is a paradoxical thing to think about, and the sermons develop this theme bit by bit, summed up in the penultimate one. We might think we understand far more about what it means to live in time, but that too is more complex than meets the eye. The sermons about engaging the issues of our watch struggle with how to live temporally while also living in eternity. The final sermon emphasizes the incarnation of the eternal within our time. The Boston University School of Theology likes to

Preface

call itself the "School of the Prophets," and I preach in that tradition; a dark cloud depressed things during my tenure as Dean of Marsh Chapel, namely, the United States' acceptance of the political philosophy of what was then called neoconservatism. Again and again, these sermons rub against that with a witness to a Christian liberal "prophetic voice." But the School of the Prophets often neglected the eternal dimension of things, likely because of its concomitant commitment to Personalism, which insists on divine temporality. These sermons set moral fervor within eternity, and eternity within time's flow.

Preaching has been the most significant spiritual road of my life so far. Given the high calling to which I have said preaching is accountable, my limitations and vulnerabilities are raw within my consciousness. But then I am not the judge of what is offered here as the result of this commitment.

This volume is dedicated to my friend, colleague and successor as Dean of Marsh Chapel and Chaplain of the University at Boston University, the Reverend Doctor Robert Allan Hill. He has carried on the ambitions for preaching that I have enunciated here and improved the quality of the University sermons. I am grateful that he is now my pastor and friend, as well as preacher.

I

The Deepest Contradiction[1]

Romans 7:11–25a; Matthew 11:11–19, 21–30

Saint Paul says in our Romans text that the good he wants to do is not what he does. What he does is the evil that he does not want to do. Paul's complaint about himself applies to us all. We know what is good, and yet so often we do something else. Here is a fundamental contradiction within the soul, and it defines the Christian conception of the human predicament. What do we need to be saved from? From this contradiction: that we know the better and do the worse.

The Christian conception of the human predicament is virtually unique among philosophies and world religions. Plato had argued that people do bad things because they do not know better, and he recommended education as the remedy. Of course we think we know what is right most of the time, and these beliefs come from our culture, our family, and personal experiences. Then we discover that our beliefs about what is right are biased, or are based on too narrow a selection of evidence. Plato was quite correct to say that much of philosophy's job is to lead us to understand what we know and what we don't know, to expand our perspectives, to embrace all that can be learned from the arts and sciences, to travel and learn the cultural perspectives and values of others. Plato invented the university, and our own university is quite explicit about the importance of university education for attaining better moral insight. Even before Plato, Confucius

---

1. Preached July 3, 2005, the seventh Sunday after Pentecost.

in China had said much the same thing. Confucius emphasized the development of moral character, noting that everyone has the capacity to be moral but that this needs to be cultivated. Although the Chinese tradition is vastly complicated, it still follows Confucius's conviction that evil comes from miseducation or a failure of development. These approaches to bad behavior that focus on education rest on the conviction that people necessarily do what they believe is best, even when that belief is selfishly framed or mistaken in fact: for, why else would they do what they do?

Christianity shares with Judaism and Islam the story of the fall of Adam and Eve in the Garden of Eden. Judaism and Islam interpret that story as a problem of immaturity and lack of strength of character in the face of temptation. Christianity makes the stronger claim that Adam and Eve knew what they should do and yet deliberately chose the temptation when they were perfectly capable of not doing so. For the Christian tradition, Adam and Eve were morally culpable, whereas for the other Abrahamic faiths they were simply immature.

Without denying for a moment the importance of knowing what is morally right, cultivating moral learning in educational institutions, and accepting the ambiguity of many moral situations, I think we have to say that Saint Paul was right about knowing the better and doing the worse. At least for myself, I do what I know is wrong far more often than I like to admit. Of course, sometimes I also do what is wrong under the mistaken belief that it is right. Many ethical situations are so complex and ambiguous that honest mistakes in moral judgment are just part of life. But my deepest concern is for those situations that are not so ambiguous, where the moral truth is plain, where I want to do the good, and I still do what is wrong. Aren't many of the rest of you like Paul and me in this? I suspect so. This is sin, which the Christian tradition takes very seriously.

The Christian conviction that sin arises from this contradiction in the soul gives rise to a conception of the human person that emphasizes freedom. Freedom works something like this. In a situation of choice we are faced with several possibilities, each with its own allure or repulsiveness. Sometimes the values of our options seem to be about equal, and choice is like flipping a coin. Other times the values of the options are so different they cannot be compared. Yet other times, we know that some options are better and others worse. The values in the options have powerful appeals, of different sorts. Some options are positive, but others are horrible and we are repulsed by them. When faced with choices, we feel the attractions and repulsions of the options and, to the extent that we understand them, we know cognitively which are the better and which the worse. Freedom consists in taking the next step, from feeling the various appeals and repulsions, to adopting one as the specific action we choose. We define ourselves as the choosers of this particular option. Before the choice, any one of the options with its positive and negative values could be made the motive of our action. All of them are possible motives, but until chosen none is *our* motive. After the choice, one of the options with its values has been adopted as our motive, and we act upon that motive. The exercise of freedom is to adopt one option with its values as the motive for our action, when any one of the options could have been adopted as our motive.

The immediate appeal of some options can be far stronger than that of other options. Physical pleasures have more immediate appeal than postponed gratifications. Options that benefit us individually are more appealing than altruistic options. But we all have the experience of knowing that less appealing options can be better in the long run, and do sometimes postpone gratification and sacrifice our self-interest for the benefit of others. Sometimes our habits reinforce certain kinds of options and make choices easier. The habit of putting others first makes altruistic choices easier. Addictions are habits with extraordinary power of appeal, apparently overwhelming the possibilities of rejecting them. Nevertheless, people sometimes do go cold turkey. Sometimes people sacrifice their interests, goods, and very lives for other causes. There is always the free act of taking the step to move from feeling the appeal of an option to making that option one's own. With our millions of little free choices we gradually build up our moral and spiritual character. Beginning with the conditions of our environment and our genetic makeup, we create the moral and spiritual character that is our ultimate identity, and we are responsible for that.

Often we are tempted to think that all choices are antecedently motivated, that we always act for some reason operative in advance of the choice, which explains the choice. This is a dangerous way to think, however, because the potential motives for our choices never are the actual motives until we choose them. We give ourselves the motives that constitute our character and guide our actions. Not to admit this is to say that we are not free, but are determined by the motives we happen to have. If we are determined by motives that come before our choices, then we are not responsible. Rather, those conditions that give us the motives would be responsible. The people who say we always do what we believe to be the best think that our knowledge determines our will.

But when we know the better and still choose the worse, we know that we, and not the configuration of our knowledge, are responsible. Of course, as Plato and Confucius knew, we are responsible for configuring our knowledge so as to know what is right and wrong so far as humanly possible. But even the choice of acting so as to improve our moral knowledge requires the free act of adopting that option as our motive. We make ourselves motivated to be morally knowledgeable. Sometimes we choose to be morally biased or ignorant, even when we know that is the worse course. Such is the human predicament.

Saint Paul's analysis was this. On the one hand, we have the law of God in our inmost self. He believed that people have a kind of innate conscience, for which the external law, as in the Bible, is only a clarification and articulation. Perhaps this was his interpretation of human beings as created in the image of God. Setting aside our concern with the genuine ambiguities of some moral situations and the difficulty of figuring out complex moral problems, we can agree that at least sometimes the moral course is clear and true. Paul says this is God in us, and that when we act in accord with this divine conscience, it is not so much we ourselves who are acting but God. On the other hand, we have this other law of irrational choice in us that makes us do the worse when we know the better. Paul likens it to bodily attractions that are not governed by a proper divinely inspired harmony; so, he says, sex is good if enjoyed properly, but becomes a kind of bondage leading us to do the worse when we know the better, when we let it dominate a proper harmony for an ordered personal and social life. Astonishingly, Paul says that when we know the better and do the worse, it is not we ourselves who are acting but the power of sin in us: the devil made me do it. The power of sin is not just the attractiveness of bad choices. Rather it is a special kind of spiritual bondage we get into when we believe that we have no responsible control over our choices, that indeed the sinfulness in us causes us to sin all the more. Where is the self in this situation? When we choose according to God's law, it is God's choice. When we choose contrary to that, it is not our own choosing but the power of sin making us sin. Our human responsibility has been destroyed. Our very self has vanished, or rather our soul has been sold to the devil, to use the old cliché. This is the human predicament: whereas we should be cultivating responsible moral selves to present to God in ultimate perspective, we are lost, vanished, utterly in bondage to the sin that we believe controls our choices. We rightly condemn ourselves for this bondage, and this self-hate binds us to unfreedom even more strongly. (And you thought British taxation without representation was bad!)

Here then is Paul's gospel. It has two steps. First, our sins are forgiven. However you interpret the death and resurrection of Jesus Christ, Paul concluded that Jesus has paid whatever moral debt we have for our wrong choices and that nothing is held against us by God in ultimate perspective. Instead of being condemned in ultimate perspective, we are loved and given a fresh start at every moment. God's love is continual creative power. Paul's second step is that we must accept the freedom Jesus Christ has given us and behave in free, responsible ways. Self-hatred is forbidden, because we are loved by God and self-hatred only gives us excuses to be irresponsible. When we accept our freedom and choose accordingly, we might still make bad choices because our understanding is poor. Even when we know the better truly and clearly, we might still choose the worse. Our habits of selfishness and giving in to addictions are not changed merely by accepting God's love. But, if we accept those choices as our own responsibility, we have been given back our own soul and have something to present to God's ultimate perspective. "Faith" is what Paul often calls this acceptance of our own freedom and responsibility. "Sanctification" is what he calls the long process of changing our bad habits and cultivating a character of high moral worth. The phrase "accepting Jesus Christ as Lord and Savior" is shorthand code for accepting the forgiveness of sins and the return of our freedom so that we take responsibility for what we do and make of ourselves.

Now I suspect many of you came here today expecting a political sermon about national identity on the Independence Day holiday. Instead you have heard some rather philosophical reflections on personal freedom and identity. These are not unrelated, for each of us citizens has a responsibility for the nation and its choices. This is not the connection I want to develop, however. Rather, I want to point out in closing that the freedom to which we are restored by accepting God's love in Christ is our small finite share of God's infinite freedom. God is like us, but without our limiting conditions. God did not create the world because God was bound by a motive. God did not create the world for a reason. God created in absolute freedom and only after the fact did God acquire the nature of being the particular, singular God who created this vast cosmos with its massive variety of things of value. Think of the difference between ourselves and God. We are free creators in small ways because we add something new to the dense set of conditions given to us as possibilities: God was given no materials or norms to work with and created absolutely everything new. We create our own moral characters but are greatly limited by the fact that our choices are about the issues given us by our environment in space and time: God creates the entire divine nature and all of the conditions that shape it. We say that our characters have a moral dimension because we have to choose between options that have morally differing values: God creates all options and the values that distinguish them, and in this sense transcends morality. God's creation is an absolute fecundity producing unlimited swarms of things of value, which is the glory of divine love. Our small creation is a constrained fecundity based on the finite conditions of our specific lives, but even in this small place we can make things of value, that is, act with love.

Do we still do things we know are bad and want not to do? Yes, sometimes. Is that bad? Yes, but if we take responsibility for it, it is an exercise of our freedom. The human predicament, according to our Christianity, is that we are born free but commonly flee from freedom by enslaving ourselves to guilts and the conviction that we cannot help but do evil. Human redemption is to receive again the freedom that has always been ours, and to take responsibility for the choices we make. To bind ourselves to Christ is to accept that freedom by which God makes us define ourselves. Happy Independence Day! Amen.

2

Heaven in Earth[1]

Genesis 29:11–28; Romans 8:21–39; Matthew 13:31–33, 41–52

Dearly Beloved, we have in our gospel text this morning five of the classic sayings of Jesus: the mustard seed, the yeast of the loaf, the hidden treasure, the pearl of great price, and the harvest of good and bad fish. Most of you have heard many sermons on each one. Gird your loins, because you are about to hear another. I should point out at the beginning, however, the special significance of this particular kind of Jesus-saying. In the last century, some influential theologians and their preacher-students argued that Christianity is to be understood in terms of a great story, a narrative. They demoted God from being the creator of all history and stories and turned God into an actor within the story, fighting against evil, which was sometimes personified as the devil. Much contemporary conservative Christianity thinks that the witness of Christianity is a story, the story of God redeeming the world from evil forces. The New Testament does have passages that present such a narrative, particularly in some of the writings of Paul and in the book of Revelation. The greater part of the New Testament Gospels, however, is not about a story like this at all. Rather, it is about our proper relation to God who holds us under judgment. We are right now in the kingdom of heaven whether we know it or not. Most of Jesus's own teachings, as in our texts today, and in the Sermon on the Mount earlier in Matthew's Gospel, and the Farewell Discourses in John's Gospel, and

---

1. Preached July 24, 2005, the tenth Sunday after Pentecost.

in the parables and admonitions throughout all the gospels, are about our proper relation to God now before whom we stand under judgment, not about a cosmic war between God and Satan. Whereas the cosmic drama can be called "Christian Narrative," Jesus's kind of teachings, and that of other books in the New Testament, can be called "Christian Wisdom." In our time, many conservative Christians take the narrative to be the primary form of Christian understanding, with the wisdom passages interpreted as support for the narrative. Many liberal Christians take the Wisdom teachings to be primary, and the narratives as symbolic or metaphorical language to intensify the points of wisdom about our relation to God.

Our texts this morning about the kingdom of heaven fall under three sorts of wisdom teaching. The first two make the point that from very small and insignificant things can come very large and spiritually important results. The seed of the mustard plant is tiny. Yet it grows into a shrub that both is large and shelters other beings. This is to say, from a tiny, insignificant beginning, a great charity can come. Those of you who think you have nothing significant to contribute to the work of Christ in the world, don't worry. You do not know what great things might come from your small gifts. We should note from this passage that small gifts in the kingdom of heaven are recognized by how they provide for others. How many of our sisters and brothers in Africa, the Middle East, Pakistan, Indonesia, and Latin America would welcome nothing fancier than a secure place to make their nests!

The second saying, that a woman's bread yeast leavens the whole loaf, makes the point that some Christian virtues need not be imposed from on high. When insinuated subtly, like yeast, they can spread throughout the whole community and transform everything. Yet they are not seen themselves. Who thinks about the yeast in bread, if you haven't made the loaf yourself? Jesus, of course, was not thinking about the Christian community when he thought of the loaf, because there wasn't any such thing in his time. He was thinking rather about his whole society, and the yeast was the gospel and witness of his small band of disciples. Speak the truth in small places, and it might well spread throughout the whole. What a hopeful message! May we have the humility to understand our gospel lives on small terms, and yet have the courage to knead them into the entire loaf of our society!

The second sort of wisdom teaching in our gospel this morning is about the unique and overwhelming value of the gospel that we hear. You stumble on some great treasure in a field, and then quickly go to buy the field to gain ownership of the treasure. Jesus's point is clear: when you discover a great treasure, you should mortgage your future to acquire it. The gospel message is that you need to be willing to sacrifice a lot or all of your previous investments when you discover the treasure of the gospel: the gospel will bring you into God's presence. Your retirement fund brings only premortem security.

The story of the pearl of great price makes much the same point, but with a significant existential distinction. Here you are, the pearl merchant, or spiritual seeker, hunting out some kind of heavenly bargain. Let's be plain about what it means to be a spiritual seeker, rather than a committed practitioner. A seeker is one who has rejected all the options encountered so far. So the seeker's mentality juggles two passions. One is the negative passion of rejecting the religious culture of birth, and also all those alternative cultures offered as possibilities. The other is the hopeful passion that keeps one moving, always looking, experimenting, risking ridicule and humiliation because of unanswered religious questions.

Suddenly you come upon a religious way of life, like the others as one pearl is like other pearls, but vastly more compelling and beautiful. At this point, you sacrifice all your other commitments and bring to the pursuit of this pearl of great price everything that you have so far invested in other spiritual paths. Jesus had a profound point here. Spiritual commitment is not divided democratically among lots of possibilities. You need one particular path. You might be able to synthesize one traditional path with other paths, but the synthesis has to add up one singular path to which you can give your whole devotion. Jesus's gospel, he was saying, is that path.

These last two sayings of Jesus make the point that religious life is ultimate. We have many important and legitimate concerns in life—making a living, helping our family, serving the nation, perhaps making a contribution to society and culture that moves beyond our immediate contacts. The religious dimension of life, however, means that in and amongst all of these concerns there is a call to an ultimate concern, something before which we would sacrifice everything else. Hopefully we will not be called upon to sacrifice our other duties and interests. Hopefully we can find the ultimate within each of them. But when push comes to shove, sell everything else and buy the pearl of great price or the field with the treasure of heaven.

The first two sayings of Jesus, about the mustard seed and the yeast, declare that we can do great things out of proportion to our powers. The second two sayings declare that this is possible only if we subordinate, perhaps to the degree of sacrifice, our other concerns to focus on the heavenly treasure and pearl. The fifth saying, that fishing nets are indiscriminate about what they haul in and that fishermen have to separate the good fish from the bad, is more complicated. This passage has lent itself to the belief of some of our conservative Christian sisters and brothers that there will come a final showdown, an Armageddon, in which God's forces of righteousness will battle it out with the forces of evil, and finally prevail. But all the passage actually says is that there is a real difference between good and evil and that this distinction will be recognized in each individual case. Each of us, sinner, schlub, seeker, sage, or saint, revealed nakedly as who we are, stands in judgment before God. Neither fudging nor excuses is allowed when we stand in ultimate judgment. Moreover, that ultimate judgment is not some distant moment when we die and show up on Saint Peter's <UltimateGoogle@Valhalla.Org >. Rather we stand under judgment every moment of our lives, and because the Hound of Heaven has our scent, we should always be prepared to give an account.

    Fortunately, the gospel of Jesus Christ promises mercy and forgiveness to all who confess their sins. We do not have to wait for a judgment on history to know that we stand before God now. We do not have to wait upon some mythic cosmic drama in the distant future, or perhaps a rapture next week, to acknowledge our ultimate relation to God. Our eternal identity within the eternal life of God is the matter of utmost urgency to us now and at every moment. Theologically speaking, it would be a religious subterfuge to say that our ultimate identity in God's perspective depends on whether God wins some historical battle with Satan and evil. That ploy is a device for escaping responsibility and displacing it onto God, as if God were a character role in a drama about the victory of good or evil over one another.

    The surprising thing about all these Jesus-sayings is that the kingdom of heaven is never represented as a hereafter in some transcendent sense. Rather, the kingdom of heaven is something we should look for in our daily lives, says Jesus. Like great plants growing from bitty seeds, or a smidge of leaven making a whole loaf rise. Like suddenly finding a great treasure in our workplace, or a pearl of great price among the things we deal with daily. Like suddenly recognizing that, though we fly with turkeys, we shall be judged as to whether we soar like eagles. Other places in the Bible refer to heaven as a transcendent hereafter. I'm sure you have many different images of a heavenly afterlife. But in our gospel text for today, there is none of that afterlife transcendence business. All of these sayings of Jesus refer to the kingdom of heaven at hand, in the daily affairs of earth, not in the by-and-by. How do they help us understand our situation to be in heaven in earth? I believe three important lessons can be drawn.

First, because we live in God's kingdom, even if we miss the point and believe we are only in our own kingdoms, there are real differences between right and wrong, like good fish versus bad fish. To be sure, sometimes affairs are too complicated to be understood clearly, and sometimes there is real moral ambiguity in the sense that what helps also hurts. Nevertheless, for Jesus there are profound and plain values that distinguish right from wrong. These are summed up as love, and are made specific in the public sphere in terms of justice, peacemaking, humility, care for the poor, and so forth. You know the list. In more private spheres love means kindness, forgiveness, nonjudgmentalism, acceptance of people different from ourselves, and you know that list too. When our politicians sacrifice justice to greed, peacemaking to belligerence, humility to bullying, and care for the poor to tax breaks for the rich, we know the net contains bad fish. When our social culture sacrifices kindness to indifference, forgiveness to retribution, nonjudgmentalism to contempt, and inclusiveness to chauvinism, we know the net contains more bad fish. Jesus says we need to behave like the good fish.

The tragedy for contemporary Christianity is that so many Christians who believe in the story of God fighting the devil think that they can be good fish just by taking on the name of God or identifying themselves by the name of Jesus Christ. They think that, if they are on God's side, then God must be on their side. But that self-righteousness so often leads them to act like the bad fish: they fool themselves into believing that the greed of our economy has God's favor, they claim that their war making is righteous because God is at war with the devil, they think that arrogance toward others is justified because they are the spokesmen of Jesus, they dismiss those who suffer on grounds that they must deserve it, and they believe that they deserve to be richer themselves. Because they think God is at war and they are on God's side, they believe that their own wars are God's battles. That belief corrupts Jesus' values of love, justice, peacemaking, humility, charity, kindness, forgiveness, nonjudgmentalism, and inclusiveness of love. Jesus said to love our enemies, not fight them. The true Christian theology is that the unmeasurable wild creator God loves even the forces of evil, and redeems them. The little apocalyptic God who wars against the devil and unbelievers is a holdover of ancient paganism, and has entertainment value only for those whom Jesus might suspect are the bad fish.

How do we behave like good fish instead? Here is the second lesson from the gospel sayings. To live with the values of the Christian gospel is likely to require sacrifice, discipline, and the focusing of our many interests on what needs to be done to live the life of the gospel. All of creation is good, we Christians say, and our lives are lived in many dimensions, with many purposes. Nevertheless, we need to put first things first in order to love properly and teach others to love as well. Christian discipline does not mean getting rid of all the dimensions and interests of life save one: it means ordering them all so that they add up to a life and community of love. Learning such discipline is a lifelong task for spiritual development, and it requires both individual and community effort. Moreover, it sometimes requires sacrifice, like selling prized possessions to buy the field of treasure or the pearl of great price. Think of the sacrifice Jesus made in order to be true to the priorities of love and redemption of enemies.

The third lesson from our collection of Jesus's sayings is that our small efforts at the disciplined living of the way of love can have enormous consequences. Like the great bush that grows from a tiny mustard seed, sheltering many birds, our small loving endeavors of justice, peacemaking, humility, care for the poor, kindness, forgiveness, nonjudgmentalism, and acceptance of people different from ourselves, can make a difference worthy of the kingdom of heaven far beyond what we see. Like a little leaven in the loaf, we can raise our whole society with the multiplier effects of love. We do not need to enlist anyone else in an army to fight God's battles as we see them. We need to model for them, and lead them into, the ways of love that have the power to redeem the worst.

The kingdom of heaven is where we live now, and our citizenship consists in being called to the disciplines of advancing love in justice, peacemaking, forgiveness, kindness, redemption and all the rest we know so well. Jesus's point is that, because this is heaven's kingdom, our small acts of faith have ultimate significance. Let us rejoice in our hope. Amen.

3

Wrestle till the Break of Day[1]

Genesis 32:21–31; Romans 9:1–5; Matthew 14:11–21

The story of Jacob wrestling with the angel or divine being—Jacob thought it was God—is a classic story of struggle to win a blessing. Sleeping in the open by himself after having sent his family, flocks, and troops on ahead, Jacob was engaged by a man or angel or god in a wrestling match that lasted all night. Jacob was ferociously strong, a point made earlier in the narrative when on two occasions he lifted huge stones that usually could be moved only by several men working together. The god could not get away from Jacob, but had to do so because, according to ancient beliefs, the god could not last in the light of day. Even after the god sprained Jacob's hip, Jacob held on. Jacob demanded a blessing, and at last the god relented and gave Jacob a new name, "Israel," which meant that Jacob would be the father of that great people, Israel. Jacob demanded to know the god's name, but the god refused; in ancient times it was thought that to know a person's real name is to have some power over him. Jacob was satisfied that he had seen God face-to-face and lived; indeed, Jacob's physical encounter with the god was more intimate than merely seeing. So, the first-level moral of the story is that you can wrestle with God to win a new divinely blessed identity, and also to see God face-to-face. Jacob is the model of the spiritual striver, indeed perhaps of the mystic.

---

1. Preached July 31, 2005, the eleventh Sunday after Pentecost.

Nurture in Time and Eternity

This incident takes on added significance when read in the context of the overall Jacob story, which runs from Genesis 25 to 35. That story is an artful contrivance based on the plot of Jacob's birth, his fleeing from home, and living for twenty years with his shifty uncle Laban while he marries two of Laban's daughters plus two concubines, and has twelve children by the four of them. He becomes vastly wealthy. Then Jacob returns home with all his belongings; the wrestling match takes place on the homeward journey. The art of the story is that the incidents on the outward journey are paralleled by incidents on the homeward journey. For instance, Jacob is born competing with Esau, his twin brother who was first out of the womb, and the end of the story has the brothers living peacefully and happily together. As a young man, Jacob cheats Esau out of their father's blessing by disguising himself as Esau. Esau is furious, and Jacob flees to his uncle Laban, ostensibly to find a wife. Parallel to this, Esau welcomes Jacob back with much forgiveness on the return home. While fleeing Esau on the outward journey, Jacob has the dream about angels going up and down on the ladder to heaven, and this is paralleled by our story of the wrestling match with a god just before Jacob meets Esau for their reconciliation. The land Jacob flees to, Haran, is the place where his grandfather, Abraham, originally came from, and Uncle Laban is the brother of Jacob's mother, Rebekah. So Jacob's wives are his first cousins, keeping the heritage all in the family, as it were. Even Jacob's flocks are taken from Laban's flocks. For our culture, all this seems a bit incestuous, and the people who say the biblical ideal of marriage is one man and one woman simply don't know the Bible. But the point of the Jacob story is to emphasize the purity of the heritage of Israel. Jacob, now renamed Israel, is the father of twelve sons whose descendents are supposed to be the twelve tribes of Israel, and the lineage goes back with purity to Jacob's father, Isaac, and then back to Abraham to whom God made such extravagant promises about the promised land. Jacob's uncle Ishmael, who is older than his father, Isaac, and, at least according to the Muslims, is the rightful heir of Abraham, is excluded from the lineage of Israel. The Jacob story begins with a long genealogy of Ishmael's descendents; Ishmael married outside the Abrahamic clan and his descendents are not part of Israel. Jacob's brother, Esau, who had a better claim by birth than Jacob to be the heir of Abraham and Isaac, also married outside the Abrahamic clan, and his descendents became the Edomites, not the Israelites. A long genealogy of Esau's descendents comes at the end of the Jacob story. Thus the illegitimate genealogies frame the story of the legitimate one. According to the Jacob story, only Jacob's lineage is kosher, as it were.

The guiding theme of the Jacob story, however, is not only legitimacy of heritage, but alienation and reconciliation. As a young man, Jacob cheats his brother, deceives his father, and provokes God. Returning home, Jacob is eventually reconciled with his brother and father, and in our wrestling incident is reconciled with God, who had blessed him rather well all the time. The point is that God is faithful to the legitimate descendents of Abraham and provides the conditions for their reconciliation even when, like Jacob, they are greedy and full of lies. Jews and Christians have long taken the Jacob story to be a parable for the reconciliation of those who deservedly are alienated from the divine heritage. Christians have often interpreted Jacob's wrestling partner to be Jesus Christ, or some kind of anticipation of Christ.

So let me say that the moral of the wrestling incident, when read in the context of the larger Jacob story, is that God comes to us when we are yet sinners and, if we hold on hard enough, not giving up even when the night is over and God has wounded us sorely, we can win the blessing of reconciliation with God and other people. Holding on to God in this struggle requires the tenacity that Paul described as faith. Although Jacob did not begin as a particularly admirable person, he clung to God in the pursuit of his own righteousness. May we all do as Jacob did: fight without giving up for reconciliation with God and our neighbors! No matter how bad we are, God comes to wrestle.

I admit that the metaphor of wrestling with God is a little sweaty for this time of year, and probably appeals to men more than to women. But you get the point.

A deeper dimension of this wrestling story needs to be investigated, however. Just who is the fellow with whom Jacob wrestles? What is his name, so coyly withheld? The text allows many answers: An angel? A primitive clan god belonging to Abraham and Isaac's clan but not to Laban's or the Canaanites? The one true God of Israel as the editors of the story have Jacob believe? The text admits of all these answers. I want to leave the historical dimensions of this question for biblical scholars and turn instead to a nonbiblical source: a Methodist hymn.

Charles Wesley, the great hymn writer and brother of John Wesley, who with him founded the Methodist movement in the eighteenth century, wrote a hymn-poem on the text of this story. He called it, "Come, O Thou Traveler Unknown." It speaks in the voice of Jacob addressing the wrestling partner, whom he calls the unknown Traveler, and the first stanza is as follows. Listen to how it fits the story:

> Come, O thou Traveler unknown,
> Whom still I hold, but cannot see!
> My company before is gone,
> And I am left alone with thee;
> With thee all night I mean to stay
> And wrestle till the break of day.

My sermon title comes from that last line.

That first stanza had a double meaning for the Wesley brothers. In addition to referring to the Jacob story, it referred to their own partnership in the Methodist movement. They often wrestled over what to do, and Charles was critical of John. But when Charles died, both of them were in their eighties, and John was devastated that his "company before is gone / and I am left alone" with God. Shortly after Charles's funeral John tried to teach this hymn to a congregation and broke down in the attempt. I suspect that many widows and widowers feel this way about the loneliness of their remaining years with God alone.

Charles Wesley's hymn gives a strange exposition of the Jacob story. It has Jacob say that he need not tell the unknown Traveler who he is himself, because his sin and misery are obvious, and besides the Traveler already calls him by name. The Genesis text does not suggest this introspection on Jacob's part, although the name Jacob meant the "supplanter" because Jacob supplanted Esau as the receiver of Isaac's blessing, and thus his name did refer to Jacob's early sin. Wesley's Jacob is desperate about his own unworthiness and does not need even to confess it. He asks, "But who, I ask thee, who art thou? / Tell me thy name, and tell me now." Not the Traveler's *blessing*, but his *identity*, is what Wesley's Jacob wrestles for. The hymn goes on with several stanzas that end, "wrestling, I will not let thee go / till I thy name, thy nature know."

Wesley's Jacob asks our central question. We all wrestle with powerful forces, forces that make us to reveal our inmost identity when we often would hide that, even from ourselves. What are those forces with which we wrestle? God? Demons? What is their nature? Greed? Ambition? Fear? Doubt? Hate? Pride? Complacency? These deep struggles define our souls. They are the things that concern us ultimately, as the theologian Paul Tillich liked to say. Our lives are shaped around them as we wrestle with them through the years.

In Wesley's exposition, Jacob becomes a Christian and asks whether the Traveler is Jesus:

> In vain thou strugglest to get free,
> I never will unloose my hold;
> Art thou the man that died for me?
> The secret of thy love unfold;
> Wrestling, I will not let thee go
> Till I thy name, thy nature know.

You see, there are a great many things with which we might wrestle ultimately that are not worth the effort. We all wrestle to make a living. But if we take it too seriously, it will deform our souls. We all wrestle to have a career. But taken too seriously, that deforms us. We wrestle to have family and friends, and we never have family and friends without long-term wrestling. But taken too seriously, that leads to dependency. We wrestle with our own character flaws, our greed, ambition, fear, doubt, hate, pride, complacency, and a hundred other vices. To be sure, we need to work on these things. But if we wrestle with our sinful selves too seriously, we will be deformed into nasty judges whose self-hate sours everything. Haven't we all known "religious" people like that? People who wrestle too much with what's wrong turn into nihilists. The only thing worth wrestling with ultimately is God.

Wesley's Jacob cries, "Yield to me now—for I am weak but confident in self-despair!" This introspective Jacob, in his self-despair, has nothing left to lose, and this gives him enormous strength. Remember the Janis Joplin song, "Freedom's just another name for having nothing left to lose"? If Jacob had hope in his own strength, getting along without victory over the Traveler, he would have given up. But he becomes more insistent. "Speak to my heart, in blessing speak, / be conquered by my instant prayer." What gall! What confidence founded upon total despair, could let Jacob demand that the Traveler be conquered by his prayer! We softer types usually think of prayer as a petition. For Jacob it is a demand that God be conquered and reveal the Traveler's name and nature. "Speak," says Jacob, "or thou never hence shalt move, / and tell me if thy name is Love." Love is Jacob's guess, or hope, for the name and nature of his intimate wrestling partner.

Love is the only thing worth a lifetime of struggle. Love is the only thing that will not deform us when we embrace it each day. Love is not always an adversary, as suggested by the reference to wrestling. But one engages love like in a wrestling match. Learning to love through all the stages of life, with all the crowd of our friends and enemies, requires holding on through the night, again and again. What more important question can we ask than whether our ultimate concern, that with which we wrestle ultimately and lifelong, is love or some fake! So easily do we deceive ourselves, that we are about God's business of love, that we need to go to the bottom of despair to ask Jacob's question: is your name and nature really love?

Wesley, of course, is alluding to the text in 1 John that says "God is love." He also suggests indirectly that the Traveler whose name and nature might be love is Jesus. But he does not say either directly. His Jacob does not ask explicitly whether the Traveler is God or Jesus, only whether his name and nature is love.

Then Wesley's Jacob hears in his heart the Traveler's whisper of his name and nature, a voice the Jacob in Genesis never heard:

> 'Tis Love! 'tis Love! Thou diedst for me,
> I hear thy whisper in my heart.
> The morning breaks, the shadows flee,
> Pure Universal Love thou art:
> To me, to all, thy mercies move—
> Thy nature, and thy name is Love.

The secret power of Wesley's song is that it speaks salvation to the individual heart because it recognizes the paradoxical universality of love: "to me, to all, thy mercies move." If the love that answered Jacob's despair were only for Jacob, healing only Jacob's vices and alienation, that would be for Jacob a fake love, a love that answers only his selfish concern for his own salvation. Wesley knew that real divine love loves everyone, the entire creation, and only an individual's recognition of the universality of that love beyond his or her own benefit has true healing for that individual. Of course the point is that being healed means loving all those others just as the saving love has loved oneself. Truly to wrestle with saving love is to wrestle for the salvation of others as much as oneself. If the apparent love with which one wrestles is not the love of those others as well, then it is fake and cannot truly address the singularity of one's own heart. Not all of the evangelicals of Wesley's time, or ours, got that point. Even John Wesley frequently said that, although he knew intellectually that Christ died for the salvation of all, real salvation means the recognition that it applies to oneself. Charles Wesley reversed this in his hymn: in order to know that saving love applies to oneself, one has to recognize that it applies to those others just as well.

Wrestle till the Break of Day

When pure universal love is the one with whom we wrestle through the night, nothing of God's business is impossible for us. Our vices will be cured and our hopes fulfilled, as these things count within God's love.

> Lame as I am, I take the prey,
> Hell, earth, and sin with ease overcome;
> I leap for joy, pursue my way,
> And as a bounding hart fly home,
> Through all eternity to prove
> Thy nature, and thy name is Love.

Amen. Let us sing the song, number 386 in *The United Methodist Hymnal*.

4

Who Was Jesus?[1]

Genesis 45:1–5; Romans 11:1–2a, 21–32; Matthew 15:(11–20) 21–28

The Jesus Christ whom we encounter in our worship and hymns, in our formal theology and stories, even in the Bible, is someone who has lived in the minds and hearts of Christians through the ages, including ourselves; we have Jesus present to us through people's memories and interpretations. We do not encounter the subjective person Jesus, any more than we encounter today George Washington or Abraham Lincoln. Some people would say therefore that we do not encounter the real Jesus, that we engage merely the Jesus of other people's memories. But the real identity of Jesus includes how he is understood and remembered by others. George Washington and Abraham Lincoln have identities that include a lot more than their personal experience: they really live in the memories of others and in the consequences of their actions long after their deaths. Everyone's identity is not merely their personal subjective experience but also how they are perceived by others and how they affect things around them, perhaps for hundreds of years. This larger sense of identity is that for which we are responsible before God, although, of course, we are not entirely responsible for how people understand us.

Jesus's identity was not limited to his subjective experience even when he was alive in the ordinary sense, teaching the disciples. They tried hard to understand him, forming tentative images and ideas of him and his

---

1. Preached August 14, 2005, the thirteenth Sunday after Pentecost.

teachings in their own imaginations. Jesus was often critical of how they understood him: witness his impatience with their lack of understanding of his parable in the Gospel today. The disciples received rather quick feedback from him when their imaginative interpretations of his identity were off the mark.

We have the same situation. You know how it is when you want friends to understand you: you can tell from what they do and say what their images of you are, and you try to correct them so that they conform to your image of yourself. Of course, sometimes we do not understand our own identity, and a friend's image might be closer to the mark. We pay psychotherapists big bucks to form images of us that reveal more deeply who we really are. Our true identity might include things we never would have thought about. For instance, we often find that we play important roles for other people of which we had not been aware—leading them astray perhaps, involving them in a dysfunctional family situation, or serving as a healthy model leading them to greater virtue and independence. Anyone who has a public role in life, and we all do in small if not large ways, has an identity that is more than the way we subjectively experience ourselves. Sometimes we can control and be responsible for elements in that public role. Other times our public life gives us an identity over which we have no control. When that is good, we rejoice in good fortune and, when that extended public identity is bad, we complain about fate.

So Jesus's identity was not limited to his subjective personal experience. Nor was it limited to his identity for his disciples who could easily check out their understanding. Jesus personally thought of himself as a Jewish reformer, not the founder of a new religion; yet the early Christians extended his identity to be the founder of a movement named after his title as Christ. Jesus personally thought of himself as chosen by God to head a kingdom of justice dominated by the twelve tribes of Israel; that's why he chose twelve special apostles, one to represent each tribe; yet Saint Paul extended his identity to be a divine agent in a cosmic narrative for conquering Satan and the forces of evil, a conception wholly alien to Jesus's personal way of thinking. Jesus in no way, personally speaking, thought of himself as divine—that would have been idolatry to any faithful Jew of his time; yet the conviction that he was divine, on the part of his followers in the early centuries, led to calling him the Second Person of the Trinity constituting God's nature. Jesus personally knew nothing about worship of himself, especially led by people in priestly garb taken from the costumes of Roman senators, which would have astonished him. He knew nothing of his role in the worship life of monks and nuns in monasteries, or in the prayer life of Protestants, or in the setting of policies in mainline churches today for charity in Africa. Yet in a very real sense, the Jesus who lives in all those movements that have taken place in his name has the identity given him by all those living roles. That is his public identity.

Of course, not every interpretation of Jesus in contexts beyond those he knew personally is valid, any more than his immediate disciples always understood him rightly. Jesus's name has been taken for causes that he would abhor. We need to remember that the ovens in the Nazi prison camps were turned off only for Christmas and Easter, a perverse embodiment of Christianity. The problem of the validity of an extension of Jesus's identity is particularly acute when the extension is to some kind of role that a human person cannot play, as when Jesus is identified with the symbol of the cosmic Christ, or the Second Person of the Trinity. Not every extension of Jesus's identity by Christian communities is valid.

The doctrine of the church in this regard is that these extensions need to be supported by the Holy Spirit. It is the Spirit that interprets for us what is Jesus Christ's true and new identity. Of course, we then need to identify the true Holy Spirit when our world is filled with so many spirits that seem to tell us what is divine. The tests of the Holy Spirit lie in its fruits, as you know: do interpretations of Jesus, and practices based on them, lead to joy, peace, patience, righteousness, piety, faith, hope, and love? Or do they lead to sourness, agitation, belligerence, self-righteousness, selfishness, denial, despair, or hate?

The feedback-testing our long extensions of Jesus's identity is more indirect and takes a lot longer than the feedback Jesus gave to his immediate disciples. Yet the feedback is exceedingly fine. We are beginning to see now, for instance, that the belief that Jesus is God's divine agent in a great cosmic drama of struggle with the forces of evil, leading to Armageddon, is a very dangerous image of Jesus. So many Christians who believe that fail to distinguish between their putative role in fighting God's battles and God's approval of their battles. When their own battles, which they assume have God's blessing, are frustrated, they fall into deep resentment of ways of life other than their own, bitter defensiveness, readiness to go to war, arrogance about their own causes, greed for power, denial of evidence that they might be in the wrong, spiteful despair of reconciliation with enemies they are supposed to love, and delight in the hate of those they brand as

God's enemies. The fruits of the Spirit test out against the Christianity that takes Jesus to be God's avenger, even when that image is in the Bible, as it is in the book of Revelation.

One of the principal anchors for our understanding of the identity of Jesus is our grasp of who he was historically. Of course, we know that our knowledge of his historical identity is limited, and always filtered through sources such as the Bible and our traditions. But our gospel text today gives us an interesting insight.

When approached by the Canaanite woman, Jesus at first declined to help her, saying that his mission was only to the lost sheep of Israel. This reflected his understanding of himself as a Jewish reformer, somewhat in the mold of the prophets. He knew about other ethnic peoples, of course. He was raised in Nazareth, which was about five miles from a new city that was being built by the Romans; since his family was in the building trades he had much connection with the Romans; the Gospels tell several stories of his interactions with them as an adult. He preached in Greek towns, and probably spoke a version of Greek. Many Semitic peoples besides Jews lived in Palestine at his time, and in our particular story he was in Syria where he met the Canaanite woman. Yet at first he identified himself as a prophet for the children of Israel alone, to the exclusion of others.

As we learned, the Canaanite woman changed his mind. So far as I know, this is the only incident in the Gospels in which Jesus is shown admitting he was wrong and learning something new. Those of you who look to highlight the accomplishments of women can point with pride to this story. Not only was she a woman, she was a Canaanite, belonging to a people whom the Israelites were supposed to have dispossessed from the land. Some of you saw the advertisement last Friday in the *New York Times* and perhaps other papers in the form of an open letter to President Bush from seven Lubavitcher rabbis and a layperson claiming that God owns everything and gave the whole Land of Israel to the Jews; they claimed that the eviction of Jewish settlers from occupied territories is a violation of God's will and that President Bush had been appointed by God to bring peace and triumph over evil by protecting God's people, by whom they meant the Jews, and their Holy Land. People today still believe that those other than Jews should be dispossessed from Palestine. Yet even in Jesus's time, it was recognized as a land for many people. Because of the Canaanite woman, Jesus came to see that his mission was not only to Israel, but to all who come seeking faith. At the end of the Gospel of Matthew, Jesus is quoted as sending his friends to make disciples of all nations, a direct turnabout from his earlier preoccupation with Israel alone.

From the beginning, so far as we can gather, Jesus had a revolutionary table fellowship. That is, he talked, ate, and drank with women as well as men, with poor people and rich people, with prostitutes, tax collectors, and various other sinners. He not only said that we should not judge others—judgment belongs to God—but that we should love them, even our enemies. In all of this, he was running against the customs and morality of his Jewish community, at least as he conceived it. Yet that inclusiveness might have been limited to people within that community. His lesson from the Canaanite woman opened the door to an inclusiveness that went well beyond the limits of the kosher. This lesson was confirmed by Saint Peter, as recorded in Acts 1 1–11, when he had a vision of unclean things that were permissible to eat and accepted the dinner invitation of a Roman.

The extension of Christianity beyond the Jewish world to the many worlds of the Gentiles was not an easy thing for early Christianity. Saint Paul argued strongly for it, and eventually won out. But the extension is still not complete today. In this day of religious as well as economic globalization, we have mastered the art of indigenizing Christianity to many cultures, even those very far from the traditional cultures of European Christianity. But we have not mastered the art of letting Christianity serve all cultures, regardless of whether people in those cultures want to become Christians. Too often, we have taken Jesus's commandment to "make disciples of all nations" to mean to recruit Christians in all nations. This interpretation is fine so far as it goes, but is too narrow. Our Christian discipleship is to offer God's hospitality to everyone. God's creative love can bring renewal and blessing to anyone, and it is offered universally. Our job as disciples is to invite people into that divine love so that they can be renewed and blessed. Jesus did not ask the Canaanite woman to sign up as his follower. He simply healed her daughter.

The first principle of offering God's hospitality is to respect people for who they are. This means accepting them in their own religions, in their own social cultures, and in their own political interests, even when they oppose our own. Of course we are not without moral standards. These standards include those values I mentioned a moment ago: joy, peace, patience, righteousness, piety, faith, hope, and love, and all the institutions of life that support these things and oppose sourness of spirit, agitation, belligerence, self-righteousness, selfishness, denial, despair, and hate. These virtues and vices are universal to all religions, and to the great philosophies of secular culture. We Christians should guide our own behavior by them. But under no circumstances can we use them to judge others. Judgment of others belongs to God alone. Our role as Christians is to host other people as they come to God, and to host God's creative love in the lives of those other people. True Christian discipleship is to give away the privileges of membership in Christian culture and to cultivate a Christian culture of conveying God's love to others, in whatever language and religious forms do the job. As Jesus came to see, when confronted by the Canaanite woman, the radical openness of God's love embraces even those whom our religion has taught us to exclude. What a radical transformation for world history!

Just how did the Canaanite woman teach this momentous lesson? She did two things. First, she demanded access to God's healing power that she saw in Jesus. Who among the world's suffering masses has not called out for relief in some language or other? Second, she used the power of humility to undermine the icy refusal of privilege. Jesus said that only the people of Israel were privileged to receive his holy meal of the healing grace of God. She said that even the dogs eat the crumbs under the table. If the people of Israel, or we self-proclaimed Christians, sit at the table of privilege regarding God's grace, she and the other outsiders will crawl to the floor to eat the crumbs. Immediately the claims of privilege dissolved in embarrassment at the arbitrary restriction of grace. Of course he healed her daughter!

What do we learn of Jesus's contemporary identity from this story from his ancient personal life? Our Lord leads us today to examine our religion to ask whether we are working to serve our religious community to the exclusion of others, or are we forming our Christian community to host others in the presence of God. How do we serve the Muslims and Jews, the Hindus and the Buddhists, the Confucians and Daoists, the secular people and the wretched of the earth who lack even any religion whatsoever? Do we ask first whether they might become Christians? Shame! Let us ask first how God can bless them. Our Lord also leads us to look for great faith in others, any longing for connection with God that might bring joy, peace, patience, righteousness, piety, faith, hope, and love. Even when we do not have that faith ourselves, we need to seek it out in others and bring it into the presence of God as we can. As for ourselves, what we learn from this critical point in Jesus's evolving identity is that the hero in the story is not the disciples, not even Jesus: it is the outsider woman whose faith led her to such humble self-abasement that Jesus's inherited sense of privilege for his own people was emptied. If only we had the power of her faith, think of what we could do!

Who was Jesus? He was a man of God who learned the universal showering of God's love despite himself when confronted by a faith whose humility undermined his sense of privilege. Who is Jesus today? He continues to be the mediator of God and the soul of the church who, among other things, teaches us to empty even our Christianity's sense of privilege for the sake of those who call upon God. This is Jesus's identity as our present and risen Lord. Amen.

5

A Living Sacrifice[1]

Exodus 1:1—2:10; Romans 12:1—8; Matthew 16:11—20

Saint Paul appeals to his Roman readers, and to us, "to present our bodies as a living sacrifice, holy and acceptable to God, which is [our] spiritual worship." Because we have become so familiar with this phrase, it is worthwhile to reflect on how radical it is. Sacrifice, in Paul's time, was a very common religious observance, practiced not only among Jews in temple worship but also by the official pagan cult of Rome and nearly every other religion in that very pluralistic environment: Mithraism, Zoroastrianism, the Egyptian religion of Isis and Osiris, Celtic religions, and the religious practices of the peoples from the Steppes of what is now Russia. Although the religions differed in the manner and context of sacrifices, sacrifices took place frequently and were an ordinary part of their world. In the official Roman religion the patriarch of the family would perform a brief sacrifice with each evening meal, according to some scholars. In the Jewish religion of which Jesus was a part, there were four major yearly festivals of sacrifices at the temple in Jerusalem plus dozens of other occasions each year in which people could make sacrifices, or pay priests to sacrifice for them.

Whereas Paul enjoins us to be *living* sacrifices, in all these religions, the thing sacrificed was a dead animal, not a living human being. Sometimes grain was offered, but that was not a sacrifice in the full sense. In the sacrifice, an animal was cut up and its parts rearranged or redistributed

---

1. Preached August 21, 2005, the fourteenth Sunday after Pentecost.

so as to reinforce what the religious group believed is the proper divine ordering of the cosmos. For instance, in the Jewish sacrificial cult, some part of the animal is burned on the altar so as to go to God, some of the meat is given to the priests, other parts of the animal to the people making the sacrificial donation, and the blood is treated as sacred, usually splashed on the altar. This division marks out the distinctions between the divinity, the servants of the divinity, the people whose allegiance is to the divinity, and the fact that the divine ordering is a life-and-death matter, a matter of lifeblood.

In some vague way, the sacrificial rearrangement of the parts of the animal not only reflects pregiven distinctions within the religious dimension, it helps to create them. In the ancient world, a great many people believed that a failure to observe proper sacrifices would let the world slip into confusion and chaos. You will remember that Saint Paul believed that the world had slipped to such a great confusion of the powers of evil and good that only the sacrifice of the Son of God could restore things to their rightful order. The ancient civilizations of India and China also were shaped with ideas and practices of sacrifices such as these.

These sensibilities are so alien to our own that we find it hard to take them seriously. Few of us sit easily with Paul's frequent interpretation of Jesus as a sacrificial lamb. Read the early chapters of the book of Leviticus to see detailed prescriptions for a variety of sacrifices that are the background of our Jewish, Christian, and Muslim traditions. Understanding what sacrifice meant in the ancient world is crucial for understanding what is demanded of us who do not take the language and practice of sacrifice seriously.

The first radical thing in Paul's admonition to us to be living sacrifices is that we are human beings, not animals. Of course, many religions, especially in times before Jesus and Paul, had practiced human sacrifice, with the same intent as animal sacrifice: to bring order to the cosmos regarding relations between divinity and human life. Given the vigor with which Hebrew Bible writers condemn human sacrifice, it probably was the case that the early worship of Yahweh included it. Or perhaps it is better to say that the early worship of Yahweh was mixed together with the worship of other gods and somewhere along the line human sacrifice was included. But the strain of Israelite religion that came down to Jesus as the worship practice of Second Temple Judaism strongly condemned human sacrifice. How daring of Paul, then, good Pharisee that he was, to advocate that Christians regard themselves as sacrifices, restoring the cult of human sacrifice! Imagine this: we Christians believe in a strange form of human sacrifice, if we take Paul seriously!

Paul's point in our epistle today, of course, is that we should be living sacrifices, not dead ones to be dismembered with our body parts rearranged. Therefore his sense of human sacrifice did not involve killing anyone. In fact, for Paul, Jesus's sacrifice unto death was the final, once-for-all, and sufficient sacrifice for the sins of the whole world. No one else ever again needs to be sacrificed to set right the relation between God and human beings, good and evil. The significance of Jesus's atoning death was that Jesus did it! We do not have to atone for our sins, only accept God's mercy. Moreover, for us to think that we do need to atone for our sins, to wallow in that guilt, is itself another sin, the sin of rejecting God's forgiving grace in Jesus. The good news of the gospel is that we are freed from the guilty life for which a sacrifice might be required to set in right order, because that sacrifice has already been made, once and for all. At least this is the way Paul saw it in his world with its understanding of sacrifice.

With this in mind, we can understand some of the Christian symbolism that is obscure to our modern sensibilities. How were the body parts of Jesus, the human sacrifice, rearranged? Most obviously, Jesus, once dead, came to life again, signifying that in the cosmic order of things, life trumps death; God is the God of the living. Jesus's resurrection and ascension into heaven signified that the way to God is open to human beings, after it had been confused or made chaotic by sin. In this respect, Paul called Jesus the firstborn of many who will get to God. Yet in another symbolic sense, Jesus left his flesh and blood with us in the eucharistic practice of his community. Each communion is a symbolic minisacrifice in which we, God's people, get a share of the body of Christ, like in the ancient Mediterranean evening meal sacrifice.

With these reflections on the background of sacrificial thinking in Paul's time, we can look more directly at his plea that Christians become living sacrifices to God. When he said we should present our "bodies" as living sacrifices, by "bodies" he meant our whole selves, not just our minds or souls or spirits. For Paul, and Christians generally, we are our visible, material bodies, and our bodies are more than mechanical bits of flesh, blood, bone, and nerve. Harmonized as living organisms, our bodies produce or embody all those realities of mind and heart, soul and spirit that we sometimes distinguish from body. A dead body, of course, is just a body. A living body is a person. Paul said to present our whole selves, our persons, to God as a living sacrifice.

But of course presenting our whole selves includes presenting our bodies, and this part of Paul's plea that we be living sacrifices has enormous consequences. We need to take care of our bodies, if not for our own enjoyment, then in order to be worthy living sacrifices. In ancient Jewish law, only animals without blemish could be used in sacrifices, and in some occasions only priests without bodily blemish could perform the sacrifices. Paul was contradicting this point of Jewish law by saying that everyone should present themselves, not only those with unblemished bodies, or even unblemished character. Remember in our epistle he went on to say that people are different in their skills and also in their degrees of faith, yet all are members of one body. So we should understand that we need to make the best of the bodies that our genes and the accidents of our lives have given us. Some people are healthy, others sickly, some strong, others disabled, some naturally talented, others klutzes, some young, others old, some beautiful, others blemished. For instance, whenever my dermatologist examines me, he mutters under his breath about all the weeds in God's garden of life. Or consider that in the history of Western Christian art, Saint Paul is always represented as bald, an affliction I take more seriously than most! We have to make do with the bodies we have. Paul's point was that we need to take as good care as possible of our bodies because we present them to God as our spiritual worship.

So fat America needs to wake up and diet if we are going to present our bodies as our spiritual worship! Starving ourselves to look like Twiggy is no spiritual improvement. Lazy muscles need to go to the gym. Those of us who do enough manual labor to stay fit need to take care that we not abuse our bodies. The poverty that makes some people starve or abuse their bodies with too much work is not only intrinsically unjust but also an impediment to spiritual worship. Nicotine, alcohol, caffeine, and other mood-altering drugs have the potential to ruin the bodies we offer to God. People with chronic conditions such as hypertension or diabetes need to take special care to remain healthy. I could go on and on, but you get the point. Our bodies are not just for us, they are our sacrificial offering to God. They are part of our ultimate responsibility, and we need to be serious in their care. The reason for this is that they are God's gift, and the only truthful way to be alive before God is to be grateful.

A Living Sacrifice

Our spiritual worship, Paul was saying, does not mean just going to church. In fact, in this whole section of his letter Paul does not mention worship in the sense of church liturgy, although I will not make too much of this point because I am very glad you are here. Rather, Paul meant that our spiritual worship is how we live in the whole of our lives. What we present to God as holy and acceptable is not our ritual liturgy but the whole of what we do and make of ourselves. Actually, one of the meanings of the ancient word from which "liturgy" comes is "work." In that ancient sense, our entire lives are our "work," our liturgies.

Paul said, "Do not be conformed to this world, but be transformed by the renewing of your minds, so that you may discern what is the will of God—what is good and acceptable and perfect." The problem with this world, Paul thought, rightly I believe, is that it is a confusion of good and evil, a debilitating mixture of the sacred and the alienated, a chaos of responsibilities considered in ultimate perspective. When we pursue holiness as living sacrifices, in our many small ways we do bring a proper divine order out of this confusion and chaos. The activities of our living members move the cosmos to better order, just as they believed about sacrifice in the ancient world. Now I do not mean that morality will ever be simple and unambiguous. What is good for some people is often bad for others, and often we need to make choices between the greater of goods and the lesser of evils. Inevitably we are guilty of wrongdoing even when we are doing our best. And sometimes we cannot even understand what we are doing. Thank the merciful God for creating a religion designed expressly for sinners!

My point, however, is that to be a living sacrifice is to sort out how we relate to God in everything we do, and to put first things first. Paul said that we should renew our minds so that we may "discern what is the will of God—what is good and acceptable and perfect." Although life is complicated and morally ambiguous, we still have guidelines for being living sacrifices. In the passage immediately following our text from Romans Paul wrote:

> Let love be genuine; hate what is evil, hold fast to what is good; love one another with mutual affection; outdo one another in showing honor. Do not lag in zeal, be ardent in spirit, serve the Lord. Rejoice in hope, be patient in suffering, persevere in prayer. Contribute to the needs of the saints; extend hospitality to strangers. Bless those who persecute you; bless and do not curse them. Rejoice with those who rejoice, weep with those who weep. Live in harmony with one another; do not be haughty, but associate with

the lowly; do not claim to be wiser than you are. Do not repay anyone evil for evil, but take thought for what is noble in the sight of all. If it is possible, so far as it depends on you, live peaceably with all. Beloved, never avenge yourselves, but leave room for the wrath of God; for it is written, "Vengeance is mine, I will repay, says the Lord." No, "if your enemies are hungry, feed them; if they are thirsty, give them something to drink; for by doing this you will heap burning coals on their heads." Do not be overcome by evil, but overcome evil with good.

You see from these guidelines about what is good and acceptable and perfect, what a difficult job we have to be living sacrifices, so that through our lives we can move the world toward a divine order.

In a society that defines love as self-interest and in a country whose government justifies heinous crimes by citing America's self-interest, we need grace to make love be genuine, to separate ourselves from evil, and cling to the good. In a society that fosters exploitation of neighbor and with a government that insists on being honored above others, we need grace to practice mutual affection and compete in honoring one another. In a society of physical and spiritual couch potatoes, we need grace to serve God with zeal and an ardent spirit. In a land where the rich get richer and the poor poorer, we need grace to sustain hope, patience in suffering, and continued prayer. When we are taught to take care of our own and to condemn people who are different from ourselves, we need grace to serve the saints and extend hospitality to strangers. In a society whose government believes that bending others to our will is macho, we need grace to bless those who persecute us. In a consumerist culture that teaches that joy can be bought, we need grace to rejoice with those who rejoice and weep with those who weep. In a political culture that believes that dominating others is the way to harmony, we need grace to live in harmony without being haughty and to know the limits of our wisdom about what is good for others. In a country that suffered evil from criminal terrorists and responded by declaring a war on terrorism and, finding insufficient numbers of terrorists willing to stand up and be warred upon, attacked two countries that did not attack us, killing more people than all the victims of terrorism combined over the last century, we need grace not to repay evil for evil and to take thought for what is noble in the sight of all. In a nation that votes in politicians who like war, it takes grace to live peaceably with all. In the richest and most powerful nation in earth's history which still believes it needs to take vengeance on those who oppose its will for them, it takes grace never to avenge ourselves and to leave judgment to God. How can we not be overcome by all this evil, but overcome evil with good, except by grace?

Brothers and sisters, I assure you that we have the grace to present our bodies as living sacrifices, wholly and acceptable to God, which is our spiritual worship. Let the witness of our lives call the world to love, goodness, affection, honor, zeal, service, hope, patience, prayer, charity, hospitality, blessing the persecutors, sharing joy and sorrow, harmony, humility, wisdom, forbearance of vengeance, and the overcoming of evil with good. These things are God's order, and our living sacrifice can make them happen. Amen.

6

Investment[1]

Exodus 12:1–14; Romans 13:1–14; Matthew 18:11–20

Let me reiterate my welcome to you this morning, especially to the new students and their families who are here for the first time. Because we are in the middle of a worship ritual, it is fair to point out that going away to college is itself a ritual act of great importance. Of course, it is not only a ritual: it is a real-life transformation. Yet it has a ritual quality to it, a culturally defined celebration of a life change. In American society, going away to college, or I should say from the university pulpit, coming to college, marks the passage from childhood in the care of family to adulthood in the care of one's own responsibility. People who do not go to college, or leave home for the military or make some other such culturally defined break from childhood often do not realize when adult responsibilities are upon them. The ritual character of coming of age by coming to college is extremely important.

The ancient Romans also had an important coming-of-age ritual, at least for the young men. Among other things it involved putting on clothes that only adult males were allowed to wear. The ceremony involved a young man being given an adult toga by his father, or some father surrogate. The Latin word for clothes is the root of our word "vestments." The liturgical vestments that Dean Olson, Dean Young-Scaggs, and I are wearing in fact

---

1. Preached September 4, 2005, the sixteenth Sunday after Pentecost and the first Sunday of the academic year.

are ancient Roman costumes worn by government officials. We today have radically different clothes for our government officials, except for judges, and the Roman vestments linger on in church life rather than government because they have taken up a liturgical role within Christian history. Worship leaders in some Christian churches wear no special liturgical vestments. When I grew up in Missouri, most of the Methodist ministers wore black doctoral gowns to lead worship; few of them had PhD degrees, although liturgical custom said it was all right for ministers to dress like PhDs when leading worship. Our own vestments at Marsh Chapel reflect an older kind of Methodism with roots in Anglicanism and before that in medieval Christianity. I doubt that the leaders of Christian worship in the first three centuries wore robes like ours, because few if any were Roman senators. Only after Christianity became the official religion of the Roman Empire in the fourth century was it likely that worship leaders dressed like government officials.

I am not stressing the importance of liturgical vestments because I think there is one right way for liturgical leaders to dress, or even because I think liturgical vestments are important for anything except contributing to a consistent and symbolically rich, historically sensitive, service of worship. Rather, I stress the importance of vestments because of our text from Saint Paul, where he says to "put on the Lord Jesus Christ." What does he mean by "putting on the Lord Jesus Christ"? He means to vest oneself in the clothing of the Christian Way. Just as a Roman adolescent boy becomes a man by putting on the tunic signifying adulthood, Paul was saying, so would-be Christians should become Christians by putting on the Way of Jesus Christ.

One of the most famous conversions in Christian history was that of Saint Augustine in the fourth century, and I follow the interpretation of that conversion given by the theologian Carl Vaught. Augustine had been raised as a Christian by a pious mother, but had fallen away from her faith. As a young man he became a successful teacher of rhetoric and, hunting for a religion, tried out, first, the religion of the Manicheans and, then, the philosophical and religious practices of the Neoplatonists. More than religious experimentation, however, he fell into a life of partying and sexual excess. (I am not suggesting that he was like anyone you will meet here at Boston University, you understand!) Augustine was tempted back toward Christianity, although he could not bring himself to affirm it. He prayed, "Grant me chastity and continence, but not yet!" One day he was in a garden with a friend, in a terribly wrought-up state of mind about whether to convert to the Christian faith. He heard some children on the other side of the garden wall chanting a game rhyme that meant "take up and read, take up and read." So he took up a copy of the New Testament lying on the garden table and read our passage from Romans: "put on the Lord Jesus Christ, and make no provision for the flesh, to gratify its desires." Suddenly he knew what he had to do. He decided then and there to put off his way of life, which Saint Paul called the way of the flesh, and to put on the Christian life. He put off the licentious way of life in which he had vested himself and put on the vestments of Christ's Way. He had not solved all of his theological problems. He did not know yet the full implications of giving up the life he had been leading to take on the Christian life. Nevertheless, he put on the Lord Jesus' Christ's Way of life from that day forward and became one of the most important Christian leaders and thinkers ever.

What is the Christian Way summed up in the phrase "the Lord Jesus Christ"? We know from the Gospels that it does not necessarily have to do with giving up partying, sex, or riches, since Jesus was positive about all those things. Augustine had to give up those things because they were holding him in bondage so that, because of them, he could not put on the Lord Jesus Christ. In our text from Paul, the Christian way is beautifully described:

> Owe no one anything, except to love one another; for the one who loves another has fulfilled the law. The commandments, "You shall not commit adultery; You shall not murder; You shall not steal; You shall not covet"; and any other commandment, are summed up in this word, "Love your neighbor as yourself." Love does no wrong to a neighbor; therefore, love is the fulfilling of the law.

That was Paul writing to the Romans. But possibly you noticed that he was quoting and glossing sayings of Jesus.

The big question for us is, how do we learn to love like that? It is one thing to say that we belong to a religion of love, and there are several such religions. It is quite another thing to put on the vestments of that religion so that we become lovers, as God is a lover. Of course, I don't mean that you have to put on religious clothing, dressing like a Roman senator or a person with a PhD. Some Christians, like some Buddhists, do wear special clothes to indicate their invested religious identity. The true vestments of Christianity, however, have a lot to do with whom you associate with in your work and leisure. Augustine immediately told his friend Alypius, who was in the garden with him, about his conversion and Alypius too converted and they began to help one another. So it will help you to cultivate Christian friends. It will help to join Christian groups. You are welcome in any of the groups we have at Marsh Chapel. It will help to read the Bible and theology, and to talk with serious friends about the meaning of the Christian life. It will help to develop habits of prayer and meditation. It will help to come to regular worship and meet people who are at very different stages in their practice of the Christian Way of love. For many people here, the true Christian vestments are brand new; for others they are nicely worn and comfortable. The Christian life is not basically about beliefs or even virtues. The Christian life is about putting on a pattern of behavior associated with Jesus Christ that leads to the cultivation of the way of love as Jesus taught and practiced.

So I invite you to invest yourselves this morning in the Way of the Lord Jesus Christ. Even the financial meaning of the word "investment" derives from "putting on" the fortunes of the company in which you invest: the future of that company is your financial future when you give it your money. For you to invest yourselves in the Way of Jesus Christ, however, is not to have a balanced portfolio. I presume all of you students will try on the vestments of different religions. Everyone who reads the Daodejing becomes a Daoist for at least as long as it takes to clean their room and drink some tea. You will make friends with people who are deeply invested in different religious traditions from your own, and you might for a while invest with them for the sake of friendship. All that is to the good! But sometime you will need to invest all your heart, soul, mind, and strength in some particular Way, such as the Way of the Lord Jesus Christ. That Way has many forms, and it might take years to find those forms that suit your own life, that lead you to greater love. I admit that some forms of Christianity for some people lead them to lives of resentment, small-mindedness, and hate. But I urge you to invest in that Christian Way that leads to life and love.

The central ritual of the Way of the Lord Jesus Christ is the communion or Eucharist that we are about to celebrate. I invite you to put on the Lord Jesus Christ by coming to his table. No membership requirements exist for you to put on Jesus Christ at this table, for Jesus did not eat only with his disciples. No virtue requirements exist for you to put on Jesus Christ at this table, for Jesus ate with sinners as well as saints. No constancy or commitment requirements exist for you to put on Christ at this table, for Jesus never insisted that people come back. If you are here just because of custom, not commitment, come put on Jesus Christ and see whether things get serious. If you are curious about Christianity and its theology, come to this table to put on its intellectual Way for a while. If you are filled with doubts and rebellion, come put on Jesus Christ and see how doubts are contained within the Christian Way. If you already have put on Jesus Christ, come to his table to celebrate with his people. If you want to become better at the Christian Way, come to his table and put on Christ's nourishment. If you are an outsider, come to the table and put on the fellowship of Jesus Christ. If you feel unworthy and ashamed, guilty and filled with self-condemnation, come to this table and put on the Lord Jesus Christ in whom there is no condemnation, for this table has the food of life. If you do not know how to love as God loves, put on Jesus Christ at this table and you will begin to learn. At this time of ritual transformation, where going to college means putting on adult responsibility, I invite you to do this by investing in the Lord Jesus Christ, our Way, Truth, and Life. Amen

7

Tolerance and Forgiveness[1]

Exodus 14:11–31; Romans 14:1–12; Matthew 18:21–35

Nearly every commentator today proclaims that our world needs more tolerance and forgiveness, even when they disagree about whom to tolerate and whom to forgive. On this anniversary of 9/11/01, we should weep to see that tolerance and forgiveness are in far shorter supply now than before that date. The American response to the criminal terrorism of 9/11 was to lash out with a "war" on terrorism instead of an international police action and criminal prosecution. Finding no terrorists who wanted a stand-up war, we then attacked Afghanistan and Iraq, neither of which had attacked us, overthrowing their governments and driving their people into chaos and devastation. We lied to the world and to ourselves about those governments' connections with al-Qaeda and about our motives for invasion. Our government simply could not tolerate those governments which did not like us. Of course, on the other side the American wars fueled the intolerance and vengefulness of many Muslim people across the globe who identify with Afghanistan and Iraq, recruiting more terrorists than Osama bin Laden's advertisements ever could. Many non-Muslim nations around the world became intolerant and vengeful against the American way of life because of our response to 9/11. So the world is in a pitiful state, now, with regard to the kinds of tolerance and forgiveness necessary for a world harmony of civilizations.

1. Preached September 11, 2005, the seventeenth Sunday after Pentecost.

Saint Paul, in our lectionary text this morning, states the case for tolerance and the forgiveness that must accompany it. "Who are you," he wrote, "to pass judgment on servants of another?" The background of his comment on not passing judgment is that the Roman Christians were a mixed community of Jews and Gentiles, lower class and upper class. The Jews were worried about being kosher, and the lower-class people were somewhat superstitious about eating meat that had been slaughtered in sacrifice to idols. In the ancient Roman world most butcher shops were attached to temples—that's where you got meat, and nearly all meat had been sacrificed to some god or other. In Paul's sophisticated view, kosher laws were unnecessary and the idols were just statues. He regarded the Christians who wanted to be kosher or to abstain from meat they believed to have been sacrificed to real competing gods as simply weak in the faith of free Christians. But they were true Christians, he believed, and therefore should be welcomed. He called on both sides to tolerate the scruples of the other, saying each side is ultimately responsible to God, not to some principle.

Our text from Exodus does not seem to have much to say about tolerance; quite the contrary. It tells the familiar story of the Red Sea crossing at the beginning of the exodus of the Israelites from Egypt, and the story is very confused. You will remember that the Israelites had gone into Egypt about two centuries previously, where Joseph, son of Jacob, or Israel, had been a high official. The land of Canaan had been in a deep famine, and the Egyptians took the Israelites in as a massive welfare case. Over the years the Israelites multiplied and flourished, and the Egyptians felt they had to suppress them with forced labor. You know the story of the burning bush when God called Moses to go to Pharaoh to bring the Israelites out to freedom. Moses called down plagues and pestilences upon Egypt to persuade the pharaoh to let his people go. Yet in each instance, God hardened the heart of Pharaoh so that he said no. Yes, the Bible is clear that it was God who hardened Pharaoh's heart. The final devastating horror was that God went through the land killing all the firstborn of people and animals, passing over only the Israelite families who had slaughtered a lamb or kid and smeared the blood on their doorposts. While the Egyptians were awash in grief, the Israelites stole their valuables and made a dash for the border. When the pharaoh learned about that, he sent his chariots after the Israelites and our text tells what happened next. God led the people in the form of a pillar of cloud by day and of fire by night. When the Egyptians approached, God whipped around to the rear to defend the column of slow-moving Israelites. He instructed Moses to hold his hand and his staff over the Red Sea, which parted for the Israelites. The Egyptians in their chariots raced in after them, but their wheels clogged and then God sent back the sea and they were drowned. The Lord arranged all this, the text of Exodus says, so that he might gain "glory for myself over Pharaoh, his chariots, and his chariot drivers," in the eyes of both the Egyptians and Israelites. To our modern sensibilities this seems like somewhat adolescent behavior on God's part, hardening the Pharaoh's heart so that God can demonstrate his military glory. In ancient warrior cultures, however, of which Israel was one for a while, such glory-seeking was a virtue. (How conceptions of God reflect their cultures is the topic of another sermon!) Of course we do not know whether any of this is historical. No Egyptian records mention anything like the escape of the Israelites or the loss of an entire Egyptian army.

The arbitrariness of God in this story was recognized by the Jewish rabbis early on. They tell about a victory party in heaven the night after the Israelites escaped through the Red Sea. Since God had done the fighting for the Israelites, the heavenly host was celebrating the victory of their divine hero. But God was found weeping. "Why?" he was asked. "Although I rejoice for my children, the Israelites," God answered, "I sorrow for my children, the Egyptians."

In the rabbis' tale lies a fundamental principle for tolerance, namely, that the feelings of all sides need to be taken into account. Or to put the point more theologically, God is as close to any one people as God is to any other. All are children of God. Of course, to understand God's dealings with people in the form of a story, as the Exodus account is a story, is always to adopt the particular perspective of the story. The Exodus is a great model of freedom for Israel, but a model of ingratitude and thievery for the Egyptians and an utter disaster for the people of Canaan on whom the Israelites fell next. The stories of the Egyptians and Canaanites cast very different lights on Israel's story of itself.

Let's think about conflicting stories for a moment, as we try to understand Christian tolerance after 9/11. We Christians like to tell a story of ourselves as spreading a religion of love, peace, and justice through a world where those ways of relating to God and to one another are in short supply. Our story includes the Christianization of the Roman Empire, of Europe, of the Americas, and many parts of Asia and Africa. When Jews tell their story of Christianity, however, with two thousand years of Christian persecution, culminating in the Holocaust, the Christian self-image can be viewed only as outrageous hypocrisy.

A few weeks ago we witnessed the bitter grief of Jewish settlers being forced out of their homes in Gaza by their own army. For many of the settlers, that was like what happened to their European parents and grandparents under the anti-Semites. Yet, whatever you think about the justice of that forcible removal, we can hope that it will give the people of Israel deeper insight into the Palestinians' insistence on the right of return to their own homes from which they were forcibly removed when the modern State of Israel was founded. Will the Israelis come to understand that the Palestinians have a similar story?

Or consider the story we Americans tell of ourselves regarding the founding of our nation. Good, upstanding, educated colonists led a revolution to separate America from the British Empire, because the economic and political policies of the Empire denied the freedom of the Americans to develop our own economic and political interests. The Americans' scrappy little standing army, led by George Washington, could rarely win a stand-up battle against the vastly more powerful British war machine, with its trained mercenaries, supplied by the best navy in the world. So the war was fought mainly by colonial guerilla insurgencies that kept the British off guard, disrupted their supplies, and finally made the suppression of the insurgency too costly, especially when the French intervened to block the British navy and the support for the war diminished in Britain. We won that war, and when the British came back in 1812, we beat them again, pretty much the same way. Americans love the underdog, the resourceful people that get around the imperial economic machines and do not let more powerful people tell them what to do. That story is an essential component of our special sense of freedom and democracy. Now you know where I am going with this point. What people have a story like ours today? The Iraqi insurgents, of course. And we Americans are playing the role of the British Empire. Many dis-analogies exist between the American revolutionary situation and that of contemporary Iraq, and these should not be discounted. Nevertheless, the positive analogy of these stories is very strong.

Tolerance requires that we disengage ourselves from our own stories somewhat and see those stories from the standpoint of the others involved. The examples I have cited illustrate different ways in which national or religious stories relate. The stories of the Israelites, Egyptians, and Canaanites about the exodus illustrate how one event can play very different and morally conflicting roles in the separate stories of the participants. The views of the Christians and Jews about Christian history illustrate how different perspectives within a single story give rise to radically different interpretations. The stories of modern Jews and Palestinians about their being forcibly removed from their homes, and the violence this justifies as countermeasures, illustrate how similar stories with heroes and villains reversed can lead to irresolvable conflicts. Northern Ireland has this kind of conflict of stories. So does the recent history of Muslims and Hindus in Pakistan and India. The similarity between the American revolution and the Iraqi insurgency illustrates the irony when one story defining heroes and villains becomes the narrative framework of another situation with the heroes of the first becoming the villains of the second.

Now I submit that tolerance is impossible so long as any group identifies itself with its story, or interpretation of a larger story, without also being able to honor the alternatives. The real problem is that God's creation is too rich to be reduced to self-identity through narratives. We are tempted to solve the problem by enlarging the stories to be all inclusive. Where that is possible is all to the good. For instance, Christian self-understanding can be enlarged to acknowledge persecution of Jews, with appropriate repentance. We Americans can enlarge our current story to see how we have betrayed our founding story of freedom and respect for the underdog in our current policies. But sometimes mere enlargement of stories is not possible. Sometimes conflicts are real, and to maintain a close hold on our own story is to be committed to an intolerant narrative. A few weeks ago I preached against what theologians call the narrative understanding of Christianity, one based on a cosmic story of God fighting the forces of evil. That kind of narrative shrinks God into a finite, parochial player in a larger cosmic drama within which God might be the biggest and best but surely not the creator of the whole. Such a narrative is also a formula for hate, because it misleads people into hating those whom they believe God hates.

The Christian gospel instead builds on the rabbis' understanding of God's tears for the Egyptians. God is the creator of the whole cosmos, and all people are equally God's children. Fundamental Christian tolerance relates to other people through our and their relation to God, not directly through our conflicting stories. Paul was exactly right when he said, "We do not live to ourselves, and we do not die to ourselves." This is to say, we do not live and die as defined by our own stories. "If we live," said Paul, "we live to the Lord, and if we die, we die to the Lord; so then, whether we live or whether we die, we are the Lord's." The same thing is true of every other people, regardless of their being Jew or Gentile, Christian or any other religion, virtuous or disgustingly sinful. Our primal identity is our relation to God in our own context, and that relation to God includes relating to other people as also first related to God in their context, and only secondarily as interacting with us in our context. Our fundamental relation to other people should be to treat them as living and dying to God, whose children they are.

No moral relativism lurks here, because we all, ourselves and all those others, stand under judgment to God. But we cannot make any deep, ontological judgment on those others, as Jesus remarked in the Sermon on the Mount. That judgment belongs to God. Because of this, our fundamental attitude toward others needs to be tolerance. Our proximate moral judgments need to be made in terms of our best understanding that is informed by stories in part, by historical, sociological, psychological, and anthropological understanding, by the critical imagination of the arts, and by experience of practical life. Most of all, our proximate moral judgments need to be informed by the conviction at the heart of our faith that even our enemies are loved by God and should be loved by us even when we have to oppose them. This is the meaning of Christian tolerance. Because we sometimes do have to oppose people, tolerance requires forgiveness, our forgiveness of them, their forgiveness of us, and God's forgiveness of all. Paul said, "Why do you pass judgment on your brother or sister? Or you, why do you despise your brother or sister? For we will all stand before the judgment seat of God."

Amen.

8

The Arbitrariness of Grace[1]

Exodus 16:1–15; Philippians 1:21–30; Matthew 20:1–16

Ever since the feminist movement has called attention to unequal pay for equal work, we have become tender about the issue raised in Jesus's parable. The vineyard owner, who is a symbol of God, pays everyone the same for very unequal work. Is this fair? It seems not to be fair, and anyone here who has supervised employees knows how upsetting it is for people to go around complaining that they are not paid enough for what they do, relative to others. Should everyone be paid the same rate in proportion to the quantity and quality of the work they do? Should this be qualified by seniority? By extra tolerance and support for the inexperienced? Should those with special needs be paid more in the form of extra support so that they can do their jobs? Should affirmative action and equal opportunity considerations enter in? Should full-time employees committed to an enterprise be paid more than part-timers hired for piece-work? Should we have government subsidies of American workers when foreign workers can do the job more efficiently? The day-work workers in Jesus's parable are closest to migrant farm workers in our society. I'd love to know what Cesar Chavez, a devout Christian, thought about this parable of Jesus. In our society our moralists and legislators have thought long and hard about these complicated issues, and the rules that now govern employment in our society would have driven Jesus's landowner up the vineyard wall. Still, no

---

1. Preached September 18, 2005, the eighteenth Sunday after Pentecost.

one thinks we have yet sorted out all the moral dimensions of the economic issues of reward for work. The globalization of the economy and the degradation of the environment make all these issues new every day.

From the standpoint of first-century economics, the landowner had a good position. He contracted individually with the workers from early morning until the eleventh hour. No one was paid less than standard wages for a day's work. From that standpoint no one had a complaint. That he paid those who went to work later the same as everyone else might not seem fair to those who started at break of day, but the early birds themselves were not cheated out of anything they had bargained for. Technically they had no complaint.

The analogy with church life is painfully clear here. We all know Christians who have devoted themselves to the church from childhood, working hard on committees, donating some of their income to the church, and defining the social shape of their lives around church activities. I'm one of these people. We want to be rewarded for this. Some of you know how in various congregations a great deal of time is spent honoring the hard workers, the Sunday school teachers, the board members, those who cook the dinners, and all the rest. Of course it is good to express gratitude, but so many of us come to expect the gratitude because of the good works that we do. How off-balance we feel, then, when the agenda of the church turns out to be serving those who have not been faithful and devoted! The parable of the Lost Sheep is comforting for those who are lost and hope that God is looking for them. But to the ninety-nine sheep who are left to their own devices while the shepherd goes to look for the lost one, that parable is not welcome. Or think about the parable of the Prodigal Son in Luke 15: the older brother was deeply provoked when his younger brother was welcomed back with a feast of a fatted calf; the older brother had worked unstintingly for his father all his life, while the younger spent his inheritance frivolously, and yet the older brother had not been celebrated with a party with even a goat, let alone a prize calf. Don't we all identify at some level with the hardworking older brother, even though we know we shouldn't? Well, we know we shouldn't because the point of much of our work in the church is to help those prodigals, isn't it?

Still, it just isn't fair. It's time to acknowledge the far greater unfairness of life as such. Some people are born in America, which at its worst is still far better than being born in Dafur. Some people are born rich and others with nothing. Some have great parents, others horrible families or none at all. Some people are born smart and others slow. Some handsome, others repulsive. Some graceful, others disabled. Some have the DNA for long life, others for susceptibility to allergies, cancer, genetic diseases, and general frailty. Some people are born in happy times, others in times of violence and chaos where no happy life is possible. Some people are lucky in daily life and others are hit by crazy drivers, chance diseases, and the bad accidents of history. I could go on and on about the unfairness of life, if fairness means that we all have equal resources, opportunities, and inner nature. You all get the point. Life is unfair and we are thrown into arbitrary situations.

Our first response to realization of this arbitrariness ought to be quick and heavy outpourings of gratitude. Everyone here and in the listening audience of this broadcast is in a greatly favored situation relative to the majority of people on the earth. Even when our careers collapse, our child dies, or we grow diseased toward death, we know that there are millions in our own time who have no careers whatsoever, all of whose children starve early, and who live diseased for so short a time that they cannot contemplate the closing down of life as if it had a normal trajectory. It should humble us to know that, no matter how unfortunate or desperate we are, people less fortunate than we exist who still give God gratitude and glory for the very gift of life itself.

Our second response to the realization of arbitrariness should be to take stock of our conception of God. Although we are inclined to imagine God in the image of the best that we can imagine for human beings, which is to be fair and just with equal benefits for all, God is obviously not that. God's creation is arbitrary from beginning to end. The Big Bang did not expand equally but clumped into galaxies. The earth was hospitable to many life forms, but most have been extinguished. People have been born all over the earth, but some were favored by hospitable natural elements and high civilization, others not. Many of you have read Jared Diamond's *Guns, Germs, and Steel*, which shows how climatic and environmental conditions favor some societies and not others; the very differences in those conditions mean arbitrary differences in the lives of people across the globe. Despite the fact that we can affirm that God loves us all equally, we have to admit that God does not provide for us equally. In part, our God's glory consists in freedom to make a tilted world.

Jesus's point in the parable, however, was not really about economic justice. Nor was it about the arbitrariness of God's creation where some people come out on top and others at the bottom, although of course he did acknowledge that and said that in his kingdom the first will be last and the last first. Rather, Jesus's point was about the infinite fullness of God's grace. Like the vineyard owner, God can reward people far more than they deserve.

The fourth-century churchman Saint Chrysostom, wrote a wonderful sermon to be preached at the Easter Vigil on the Saturday before Easter morning. At that service, people are at the eleventh hour, a phrase he elaborated repeatedly, awaiting the celebration of the resurrection. Everyone is tense for the resurrection moment. In his day, and in ours at this service that we do in Marsh Chapel each year, we have lit the candles symbolizing the light of Christ against the darkness, listened to the Scriptures of the promises of God for salvation, and sung the hymns that incorporate the people into God's work. The catechumens have been examined, just then baptized, and accepted into the church, and we anticipate closing with the Eucharist by which we participate in Christ's death and resurrection. Then comes Chrysostom's sermon. If you began the Christian life in the infancy of your days, Hallelujah, welcome! If you came at 9 a.m., like the beginning of adulthood, Hallelujah, welcome! If you came at noon, in a midlife crisis, or in the afternoon, facing old age, Hallelujah, welcome! And if you come at the eleventh hour of the workday, when you really can't do much good at all any more, do not hold back. Come! Hallelujah! You are welcome! The grace of God is as full for you as for those who lived bathed within it since the dawn! For God's grace, the eleventh hour is as good as the first!

Now I suspect that Saint Chrysostom's sermon was as upsetting to the good folks of his own time, the acolytes, deacons, and proper established Christians, as it is to us. His was a doctrine of radical grace, grace that does not demand that it be deserved, but offers to transform those who do not deserve it and yet accept the grace. In our own time, when people feel so strongly the requirements of good behavior, this is a strange and strong gospel. We are never too late. Amen.

9

Face-to-Face with God[1]

Exodus 33:11–23; 1 Thessalonians 1:1–10; Matthew 22:11–22;
Luke 1:41–55

The Magnificat of Mary summons our attention to what it means to be face-to-face with God. Our primary text this morning is part of that remarkable story in Exodus of God coming to Moses on top of Mount Sinai to give him the covenant for Israel. One of the most remarkable contrasts in the story is, on the one hand, its extremely anthropomorphic depiction of God and, on the other, its declaration of the utter transcendence and transformative character of God.

The anthropomorphic elements are obvious. God and Moses have a conversation as if between two people. In an earlier passage that we read last week, God was depicted as flying into a fury because the Israelites had made the golden calf, and he was about to destroy them. Moses calmed him down and persuaded him to change his mind by saying that the Egyptians would laugh at God for going to the trouble of rescuing the Israelites from bondage in Egypt only to slaughter them in the desert. In our text for this morning, God, who is always audible, takes on visible form, first as a shimmering cloud of glory and then in the form of a rather large human who is still shimmery. When he passes by Moses, God puts his hand over Moses' face and lets him see only his backside. Now at this point in their history, the Israelites were polytheists. The overall point of our passage and

1. Preached October 16, 2005, the twenty-second Sunday after Pentecost.

the surrounding ones in Exodus is that this God was establishing a special relation with Israel, like that which other gods had with other nations. God promised to attach himself to the Israelite people in their march toward the promised land if they would be loyal to him as their god and not suck up to the gods of those other people. Of course, they did get involved with those other gods, and God was jealous. This is the anthropomorphic extreme of the biblical story.

On the other hand, God is the Holy One of Israel who transcends all human depictions. God told Moses that no one could see God's face and live. The symbols of God's descent to Mount Sinai in fire, smoke, 7.5-Richter-scale earthquakes, and sound that gets ever louder with no maximum, mean that no anthropomorphic ideas are ever adequate. After all, God is the creator of everything that has a determinate form. If anything is a thing, a "this" rather than "that," God is its creator. If God has a determinate nature, an image, this is the result of creation, not something we can know God to be prior to creation: God's creating determines God's nature as creator. Our best science says that the cosmos we know began in a Big Bang, and if that's so, then God created the conditions for the expanding universe with an intensity of energy we cannot imagine save through pallid mathematical formulas. The immensity of God's creation drives our imagination beyond any anthropomorphism.

To note but a few points: the Big Bang Blast began motion as such, and therefore time. Before motion, there was no time. Nothing existed before creation. There was no "before" creation. The initial Blast defined space and time as characters of the expansion of energy. The early expansion of cosmic gasses was chaotic and idiosyncratic. Those particular configurations that found reinforcement in their cosmic environment steadied down to have the regularities of natural law, and the others dissipated in nanoseconds. Billions of years later this "let there be light" cosmic Blast steadied into galaxies, solar systems, and the Earth, third planet out from Sol, on the edge of the little Milky Way Galaxy. Finally, human societies evolved.

Over the last three thousand years we have come to see that the simple anthropomorphism of Exodus opens on to a much more complex picture of God the Creator of space, time, and everything definite. The Holy, Mysterious, Transcendent character of God as Creator of everything that has form, turns all anthropomorphism into symbolic speech, not literal description.

So then what are we to make of the encounter with God face-to-face, if God has no face? I know of no more important spiritual question than this if you are interested in anything deeper than the social aspects of religion. Two answers define the Christian faith. The first is that we encounter the face of God in Jesus Christ. This was the answer given with the formation of Christianity in the first century when they already knew that God the Father transcends all imaginable description. Colossians says that Jesus Christ is the "image of the invisible God." And what an image he is! God the Almighty Creator fits into a humble man, not a proud king who imagines God must be like himself only better. God the Almighty Creator fits into a charismatic person who welcomes everyone, the rich, the poor, the virtuous, the villains, the smart, the slow, the brave, the cowardly, the loyal, and the betrayers. God the Almighty Creator fits into a lover who can be intimate with anyone, even sinners, even us.

Because Jesus is the face of God he is God's love that atones for our sins. Because Jesus is the face of God he is the Cosmic Christ who shows us how to be at home in the universe. Because Jesus is the face of God he is the revealer who brings us to God. Because Jesus is the face of God he is for us the Way to live before God, the Truth of what is important in human life before God, and the very Life in which we participate to find God's life abundant. Because Jesus is the face of God whom we can come to know as we meditate on the Scriptures, learn his teachings, and understand through his deeds and legacies, we can imagine him as our friend, our honest comrade in the peaks and valleys of life, our companion in daily life, our intimate beloved. The imagination is the Holy Spirit working in our subjective experience, and we can imaginatively come face-to-face with Jesus, and thus with God, as we focus our devotion on him. This part of the Christian tradition, this devotion to Jesus as the face of God, is not for everyone. But for those who enter into it, the devotion leads to an immense, profound, shattering, and healing love.

The second answer to how we can be face to face with God is more complicated, I fear. We should acknowledge, of course, the ancient point that no one can see God face-to-face and live. What this means, minimally, is that our old identity will be deconstructed. Nevertheless, in the Exodus passage assigned by the lectionary for next week, it is said that Moses did see God face-to-face and did live, forever changed. His skin glowed with such transfiguring light that he had to wear a veil when he was around people. How can we see God as Moses did, or even a little bit like Moses did? We need to learn God's name. In our anthropomorphic story, God recited his name for Moses, spoke it for him out loud. The belief in those days was that knowing someone's name gives you some magical control over them, and so God was allowing Moses to become intimate with him. God knows Moses's name too, the text says.

For us to know God's name is for us to have the ideas, the signs, the symbols, the concepts by which we can meditatively engage God in prayer. Meditative prayer is not the recitation of words, not the begging of petitions as we do in liturgy, or the voicing of praise. It is the opening of oneself to God's transcendent ultimate reality and the engagement of it. Without the capacity to discriminate colors, we cannot see colors. Without the capacity to identify and discriminate God, we cannot see God. With what symbols can we see God? The anthropomorphic symbols of God as a large finite being participating in a human drama do not take us far, because we know immediately that they are too small. More than those story-symbols, we need the clear ideas of a thoughtful theology. Perhaps you do not want me to say that you have to be a thoughtful theologian in order to pray in a way that takes you to God, but I'm afraid it's true. Theology provides ways to conceive the eternal and immense God as creating time and space and teaches the limitation of our symbols. But then we need to move on to live with the great symbols of the faith, God as Creator, Redeemer, Wild Spirit. We need to so live into these symbols so that we can see how this great creating God is present in the blast of the Big Bang, in the evolution of human life, in the glories of fall mornings and the horrors of earthquakes and typhoons. Then we need also to live into those even deeper symbols that break the best work of our imagination and push us out on the other side into God's infinite depth. We need to love God named as the Abyss of Nothingness, God the Primal Fire of Creation, God the Deep River on whom we must launch ourselves to get home. The mystics know the mortal force of these deepest symbols. They pull us from our moorings and tumble us into God so that our mortal lives are of no consequence. The Awesome, Beautiful, Terrible, Lovely, Beloved Depths of God call us to meet the Almighty Creator face-to-face. Since God's face is infinite, we die to any significance in the finite identity of our own face. We give ourselves without remainder to our Beloved.

Now I do not ask you to join me in growing into God. To live a life of justice and mercy is enough. To be a disciple of Jesus, carrying his ministry into our time and place is enough. To worship under the pretense that God is a big spiritual King who wants our praise and our confession, who deals out pardons and bestows blessings, who likes us to preach and sing about Him (or Her), who likes our offerings and sends us out to live in this glorious, difficult, and ambiguous world, is enough. This is the pattern of the Christian Way of life, and it is enough. But this is not to come to God face-to-face.

I welcome those of you who want also to come meet Jesus as the face of God. Stabilizing your life with justice and mercy, ministry and worship, come into a devotional journey in which you come to know Jesus personally. This is a dangerous journey, because to know Jesus close up you will have to discover and acknowledge unsavory things about yourself. To know Jesus is to expose yourself to such a penetrating, honest eye that you cannot hide. But you will accept yourself as loved by one who knows your worst and joins you in your best. If you come to know Jesus, you will become a true lover, the better lover the more Jesus lives in your heart as your best friend. Welcome if you want this journey with Jesus, the first, visible, face of God.

With trepidation I invite you to come farther and engage God in the depths of the divine mystery. This will require setting anthropomorphic religion at some distance by knowing it in its historical context. This farther journey will require thoughtful theology to develop sophisticated concepts and know their limitations. This journey becomes serious when you learn to live and pray through the great symbols of the faith. God is the glorious Creator, but in that creation God is also the Great Destroyer. God is the gracious Redeemer, but in that redemption is also the Terrifying Judge. God is the Holy Spirit by which the divine energy pervades absolutely every part of creation, but that Holy Spirit is wilder than the cosmic gasses and blows where it wills, not where we want. Those of you with the passion for it can learn to love this Creator and Destroyer, Redeemer and Judge, Bringer of Glory whose wildness knocks us about. It is hard, but you can do it. You have to learn to love your enemies first, which is the topic of next week's sermon. Nevertheless this further journey does not rest here. It moves on into the mystical depths and I invite you with my whole heart to come. Let those grand positive symbols of the faith lead you to the river's edge at which you can launch yourself over the infinite depths of God, leaving the known shore behind. Climb to the verge of your life's struggles and throw yourself into the Abyss of the Divine Mystery. Plunge into God's Holy Fire and let that raw creativity burn away the features of your finite face so that you can meet the Infinite face-to-face. This journey is not required. It is not for everyone. But it leads to the bliss God offers. Is ordinary life, then, like living behind a veil? No, it is like living in divine clarity and love for the world. Amen.

10

The Great Commandment[1]

Deuteronomy 34:1–12; 1 Thessalonians 2:1–8;
Matthew 22:31–46

During the last week of his life, Jesus entered into Jerusalem on Palm Sunday, spent the subsequent nights in Bethany, probably at the home of Lazarus, Mary, and Martha, and taught in the temple on Monday, Tuesday, Wednesday, and part of Thursday. He was arrested Thursday evening after dinner and crucified the next day. He knew he was walking into danger when he came to Jerusalem in the first place.

Our gospel today takes place on Monday or Tuesday of that week, when the Pharisees, Sadducees, and members of the royal house were trying to trick him into saying something religiously heretical or politically rebellious against the Roman occupying authority. The Pharisees sent a lawyer to ask him, Which is the greatest of the commandments? The trick in the question is that all the commandments are binding, and any one that Jesus would choose as greatest could be challenged on behalf of the others. Jesus answered with none of the Ten Commandments. Rather, he misquoted Deuteronomy 6:5, which said, "You shall love the Lord your God with all your heart, and with all your soul, and with all your might." According to Matthew, Jesus said heart, soul, and mind, rather than might. The parallel passages in Mark and Luke fix up Jesus's misquotation by having him say to

---

1. Preached October 23, 2005, the twenty-third Sunday after Pentecost.

love God with all your heart, soul, mind *and* strength, or might. The point is, the greatest commandment is to love God with everything you've got.

Without stopping Jesus went on to say, "This is the greatest and first commandment. And a second is like it: 'You shall love your neighbor as yourself.'" On these two commandments hang all the law and the prophets." The phrase "You shall love your neighbor as yourself" comes from Leviticus 19, which is in the middle of what scholars call the Holiness Code, designed to give a special ethic to the Israelites to distinguish them from their neighbors. Generally, the Holiness Code is a bunch of "you shall nots." "Thou shalt nots."

The astonishing thing about Jesus's answer was that it transformed the whole issue of commandments, which usually had meant negative prohibitions that articulated the special covenant Israel had with God, to the positive commandment to love, first God and then neighbor. Of course, love was not alien to his Jewish heritage—Jesus after all was quoting the Hebrew Bible. But the transformation of the meaning of commandment from prohibition to the positive skill and habit of loving is extraordinary.

Was Jesus going too far? It is always possible, if difficult, to avoid doing prohibited things. But how can we be commanded to love? How can we command our hearts? Jesus's commandments about love were radical and rigorous. Christians are supposed to have been living under the commandments to love from the beginning, but our history has been just as filled with holy wars as that of the Muslims who now preach jihad or the ancient Israelites who tried to exterminate the residents of Canaan in order to possess that land. In historical fact, ours is a religion of violence as much as a religion of love. Was Jesus just unrealistic?

No, Jesus knew that the commandment to love God wholly, with everything we have, and with no reserve, was the first and greatest commandment. Jews would not disagree. But Jesus also believed that such love of God is impossible without the radical love of neighbor. Not only is love of neighbor *like* the love of God, it is a condition for loving God. If you cannot love your neighbor, then you cannot love God.

Part of what Jesus had in mind was hypocrisy. We say we love God but we treat God's children unjustly. We leave them in poverty, exploit them, make war on them, behave arrogantly toward them, demean them, and despise them. This was Jesus's criticism of the religious leaders during his last week, when he said that they called people to follow the law, including loving God, but themselves were selfish, lying hypocrites. So are we all when we profess love of God but tolerate injustice, poverty, exploitation, war, arrogance, cruelty, or hatred. We are hypocrites if we think or say we love God but do not love our neighbors.

Jesus's position has a deeper reason, however. God, you see, is unlovable by most standards. To love those who are good to us is easy. That is why loving friends is so much easier than loving enemies. In the case of God, our initial impulse to love God is usually premised on the understanding that God is good and worthy of our love, especially good to us, if not others. So much of our theology pumps up the belief that God is really good to us and that the bad things that happen are our fault. We can be grateful and loving to the God who gives us health and wealth, great weather and a flourishing economy, great talents and a job market just waiting for them. Who could fail to be grateful and loving for all that? Much of our popular religion imagines God as an immense spiritual moral agent who, by nature, does only good, and who rewards people who are good and punishes those who are bad.

Yet we all know that this is vain fiction. However healthy we are at some point, we all sicken and die. Blue skies are fine, but hurricanes, tsunamis, and earthquakes devastate our lives. A few are rich, but most people in the world are dirt poor and live in degraded, oppressed, exploitative conditions. Some of us are talented, but most of us are not and some of us are just klutzes. The market rarely wants what we have in our hearts to offer. If we are to be faithful to the fundamental doctrine of creation, then God creates the disasters as well as the delights. This is a terrible truth, one which religious people go to great lengths to deny. Consider three dodges.

First, some people say that there is a countergod, a devil or Satan. Whereas God is responsible for the good, Satan is responsible for the evil, they posit. Often these people see the world as a battleground between the forces of good and evil, a view that too easily leads them to see their battles as God's battles and assume divine sanction for them. Many conservative Christians and Muslims think this way, though oppositely in terms of their sides. But if Satan is equal to God, then God is not the creator; if Satan is subordinate to God, then God is Satan's creator and is responsible for Satan's evil. To say, as many do, that God allows Satan to cause vast evil and suffering so that he can beat Satan up in the end, is to attribute to God a morbidly adolescent and vicious character. This theological dodge fails.

Second, some people say that God is not the omnipotent creator but is only a finite good spirit, perhaps surpassing all others but still impotent to prevent evil and ensure that only good things to happen. God is doing the divine best, but that is insufficient to conquer evil. This is the position of most personalists and process theologians. Aside from abandoning the fundamental affirmation that God is creator of the whole world, this advocacy of the finite, benign, struggling, but weak God leads to unbelief. Why believe in such a God at all? That theology does not explain why or how there exists the cosmos, nor does it provide ideals that do not come from human experience itself. This theological dodge also fails.

Third, some people say that God really is good and in charge, and we merely do not see it. They say that when people suffer, they somehow deserve to suffer, however innocent they seem. And when the evil people flourish in this life, and the good do not, all this will be reversed in heaven. After the Holocaust, however, or the recent Pakistan earthquake, or the devastations of Katrina, or the tsunami, or the Rwandan massacres, or the Armenian genocide, or the medieval Black Death, or Noah's flood that killed all those animals and innocent children, who can believe this dodge? The proportion of injustice and suffering in this world simply defies any balancing act of moral deserts or rectifying pie-in-the-sky by-and-by. After the twentieth century, no one can believe that a morally good God is really in charge of history.

The tough point is, the glorious God who creates also destroys. The God who gives us life, gives us a life with pain and suffering as well as joys. The God who creates a world with moral standards that are recognized in every civilization does not behave like a moral agent within that world. While we are filled with gratitude for some things, if we conceive of God to be a moral agent, we must also be filled with hate for the cosmic violence of creation. It is hard, hard, hard for us to love that God.

Love of neighbors is therefore training for love of God. Some of our neighbors are good and friendly folks, building up our community and helping us in our particular projects. But a lot of them are indifferent, incompetent, unproductive, dependent, or hostile. Some are even competently organized to oppose us. Some are hell-bent on wreaking evil where they can. A great many people are conditioned by cultures that make them burdens on the larger society to which they are hostile anyway. How can we love such people, especially those who are effective and powerful enemies? Jesus has a way. It is difficult and is likely to endure crucifixions of many sorts. But he has a way. The Gospel of John does not tell of Jesus quoting the Great Commandment, but it is about love all the way through. In the conversation after the Last Supper, Jesus tells his disciples, who generally are a bunch of losers as they are about to prove in the next twenty-four hours, that he has taught them to love one another by loving them himself. And, because of this, God loves them and they are able to love God. The way to treat enemies, Jesus taught, is to love them so that they become lovers too. That is what love really means—to turn the beloved into a better lover. If we can learn to love our enemies, then we have a chance to be honest about God and still love God.

If we are to love God with all our heart, soul, mind, and strength, then we need to get beyond the cheap love of God for material benefits and also the corresponding hatred of God for material pain. We need to accept the mixed life God gives us, with both beauties beyond compare and suffering beyond merit. The loveliness of God, like the loveliness so hard to see in our enemies, consists in the glorious freedom of creation. Whereas we human beings, enemies included, create within very circumscribed limiting conditions, God creates with no limiting conditions. God is the source of the vast, wild cosmos, of the evolution of the earth as our fragile habitat, of the burgeoning of species and human communities that fight one another for living space, of our biology and social bonds that make civilized life possible, but also require decay and death, competition and contention, spite, revenge, and hatred. Jesus' contribution was to show a way to accept all these conditions of life while living so as to turn away hatred, revenge, and spite, to work through contention to friendship, to turn competition to cooperation, to rejoice that life trumps death, and to accept decay as the work of the Holy Spirit on the way to new things. While life is never to be unfragmented and unambiguous, it need not be alienated from its Creator.

So I invite you to bind yourself to the two commandments, so like one another, to love unlovely neighbors and to love unlovely God. In both cases, what begins as unlovely turns to glorious beauty and loveliness. Though we glimpse God as Creator and Destroyer, Redeemer and Judge, Wild Spirit of construction and destruction, we are lured to rapture by the deeper glimpse of God as the fiery abyss of creation out of which we come to be together with the vast cosmos and on whose energy we take life. God is the deepest part of our soul, connecting us in creation with every other creature at the deepest level, friends and enemies alike. Our own creative love, like that of our neighbors, is a spark of God's creative fire. Even to know this about ourselves already is to love the God loving us into being. Amen

11

Hypocrisy and Humility[1]

Joshua 3:1–17; 1 Thessalonians 2:1–13; Matthew 23:1–12

Our gospel today is one of the classic statements of Jesus's twin attacks on hypocrisy, which undermines truthfulness before God, and arrogance, which abhors the divine trait of humility. The passage begins with a scurrilous condemnation of his religious leaders, who "sit on Moses's seat." They do give proper instruction in the law, Jesus said, and therefore are to be heeded in that. But they themselves "do not practice what they teach." They delight in placing the burdens of the law on others, but do not follow the law themselves. Moreover, they are arrogant in their posturing and demands to be shown honor and respect. The passage ends with a broadside typical of Jesus as cited throughout Matthew, Mark, and Luke: "The greatest among you will be your servant. All who exalt themselves will be humbled, and all who humble themselves will be exalted." Weighed on the true scale of things, the first will be last and the last first, as he so often said.

We live in a time when hypocrisy and arrogance in our national public life have reached astonishing proportions. Representing themselves as religiously righteous in the promotion of open democracy, our leaders mislead us about reasons for war, about global warming, about threats to the environment, and about political advertisement disguised as news. They intimidate the people who would speak the truth, expose their secret agents for revenge, and may well believe their own lies. Their arrogance

---

1. Preached October 30, 2005, the twenty-fourth Sunday after Pentecost.

Hypocrisy and Humility

in withdrawing from international treaties, in opposing a world court that would hold the United States to the same standards as applied to other countries, and in invading other countries for no justifying reason have made our national character that of a bully. Probably all leaders are tempted to hypocrisy and arrogance, and most succumb to some degree. But the scale of these vices among many of our governmental and religious leaders has transformed the moral fabric of our society. Hypocrisy and arrogance are alive and well in our public life, while truth and humility are in short supply.

My concern this morning is with our spiritual lives, however, not with public life. Some of you have heard me speak before about five special virtues for Christians, not that other religions do not also prize them. They are righteousness, piety, faith, hope, and love. Righteousness is the virtue of discerning and pursuing just ways of ordering our lives, especially our lives together. Piety is the virtue of deferring to the intrinsic worth and dignity of each part of God's creation, considered in itself. Faith is the virtue of courage in embracing the particular circumstances of our world and living within those circumstances with righteousness, piety, hope, and love. Hope is the virtue of intending to give an ultimate account of ourselves no matter what obstacles and failures come our way. Love is the virtue that combines all the others with a creativity that magnifies the value of those loved with righteousness, piety, faith, and hope. Love that lacks righteousness, piety, faith, and hope is deficient.

Now hypocrisy and arrogance are vices that particularly corrupt faith, although they are not good for any of the other virtues either. Faith is important because so many aspects of life are difficult and filled with suffering. On the personal level, our fortunes are always mixed. Our families are wonderful, and also venues of conflict and destruction. Our careers are sometimes exciting, but also sometimes frustrating, occasionally devastating. Our communities can be places of growth and enjoyment, but also places of violence and terror. Our health is sometimes good and we can enjoy the vital surges of nature, but even the healthiest of us will die, usually after illness. When things get tough in our personal lives, we are tempted to live in denial, to pretend to be something we are not, and in a situation different from the true case.

On the social level, the mixture of good and evil is even more complex. Despite the tenuousness of the stock market and the madness of the taxless/spend-more government that makes tax-and-spend liberals look like fiscal conservatives, our economy is healthy and vital compared with places such as Afghanistan or the Sudan. Yet the health of our economy is based on measures that make other economies less competitive, and it rewards the rich far more than it does the poor. How can we live with the exploitation of other economies and the poverty in our own land, without being in denial? We have a pluralistic, vigorous, society, filled with opportunity and embracing cultural groups that have immigrated from all over the world. For all the current hostility to America as a hypocritical bully, to come to make a life in this country remains the dream of many people in nearly every other society. Yet without being in denial, how can we remember that our immigrants from the beginning dispossessed and nearly exterminated the Native Americans, and that many of them enslaved the Africans who were brought here in chains whose descendents still bear a disproportionately large burden of our poverty, ill-education, and cultural self-hate? It takes great courage, great faith, to acknowledge the underside of our great flourishing democracy and address those issues with righteousness, piety, hope, and love.

Hypocrisy is the great instrument of existential denial. Hypocrisy lets us say that we are engaged with our world while in fact we are in full flight. Jesus thought at least some of the religious leaders of his time talked a good line about faithfulness to the covenant and yet were in egregious contradiction to it. Leaders in our time tout democracy yet impose governments on others with the barrels of guns, lie, conceal, and distort the truth necessary to democracy, and blatantly hand over increasing power to the wealthy at the expense of everyone else. That is hypocrisy, and the truth is something else. This hypocrisy masks the fact that so many of our policies are in full flight from fostering real democracy, helping the poor, and representing people honestly. The reality of the situation is that we are making enemies and strengthening them, we are selling out the future of our economy to short-term gain for those in power, and we are ruining trust in the institutions we should be able to count on for honesty. So much of our religion is escape to dime-novel fictions.

How many of us in our own lives spin little stories about ourselves that hide from us the true realities we need to face? Most of us have little conversations on mental tapes that we run through our minds throughout the day, conversations that tell us what our identity is, what people think about us, what our skills are, and what our situation is. These conversations cannot be entirely false, or we would be run down crossing the street. But

Hypocrisy and Humility

they often are largely false, or highly skewed, to keep us from facing the truth about ourselves and our situation. Some people are clearly pathological liars to themselves. Some other people are very realistic indeed, with little fiction in their sense of ego. Most of us are in the middle, however, using these fictional inner stories to let us live in denial about crucial aspects of our lives.

The first horrible thing about such hypocrisy in our inner stories is that we deceive ourselves by them. Other people can see through our hypocrisy rather easily. Or should I say, we can see through other people's hypocrisy. But we are blind to it in ourselves. Try as we might, we cannot live honestly. We fool ourselves into thinking that we are honest. Sometimes a good friend can call us to account, but denial is stubborn. Usually it takes some kind of ontological shock, some brutal encounter with the tough side of the divine to shake us out of our ego-driven hypocritical denial.

The second horrible thing about this kind of hypocrisy is that, although we fool ourselves, we have a bad conscience about that. At some deep level we know we are believing our own lies. And in reaction we become arrogant. Arrogance is a kind of deep whistling in the dark that attempts to reassert the lies we live by and force others to acknowledge them. Arrogance is the drive to bend others to our will and force them to acknowledge the virtue we claim for ourselves because we secretly fear that they see through us. We behave arrogantly to call attention away from what we are denying about ourselves and our situation. Of course, that is a self-defeating strategy. People see through our arrogance more easily than they do through our hypocrisy.

Jesus was quite direct in saying that hypocrisy and arrogance are easy to name, and once named they become self-defeating. The hypocrites who have the arrogance of power will be brought down, and the humble will be exalted. The true power of humility, you see, is its honesty. Humble people do not have to tell stories to others or themselves. They simply accept themselves with all their weakness. They look clearly at their situation with all its fragmentation, suffering, and bad luck. They know they can do what they can do, and that's that. Humble people are not only the opposite of the arrogant, they have no need for hypocrisy. Humble people engage their lives fully and realistically, while arrogant hypocrites live in a dream-world.

How, then, can we be humble? It is not easy to turn off the mental tapes that tell us our hypocritical stories. The truth is too terrifying. In order to be humble, we need faith. Faith is the courage to engage our world without hypocrisy and arrogance. Faith is not an easy virtue to cultivate. It does not mean simple belief, because our religious beliefs are so often among the most hypocritical elements of the stories we tell ourselves. Yet faith does mean believing in our encounters with the divine that shock us out of our hypocrisy. Jesus, the man who was humble to death, is an astonishing shock when we think of what he did. On the cross, he gave up his last illusion, that God was going to rescue him with angels, and still commended his soul to God. What greater faith could one have?

Faith is not just adopting a belief that is honest, it is also the putting on of the way of life that goes with radical honesty before God. Faith is establishing the habits of being faithful to honesty. Faith is organizing one's life with steady courage that does not flinch in crises or become distracted in ordinary life. Faith is clinging to the realities of our world because this is the world God has given us. Faith is being truthful before God. Faithless life is living a lie before God.

Halloween celebrates the dead in grotesque ways—skeletons, monsters, and witches, of course dandified for children. Among the dead are both hypocrites and humble people. Halloween is a carnival that overturns the usual order in which the hypocrites with arrogant power run things and the humble, honest people are beaten down. In death, as celebrated by this Holyday, things are turned upside down. The hypocrites are seen for what they are—foolish bones, ghosts of unlived lives. The humble too are seen for what they are—saints who live in harmony with the world in which they were created, and thus in harmony with God. Hypocrisy and arrogance give us half-lives. Faith gives us whole lives to engage the world.

Jesus loved the humble, who live with and in the truth. Thanks be to God, Jesus also loved the hypocrites and bullies, and wooed them with his winsome honesty and humility. The divine transparency of his honesty could be ours if we give up our hypocrisy. The world-redeeming strength of his humility could be ours if we give up our arrogance. I invite you to the faith that accepts God's love for us, in which love we can live in truth without the pathetic self-defense of hypocrisy and arrogance. I invite you to the exalted status of the humble. Take the hand of Jesus. Amen.

12

Wakefulness and Different Talents[1]

Judges 4:1–7; 1 Thessalonians 5:1–11; Matthew 25:11–30

Our text from 1 Thessalonians warns about the unpredictability of the time of judgment—anytime, like a thief in the night. But for what shall we be judged? Jesus's parable of the Talents in Matthew gives a disturbing answer. For it seems to rest upon an unjust premise.

The slaveholder is going on a journey and entrusts at least part of his estate to three slaves. To one slave he gives five talents. A talent was a unit of money that in those days equaled about fifteen years of wages for an ordinary laborer. If you figure a minimum hourly wage of about $6, times forty hours a week (of course they worked much more than forty hours then), times fifty weeks (of course laborers didn't get two-week vacations then), times fifteen years, five talents was worth about $180,000. If you figure a fifty-hour week and a fifty-two-week working year, the sum of five talents is about $234,000. Either way, that is a hefty sum of money for a responsible slave to invest. Two talents, which went to the second slave, was worth about $93,600, and one talent for the third slave amounted to about $46,800. Being a one-talent fellow myself, I would be glad for a $46,800 sum to invest and prove my worth.

The rub in the parable, however, is its allegorical meaning. The slaveholder is God, and the slaves are people like us. God gives some of us a five-talent endowment, some two talents, and some just one. Then God

---

1. Preached November 13, 2005, the twenty-sixth Sunday after Pentecost.

goes off and lets us lead our lives according to the resources of our talent endowment. At the end God returns for an accounting. Those of us who started off supertalented—you see how I am playing with the happy ambiguity of that word—end up with the richest life. Those moderately rich in talents end up doubling their moderate riches. The one-talent people seem to be so fearful of losing what little they have that they hide it and in the end, when God comes, even that is taken away.

Isn't it fundamentally unjust that some few of us are born really rich, with welcoming, supportive, and challenging families, with easy access to the best schools and universities, and all the connections to get good jobs and earn respect and worth for a life well-lived? Of course, some of the best endowed people are screw-ups, but that was not the point of Jesus's parable. Compared with the really rich are those two-talent people, like most of us, who are moderately endowed and who need to work through somewhat ambivalent families, go to second-tier schools and universities, and work really hard to rise through careers the hard way. Although life is not a breeze for us, we can still make significant contributions and enjoy rewards twice that of our parents. Then there are those of us whom life has dealt a bum hand, with seriously broken and dysfunctional families, lousy schools and no home support for education, a future of marginal employment, ill health, and vicious neighborhood connections bound to drag us down. Of course, people from the worst of circumstances can rise heroically to great things, but that does require heroism compared with the superrich, who can pretty much coast to a decent and abundant life. Is it not unfair that anyone should be born with the one-talent burden? Is it not unfair that some people start off with all the advantages? How could Jesus have spoken so approvingly of the unfair distribution of the world's resources? Then, to make matters utterly intolerable to fair people, he said that to those to whom much is given, even more will be given, and to those to whom little is given, even that little will be taken away. What happened to Jesus's support for the little guy, the loser who is supposed to come out on top?

In Jesus's defense, I have to point out his realism. He knew that life simply is not fair in terms of the originating conditions of our lives. Some people are born in prosperous and peaceful countries, and others in wretchedly poor and war-torn nations. Some people are born in historical periods of peace and creativity, and others in times of violence and social collapse. Some are born rich and others poor. Jesus acknowledged slavery as a condition of his society and did not complain about it. He pointed out that God

Wakefulness and Different Talents

sent the sun and the rain on the just and unjust alike. Nature and history are not fair. This does not mean we should not try to make them as fair as possible: we should. But that is because of our obligation always to do the best, not because our moral life aims to stay true to the originating conditions of our lives. Most often we need to alter the originating conditions of our lives.

Some people like to think of God as a really big spiritual moral agent. The unfairness of life is a serious problem for these folks, because such a divine moral agent should be held responsible for creating an unfair world. Sometimes believers who treat God as a finite moral agent try to exonerate God by saying that the victims of life's unfairnesses must deserve it somehow. When Israel was smashed by the Assyrians and Judah by the Babylonians, some of the prophets tried to argue that this was their punishment for being unfaithful to the covenant with Yahweh. But too many innocent people in Israel and Judah were devastated for that to be a fair punishment. No matter how sinful European Jews might have been, to say they deserved the Holocaust is outrageous. The fishermen and vacationers killed by the tsunami did not deserve that. The innocent people of New Orleans did not deserve Katrina. The fault of all this blaming-reasoning lies in the conception of God in the first place. God is the creator of the distinctions between good and evil, not an agent morally bound within the system of good and evil as we are. This theological point is important to bear in mind when attempting to understand Jesus's parables.

Jesus was not at all concerned to judge the man who owned the slaves who loved investing. He didn't even point out that investing for the sake of gain was condemned as usury by Jewish law. Rather Jesus was concerned with how the three slaves responded to the conditions and responsibilities placed upon them. That is, he was concerned with how we react to the conditions of life given us, however unfair they might be. It's what we do with what we are given that counts in life, not what we are given in the first place.

This parable is about what counts in what we do with the hand we are dealt. The two slaves who were approved by their master used what they were given to create more. They risked what they had in the adventure to double the master's money. Of course, they might have failed, and knowing their master's reputation as a harsh man, they knew the risk they took. But apparently it did not occur to them to fall back on the third slave's strategy. The strategy of the loser was to guard against losing. Fearing loss, the loser-slave buried the money and returned it safe but unused. The master was furious and took away what little the loser had. The point is, the loser was given a life. But he did not live it. He buried it. And when his life came to an end, it was as if he had not lived at all.

Now you have heard many sermons about the pitfalls of spiritual death, and the need for spiritual resurrection. Sin kills you spiritually, and Jesus's atoning love revives the soul. Well, good enough! Jesus here points out something far more serious: the failure to take up spiritual life in the first place. It wasn't that the loser was wicked. On the contrary, he was trying extra hard to be good and safeguard the property placed in his care. His problem was that he had never accepted the life given him in the first place as his to live. He did not see that he had a contribution to make, and that burying his talents was to avoid making that contribution. Perhaps this way of putting the point is too utilitarian. Instead let me say that he did not see that he had a life that needed living; he saw only a loss to avoid. So out of fear of loss he never came alive.

When we think of ourselves in this regard, we quickly come up with many excuses for the loser. The very poor have so little they cannot be expected to do anything but hunker down. The oppressed have so little hope they can't be expected to leave their bunkers. The person beaten down by a long string of bad luck cannot be faulted for hiding from life. The clumsy person who is embarrassed in most social contexts must be excused for fleeing interactions. Those who have little should not be expected to risk what they have when unjust social structures are responsible for the meagerness of their life. The victims of injustice cannot be expected to stand up for themselves. The unfairness of life means that the losers are entitled to demand that the two-talent and five-talent people take care of them. You know what Jesus would say to all this: Sheepdip! The only way to live your life is to live it yourself.

Of course, the well-off do have a responsibility to care for the poor and to correct injustice. That is part of their lives. To evade that responsibility is a failure on their part—on our part—to take up life. To take up that responsibility is the vigorous living of our lives. The life of real responsibility is not the exclusive preserve of the rich and middle-class, however. That is just another way of saying that the losers do not have to come to life. But if the losers do not come to life, Jesus said, they lose even what little they have.

The parable's real point is not about poverty in the economic sense or injustice in the social sense. The real point is about spiritual loss. Even superrich people might never awaken to the need to live life in creative risk. The social benefits of five-talent people might in fact provide such a simulacrum of life that they never awaken to the need to double the talents they are given. As God creates the world, so we are all called to a life of creativity. But it is possible to go a long way in life without waking to that fact. St. Paul in our Thessalonians passage calls us to be awake, to emerge from the dark to live in the light of the great expectations put upon us. The spiritual message here is not a repair job for something broken. It is a call to waken to something defining life that has been there all along but that we had not noticed. If we are not wakefully creating our life as a finite version of the way God creates the world, then we are denying the divinity that lies within us and defines us.

So I invite you to invest your life and make it grow. Do not let yourself be defined by the originating conditions of your life and their inertial consequences. If you live in some unfair quadrant of life, do not accept failure as defined by that quadrant's unfairness but go in a different direction. If you are a student in fear of failing, do not neglect to study but aim also learn more than is required. If you are a faculty member seeking professional recognition, do not accept the profession's standards but redefine them by your own project. If you are in business seeking greater wealth, work hard but think outside the box about how to achieve wealth. If you think wealth is all that matters, invest your resources but reevaluate what counts as wealth—it's not just money. Being truly alive is about the risk and adventure attendant upon creativity. All creativity is God working within us. To seize the creative life is to embrace the divinity that gives us life in the first place. There is no losing in the life of creative risk. It is God all the way down and all the way up. That this might lead to failure in the ways the world measures success is an old story. The divine judgment on worldly measures is that the first will be last and the last first. The divine measure says that the only losers are those who refuse to live the life they are given. I beseech you to invest in life. Amen.

13

The Day of the Lord[1]

Isaiah 40:1–11; 2 Peter 3:1–15a; Mark 1:1–8

What a treat it is to be back with you after missing two Sundays in a row! You should know that worshiping with you on Sunday mornings is the highlight of my spiritual life. I usually get here around 7:30, weather permitting, and go up to the balcony to pray until my presence is too inhibiting to the people who need to set out the music and paraments. Then I go work through my sermon one more time and study the order of service. By 9:30 I'm ready for my Sunday Morning Theology class, which takes place while the choir rehearses, and we begin here at 11. For me the service builds up to the postlude, to which I listen from the back of the center aisle while waiting to greet you all after worship, nervous that we get out in time for the Catholics to set up for their 12:30 service. For all the regularity of my Sunday morning routine, however, there is an edginess to it, a mystery, because all parts of that routine touch the immense God who is not domesticated within it. Our Lord's Day here often throbs with the uncanny presence of God. Like catching a glimpse of someone out of the corner of your eye, you can sense a divinity in the music, the words, and the prayers, a divinity that plays with us through our routines. What an amazing grace we have to celebrate the Day of the Lord!

Of course, our texts this morning have a somewhat more portentous view of the Day of the Lord, a phrase Peter quotes from the prophets Amos

---

1. Preached December 4, 2005, the second Sunday in Advent.

The Day of the Lord

and Joel. For the prophets, the Day of the Lord is the time of last judgment. Because this is the second Sunday of Advent, we should recall that Advent is not about the first coming of Jesus, which we celebrate at Christmas with all the symbols of the infant Jesus. Advent is about the second coming, which is a time of judgment.

Peter's approach to divine judgment was one of which I am not fond. He was preoccupied with ecological disasters. Earlier in his letter he had remarked about how God had once destroyed nearly all the world with Noah's flood. Although many lessons are to be learned from Noah's flood, I join with those who believe that the slaughter of all those animals and innocent children is not a good illustration of the fairness of divine judgment. And in our passage, Peter gets excited about the final judgment, when the world burns to cinders. In the centuries since Saint Peter, we have come to understand that the cosmos is far vaster than the plane of human affairs. Although our planet might well be blasted to cinders by an encounter with a great comet, or by our sun going supernova, that would not be in order to punish evildoers. Peter's final point, that "we wait for new heavens and a new earth, where righteousness is at home," can be made without speaking favorably of such ecological violence.

Isaiah's rendition of God's advent in judgment is also not ecofriendly. Mountains shall be razed and valleys filled in to make a straight and level highway for God to come. It sounds a little like the nineteenth-century urban planning in Boston in which they leveled the three mountains downtown, which we remember now only in the name of Tremont Street, leaving only Beacon Hill. They used the earth to fill in Back Bay so that we could have Commonwealth Avenue as the straight and level highway it is. Compared with Peter's universal flood and world-incinerating fire, however, Isaiah's Army Corps of Engineer approach to level roads for God is a relatively benign image. The context for Isaiah's remark was that Cyrus the Great had just sent the Jewish exiles home from Babylon to Jerusalem, and they must have had festive roads on their mind. The coming of God in judgment, for Isaiah, meant God's going to Jerusalem to establish a reign of peace and justice. Isaiah's two images of God in our passage are striking. On the one hand, God is a warrior who comes in might to rule by his arm. On the other hand, God will feed his flock like a shepherd, gathering the lambs in his arms and gently leading the mother sheep. The first image of God as warrior is an old one in Israelite religion. The second image, that of the shepherd, is one that Christians will pick up for Jesus. Isaiah precedes both of these anthropomorphic images of God with a testimony to God's eternity in contrast to our evanescent temporality. And he follows our text with a description of God as creator of the ends of the earth, far above human warriors and shepherds. Isaiah knew how to set limits to his symbols.

The most striking element of Isaiah's vision of God's advent in judgment is that it is a gospel of comfort. "Comfort, O comfort my people, says your God. Speak tenderly to Jerusalem, and cry to her that she has served her term, that her penalty is paid, that she has received from the Lord's hand double for all her sins." This is not to say that God does not take sin seriously, in Isaiah's view. On the contrary, Isaiah construed the terrible experience of the exile as a punishment for failing to keep the covenant. But in the end there is reconciliation. The immense, eternal God comes down that straight highway with comfort, like a shepherd who carries the lamb in his arm. I much prefer this gentle image of judgment to Peter's.

Mark's approach to judgment returns us to the Christian advent theme. He cites Isaiah's line about preparing the way of the Lord, making his path straight. But instead of saying that the Lord will come, Mark says that a messenger will come, meaning John the Baptist. He says this by citing a line from the prophet Malachi. The whole of Malachi's line is the following, which many of you will recognize from Handel's *Messiah*: "See, I am sending my messenger to prepare the way before me, and the Lord whom you seek will suddenly come to his temple. The messenger of the covenant, in whom you delight—indeed, he is coming, says the Lord of hosts. But who can endure the day of his coming, and who can stand when he appears? For he is like a refiner's fire." Malachi meant that the prophet Elijah would return with a warning before the final judgment. Handel interpreted the messenger to be Jesus himself, the judge. Mark says the messenger is John the Baptist. What do we make of all this, when we contemplate all these symbols of the second coming of Jesus? We can appreciate the rich interplay of symbols as different traditions take them in different directions. But what do they mean for us?

The first thing they mean, all of them, Isaiah, Peter, Malachi, and Mark, is that sin is serious and that we need to repent. Perhaps they differed amongst themselves as to what constitute the worst sins. We surely know what our sins are, lying and self-deceit, selfishness and greed, lack of discipline and direction, enjoying social structures that involve much injustice, forgetting the poor, making war rather than peace, national arrogance, contempt for neighbor, and all the rest. John the Baptist calls for us to analyze these sins honestly and thoroughly, take responsibility for them, repent, and amend our ways. This must be done clearly enough that we can undertake some kind of ritual recognition of putting ourselves outside the power of sin, a ritual like baptism.

The second thing the symbols mean, in their various ways, is that with repentance comes forgiveness. Forgiveness means that God reconciles us to the divine life and restores us to right relation with all the dimensions of ultimate reality. From the Lord's Prayer we know how complicated forgiveness is—God forgives us in the measure that we forgive those who sin against us. So sin is not just sin against God—it is sin against neighbor. Repentance too is not just a matter of our relating to God. We need to repent to our neighbors, and accept them with forgiveness when they repent to us what they have done to us. How could this be more complicated, this snarl of hurts and wounds, gripes and grievances, demands for forgiveness and merciless self-condemnation, loving neither neighbor nor ourselves? The gospel says all this can be worked out.

Third, Mark is very clear that the business of repentance and forgiveness, though essential to our relation to God and one another, is the concern of a lesser figure, John the Baptist, who heralds one greater than himself. In what sense is Jesus greater than John? John baptizes with water to wash off sin. Good enough! Jesus baptizes with the Holy Spirit, God's very presence. John is about us, and our forgiven sins. Jesus is about God whom he brings into our lives. How does Jesus bring God? By bringing God's love!

What is the logic of the situation? You would think that the steps would go, first, that we acknowledge our sin; second, take responsibility for it; third, repent; fourth, thereby get forgiven; and fifth, with forgiveness come into harmony with God. But it does not work that way. Precisely because of sin we deceive ourselves about our sin. We deny responsibility for it, or at least seek to share the responsibility with plenty of excuses. We are unable to repent except for relatively trivial things. Because we feel deep in our hearts that we have not repented, we are unable to accept forgiveness, except for relatively trivial things about which we congratulate ourselves on being forgiven. Even if we know intellectually that God forgives us our worst, we are unable to take that seriously. Even if we have made every possible profession of faith that God forgives us, we know that is whistling in the dark and leap for one more profession of faith. We seek trivial sainthood because we are unable to face the serious depths of our heart's darkness. This is the logic of defeat.

The logic of the good news of Jesus Christ, however, says that the first step is upfront confrontation with the love of God. That love beats us over the head. That love is not the love of a politically correct blind God, but the love of God the judge who sees into our hearts as we cannot. That love is not the management love of a God who wants to run a just kingdom and knows that being kind is a more effective management style than being punitive. No, that love is the wild love of the Creator, it is unmeasured, undeserved, never without resources, overwhelming, and blows away our guilt and self-pity. God's love does absurd things, such as sacrifice itself. Once we have encountered that love, in Christian symbolism or in the concrete form of love in other people, we are given the power to acknowledge our sins, to repent, and accept forgiveness. And if we can accept forgiveness, how can we hold it back from others? We cannot wait for them to repent and ask for forgiveness. We have to love them first so that they will have the power to do so. And then forgiveness comes generously in passing.

Jesus Christ, present in his teachings, in the symbols applied to him, in his roles in our history, worship, church life, and discipleship, manifests God's love so that we can touch it. As our text has it, Jesus buries us in the Holy Spirit, which is the spirit of love, the way John buried sinners in the waters of the Jordan.

So, Beloved, do not wait for Jesus's second coming in some distant future advent with fire and brimstone, nor in an expectation that history is suddenly going to become unambiguously just and prosperous like a level road. No, look for Jesus in all the love around you now. If you see only pain and no love, then it is up to you to provide that love. This is what it means to be "in Christ." It only seems that Jesus is gone. He said he would be with us until the end of the age. He comes to us when any Christian smiles. Or when any person of any faith loves, for love is of God. The love we see around us seems confined, perhaps even sentimental. But that love, every bit of it, is a window opening onto the uncanny, wild, absurd, unmeasured love of the Creator. I can sense this at 7:30 on Sunday mornings looking at that Rose window. You can sense God's wild love in the music, prayers, and words of our worship. You catch it when you glimpse your neighbor's loving soul out of the corner of your eye. God's wild love is in your own soul, growing tumescent in your smile, your handshake, your passing of peace, your giving of bread, your word of comfort, your song of joy. Do not wait for Jesus. The kingdom of heaven is at hand. Jesus is here still and again. Let yourself be in love with him, and God's love will sweep away your sins like baptism in a raging torrent. Amen.

14

God with Us[1]

2 Samuel 7:1–11, 16; Romans 16:21–27; Luke 1:21–38, 41–55

The story of Gabriel informing Mary that she would bear the Messiah, and her response in what we know as the Magnificat, are great treasures of Christian literature. Scenes of the Angel Gabriel talking with Mary are among the most popular in medieval and Renaissance art. Although some of the gospels indicate that Mary later was doubtful about Jesus's religious mission, here she is presented as piously accepting the role given her. Actually, in Luke's Annunciation scene, our text this morning, Mary showed no interest in Jesus being the Son of the Most High or in his being the rightful heir of King David who would rule Israel, as Gabriel was saying. Rather she was interested in how she would get pregnant. Perhaps that is the more relevant question for a young girl in that circumstance.

Scholars say that these scenes concerning the birth of Jesus were a later interpolation on the original telling of the gospel story. Stories of gods being born miraculously, often enough of a virgin, were common in ancient times; even Buddha was given a miraculous virgin birth, according to legend. On the Christian side, neither Mark nor John mentioned anything about a miraculous conception and birth. Matthew said that Mary got pregnant by the Holy Spirit while engaged to Joseph but reported that the angel appeared to Joseph, not Mary, urging Joseph to accept the baby.

---

1. Preached December 18, 2005, the fourth Sunday in Advent.

The angel came back later to Joseph and told him to get out of town because the authorities were seeking to kill a newborn reputed to be the Messiah.

Mary's response to Gabriel's message, the Magnificat, has been the subject of many Christian musical compositions. Only a few weeks ago we had a musical service devoted to Bach's setting of the Magnificat. Actually, the Magnificat in Luke is a streamlined version of Hannah's song in 1 Samuel. Hannah was the mother of Samuel, the great prophet and judge who anointed Saul and David. Before Samuel's birth, however, Hannah had been barren many years, praying for a pregnancy. When Samuel was born, miraculously it seemed, given her age, she dedicated him to God. Sometime after the basic narrative of Samuel's birth was written, scribes inserted the following song, which became the paradigm for Mary's song. It is worthwhile hearing it because it gives a context for understanding Luke's Gospel:

> My heart exults in the LORD; my strength is exalted in my God.
> My mouth derides my enemies, because I rejoice in my victory.
> There is no Holy One like the Lord, no one besides you; there is no Rock like our God.
> Talk no more so very proudly, let not arrogance come from your mouth;
> For the LORD is a God of knowledge, and by him actions are weighed.
> The bows of the mighty are broken, but the feeble gird on strength.
> Those who were full have hired themselves out for bread,
> But those who were hungry are fat with spoil.
> The barren has borne seven, but she who has many children is forlorn.
> The LORD kills and brings to life; he brings down to Sheol and raises up.
> The Lord makes poor and makes rich; he brings low, he also exalts.
> He raises up the poor from the dust; he lifts the needy from the ash heap,
> To make them sit with princes and inherit a seat of honor.
> For the pillars of the earth are the LORD's and on them he has set the world.
> He will guard the feet of his faithful ones, but the wicked shall be cut off in darkness;
> For not by might does one prevail.
> The LORD! His adversaries shall be shattered; the Most High will thunder in the Heaven.
> The Lord will judge the ends of the earth; he will give strength to his king,

And exalt the power of his anointed.

See the similarity to Mary's song?

I take pains to point out the literary position of our texts because most of you in a university church are going to regard this as legendary material anyway, not a serious historical report. The church has taken these stories very seriously, however, and often literally as history. But we cannot let that distract us from the gospel message contained in them. Whether you take the stories literally or as mythic legend, they are in the Bible because of their religious message. What is that message?

The message is that God comes to us. We do not have to go to God. Every one of the gospel writers is clear about this. The message is not that we have to find some divine wisdom or perform some divinely approved act in order to be saved. We do not have to leave the world for salvation. Rather God comes into the world and changes it. We should not expect God elsewhere, but in our daily lives. Moreover, God is not going to be a superhero whose sidekicks we are. No, God is going to impregnate us and we are going to have to deal with that.

So the question is, what does it mean to be pregnant with God? Here is where Mary's response in the Magnificat is so important, and why seeing its derivation from Hannah's song so reinforces its importance. Both say that when God comes into our lives the usual order of power and wealth is overturned. Think of the items in Mary's song.

First, God is in charge, not those who think they are in charge: "He has shown strength with his arm."

Second, he has scattered the proud, turning them into nothing more than "the thoughts of their own hearts."

Third, he has brought down the powerful from their thrones and lifted up the lowly.

Fourth, he has filled the hungry and sent the rich away empty.

Fifth, he has remembered his people, when the world's events seem to make them losers. Hannah's song has all these elements and adds that God determines life and death, and guards the faithful. Hannah, like Mary, praises God's power and rightful reign over the earth.

So if we think God is coming to us, then we need to think about these power relations. We are a people of extraordinary arrogance who believe we can impose governments on other people. But God is ultimately in charge. We are a people who pride ourselves in the righteousness of our history of helping the underdog, and that pride has turned now to pure hypocrisy as we beat down everyone who stands in the way of what our government calls our "national interest." After pride comes the fall. We flaunt our military and economic power, but should God come that will be overturned. We withdraw support from the poor and favor the rich, but should God come that will be revealed. We say that those who oppose us count for nothing—we do not even report the numbers of the Iraqi and Afghani dead. But God remembers all God's people, and also those who demean them, by the way.

Perhaps it was a good thing that Mary was distracted by obstetrical concerns about how she would get pregnant. Had she thought about the real meaning of divinity suddenly coming into human affairs, she might have been less docile about accepting it. Not many of us, not even those who agree with the list of injustices I just cited, are ready for the overturning of power relations that God's presence entails. Of course these power relations are very complex and subtle. I've oversimplified them in order to echo the Scriptures. The clever among us can always rationalize the current state of affairs and policies as expressive of the very ways by which the meek inherit the earth. No one fails to be morally ambiguous, even the meek, poor, and downtrodden. That the Iraqi insurgents are patriotic defenders of their land and religion against foreign invaders does not mean that they are not also often terrorists and desirous of using the patriotic conflict to win special advantage for their own faction over against other factions. False righteousness from the arrogant top down is worse than the false righteousness of the embittered victims, but only marginally so. All of us are guilty of the abuse of power, even those who have little of it. All of us will be caught up short when we realize that God is in charge. All of us fail greatly when we caricature our opponents and make them seem to be the only unrighteous ones among us. The coming of God to be with us, of course, is good news. But it is also bad news. So it should be with the greatest caution and fear of the Lord that we celebrate God's coming to us in the form of that revolutionary baby.

Given these warnings, how should we think about God coming to us? The image of God coming to us riding on clouds of glory and separating the sheep from the goats, the wheat from the tares, the righteous from the wicked fails to register the subtlety of the ambiguity of human life, the inextricable mixture of good and evil. The better, and far more shocking, image is that God comes to impregnate us. God enters our fragile, frail, frames and makes us fecund with divine children. What Gabriel announced to Mary is a message for us: "Do not be afraid . . . you will conceive in your womb and bear a son . . . The Holy Spirit will come upon you, and the power of the Most High will overshadow you; therefore the child to be born will be holy."

Now, my *brothers* in Christ, you might not be comfortable with this imagery, this lesson that gives us wombs, tells us that what the Holy Spirit would do to us is to impregnate us, and calls us to say, "Here am I, the servant of the Lord; let it be with me according to your word." That grates against the male ego even more than the male anatomy. Our sisters in Christ, however, have had to put up with a lot of male imagery, inapplicable to them, for millennia, and we can very well do some adjusting here. Besides, Christians have thought of themselves individually and the church collectively as the bride of Christ almost since the beginning. So we can put aside our machismo and imagine ourselves, for a moment, all of us, men and women alike, to be wombs for God.

The fruit of our wombs, of course, shall be Jesus if in fact we submit to be overshadowed by the Holy Spirit: Jesus the merciful who is present in all our acts of mercy, Jesus the peacemaker in all our efforts at reconciliation, Jesus the humble when we shame the arrogant, Jesus the nourisher we feed the hungry, Jesus the friend when we companion the lonely, Jesus the lover when we embrace all those who can be made whole by our love. The fruit of our wombs when God comes upon us will not be an obedient child. No, Jesus our issue will turn things upside down, upsetting bad rulers, scattering the proud, lifting the lowly, nourishing the lost, dismissing the established. The divinely inspired deeds of our lives will get us into trouble, praise God! Look what happened to Mary's Babe!

Nevertheless, here is the meaning of Advent. When we sing, "Come, O Come Immanuel," we should not mean that we want Jesus to pop into Copley Square suddenly. We should not mean even that we want Jesus to come into our hearts and make us feel repentant and forgiven. We should mean that we want Jesus to come into our wombs and be born in deeds of divine action that are flesh of our flesh, bone of our bone. The seriousness of the incarnation requires that we spread ourselves open so deep and dark to God as to feel the impregnation of the midnight hour, the travails of birth, and the hopes and heartbreaks of sending children into the world that is healed by them and then flays and hangs them. Imagine Mary's heart! Gabriel announced, this is our heart. Come, O Come, Immanuel! Amen.

15

The Word Became Flesh[1]

Isaiah 52:1–10; Hebrews 1:1–4 (1–12); John 1:1–14

What a joyous day Christmas is! Some people prefer Easter as the central Christian holiday, because it celebrates Jesus's victory over death, and consequently our own victory over death. But I prefer Christmas because it celebrates God's incarnation in the world. God's taking on flesh in the world is the precondition for Easter being a meaningful holiday. Our gospel, from the famous Prologue to the Gospel of John, shows some of the astonishingly rich complexities of the incarnation, the "enfleshment" of God. Let's unwrap some of these complexities, as we all have been unwrapping presents these days.

The first point to make, and perhaps the most surprising, is that only in creating the world does God have any flesh at all. "Flesh" in this context means determinate character. Apart from creation, God has no determinate character, no "nature" about which we might know. So in creating the world, God makes God's own divine nature as creator of this world. Only as Creator does God have the flesh of a divine character.

Now this is surprising to many people because we are accustomed to projecting our ideas about things within the created world onto God, as if God were another thing within or alongside the world. Such a projection is perfectly appropriate in many dimensions of spiritual life, but it obscures the astonishing grandeur of the incarnation. Space is itself created. So apart

---

1. Preached Christmas Day 2005.

from the creation, God is not anywhere, not alongside anything, not alone as if there were room for something else. Time also is created. Apart from creation God is not in time, does not have a date, does not endure, or anything like that. Apart from creation God cannot be a thing that possesses properties in a place or holds a constant character through time. Only because God does create can God have a nature and endure through time. The Bible, of course, never mentions anything about God apart from creation, only that God is the creator of this world and has a meaningful character in relation to the world. When Genesis says, "In the beginning God when God created the heavens and the earth . . . ," that means that time and space began with the creation, and so did God's character. The creation of the world is what gives God flesh. The first and most profound meaning of Christmas is that God takes on the character of being our creator.

This means that God is in us, creating us. We are among the end-products of God's creative act. God cannot create us and withdraw, because there is nothing outside of space-time to withdraw to. God is incarnate in each creature, our own true inner nature.

The Gospel of John calls the character of God the "Word." When with the creation God became God, it was because of the Word through which all things are created. The Greek word for Word is *logos*, from which we also get the word "logic" and all of its cognates. In the ancient world, the *logos* was the fundamental rationale or intelligibility that allows finite determinate things to exist, and philosophers and theologians have debated in what this might consist. I believe myself that the *logos*, or Word, or divine nature that arises through creating, involves four elements. One is that to be a thing, a created thing has to have a form or pattern. A second element is that created things have parts or components that are integrated by their forms. A third element is that created things have location in space and time; they exist somewhere and somewhen. A fourth element is that a created thing has value, namely, the value of having all its components together in its particular form at the spatiotemporal location in which it exists. Its value would be different if it had a different form, some different components, or were existentially located elsewhere. These four elements together add up to the fact that every created thing is a harmony of some sort, perhaps with an unfolding form like a melody, diverse in its components, and particular in its existence. They also indicate how every thing is related to all the other things that connect with its form, its components, its existential location, and its value. God's incarnate nature is to be the Creator of the ecology of harmonies that constitute our cosmos.

This might seem to be a lot of metaphysics for the Word of God. But remember, it is this Word that became incarnate in the man Jesus, according to John. How can this be?

Inanimate things play their roles as parts of God's creative act in simple ways, compared with human beings. We have freedom, and thus exercise some control over what we do and are. Being free, we have a problem to find and embody the best forms for our lives. In moral terms, this means we should be righteous, forming our lives justly, although we can choose unjust forms, which is to be unrighteous. Being free, we should honor all the components of our lives—our bodies, our use of resources, our neighbors, our traditions—as we bind them together into the forms for which we are responsible. In moral terms, this means we should be pious toward, or deferential to, the things that we manipulate to form our lives, although we can be callous and abusive instead. Being free, we should engage the issues and problems of our existential location, our politics, our family problems, our social issues, our personal trials. In moral terms, this means that we should have the faith to engage our existential location, although we are so often tempted to live in denial and escape. Being free, we should be concerned to achieve the best possible value for our lives, viewed in ultimate perspective, given the life-forms available to us, the components, and the existential realities of our location. In moral terms, this means we should live in hope that we might be acceptable players in God's cosmic creative act, although there are many temptations to despair. Righteousness, piety, faith, and hope together add up to love: love is the creativity with which we address harmonies, making them more harmonious where we can and always enjoying them for their beauty. A stone automatically has its form, components, existential location, and value. By contrast, we human beings are responsible in part for achieving the best form, for honoring the parts of our lives, for engaging our existential location, and for holding out for the most divine-worthy value.

To be sure, we customarily screw up. We are unrighteous, impious, faithless, and despairing, at least some of the time. We are not perfect in love. All this is to say we are sinners. Christianity sees sin as more serious than merely failing, however. In addition to screwing up, we take our failures to be reasons to alienate ourselves from God. We refuse to accept our responsible roles as parts of God's great creative act. We turn from the joyous tasks of manifesting and multiplying the harmonies of God's creation and work against that. We hate rather than love, and in this we magnify our unrighteousness, impiety, faithlessness, and despair. Of course all this alienation is vain. Our very existence is part of God's creative act. Nothing exists except God's creating us and the others. So to accomplish alienation we blind ourselves to the reality of our existence. We tell ourselves that we are separate individuals, existing our own, so that we can be selfish. But in fact we all exist together in the seamless ecology of creation. We can no more exist apart from God than a dance can exist without a dancer. God's dance includes the whole of creation. This is God's incarnate life. When we blind ourselves to the ecology of our creating God, we live in the darkness to which John referred. But our darkness did not overcome the Light of the Word in Jesus.

How was Jesus the incarnation of the Word? For starters, he showed people how to be righteous. He preached and lived out a life of justice. He also showed people how to be pious and deferential, accepting the value of God's creation even when parts of it are inconvenient. Jesus demonstrated extraordinary faith, accepting the tragic existential location that brought him to the cross with heroic courage. And Jesus delivered to his disciples and, through them, to us the hope that we might live as blessed creatures in God's ultimate, creative life. All of this Jesus summed up in his teachings and practice of love. John's Gospel especially is filled with the work of Jesus making love happen. Jesus was the model of how a human being can embody the Word, with the right forms of life, the right deference to life's components, the right engagement of existential location, and the right way to human value.

These things Jesus did constitute an astonishing achievement. Yet I have to say that they are the sorts of things we attribute to many of the great religious teachers and founders, the Buddha and Confucius, for instance, or the prophets to whom Jesus was so often likened. Something else about Jesus is what makes him the incarnation of the Word, namely that his historical appearance provided a way to reverse sin's deep alienation from God. Jesus is a special part of God's creative act reversing the alienation into which so many if not all people had fallen. To put it more bluntly, Jesus is God saving the world.

This divine saving activity is not so much Jesus the man doing something, although of course it would not have taken place if Jesus had not done pretty much what he did. Rather, the saving comes through our response to

Jesus. That response is to see that God loves and accepts us despite our sins. It is to see that our alienation from God is just stupid and self-destructive. It is to see that in following along Jesus's way we can indeed play our roles as parts of God's glorious creation even though we still do unrighteous, impious, cowardly, and fainthearted things sometimes.

Our response in these saving ways is, of course, also part of God's creation, and the official theological term for that response is the work of the Holy Spirit. The Holy Spirit is God in us interpreting the life of Jesus in such ways that reconcile us to God. Jesus would be only a man, however great a teacher, if the Holy Spirit did not also let us see him as the Way, the Truth, and the Life before God. The Holy Spirit worked in the disciples, the New Testament writers, and in the saints of the church from the earliest days down to us to interpret Jesus's life in a phantasmagoria of symbols so that we are reconciled to God. The Holy Spirit, God working in us, delivers us from our vain alienation and gives us joyous ways of living out our roles within God's creation. I'm sure that Jesus, the Galilean teacher, would have been amazed and perhaps dismayed at some of the interpretations laid upon him. No faithful Jew like Jesus would have been comfortable being called divine, for instance: that would seem like idolatry. But by thinking of Jesus as divine, as God's own divine Son, come to pay for our sins, loving us despite our sins, showing us the way to love and justice and piety and faith and hope, our salvation is accomplished. What counts for salvation is not the details of Jesus's life but rather the work of the Holy Spirit in the believers to interpret Jesus to us so that we are transformed. The real Jesus is not only the man, about whose legends we might have doubts. The real Jesus is the interpreted Jesus who delivers us from bondage to sin and alienation from God, whom we know as King of Kings, and Prince of Peace.

The lesson of the incarnation, my friends, is not about Jesus alone. No, it is about the Holy Trinity. God becomes the Father in creating the world. God's nature as creator is the Word through which all things are created and which was embodied in human form in Jesus. God's Holy Spirit completes the creation in us, overcoming our alienation and bringing us to God's joy by making Jesus Christ the Redeemer God for us.

So who is this baby whose birth we celebrate today? It is God coming to glory in the cosmic creation. It is the divine nature fitted into human form in Jesus. It is the Spirit of holiness that allows us to embrace God's saving love in Jesus. The cosmic drama of creation and redemption pivots on this baby boy, divinely conceived, born in a stable, surrounded by beasts, adored by shepherds, hymned by angels, honored by wise men, exiled to safety, trained in his traditions, followed as a teacher, sought as a healer, loved by his friends, betrayed by his enemies, crucified for our sins, raised for our redemption, and ascended into heaven, which is God's unambiguous creating activity in every creature in the divine ecology, deeper in our hearts than our separate selves, the common root of us all, the divine life itself whose song is incarnate in all reality. Lord of Lords! King of Kings! Prince of Peace! God with Us! Redeemer! Amen.

16

A Time for Everything[1]

Ecclesiastes 3:1–13; Revelation 21:1–6a; Matthew 25:31–46

Everyone here is conscious of the fact that this is New Year's Day, the beginning of the Year of Our Lord 2006. With just a quick reminder everyone gets the point that this is the first Sunday of the liturgical year when Christ is with us. We call it the Sunday of Epiphany, which is the season in which we celebrate the appearance of Jesus Christ to the world. *Epiphany* means "appearance." The alternate lectionary reading for the first Sunday of Epiphany, which is used when the Sunday does not fall on New Year's Day, is the visit of the three wise men to Jesus, who appears to them as the king.

For many people, New Year's Day is a ritual time for marking the change of the times, for turning over a new leaf, a new page in the book of our lives. Many of us have New Year's resolutions, which usually begin with a program to lose the weight gained in the festive season about to end. What a blessed relief to know that most gyms are closed on this holiday, and many also on Monday; so workouts can be postponed until Tuesday, at least. My own New Year rituals include packing up the bills and check stubs for 2005 and putting them in the tax file for later. I go around the house replacing batteries in clocks and smoke alarms that otherwise would fail at inconvenient times. Of course it is legitimate to take a ritual nap in the afternoon to recoup from the celebration of New Year's Eve. Many of us have ritual house parties to host or visit. Usually I also take time to make

---

1. Preached New Year's Day, 2006, the Sunday of Epiphany.

a reflective entry in my journal. I hope everyone reflects a while on what it means to move from 2005 to 2006.

Our familiar text from Ecclesiastes says that for everything there is a season. "A time to be born, and a time to die; a time to plant, and a time to pluck up what is planted; a time to kill, and a time to heal; a time to break down, and a time to build up; a time to weep, and a time to laugh; a time to mourn, and a time to dance; a time to throw away stones and a time to gather stones together; a time to embrace, and a time to refrain from embracing; a time to seek, and a time to lose; a time to keep and a time to throw away; a time to tear, and a time to sew; a time to keep silence, and a time to speak; a time to love, and a time to hate; a time for war, and a time for peace." This litany has an unsettling effect on Christian ears, for most of these contrasted pairs have a preferred member. Christians like being born, and go to great pains to say that death is not what it seems. We like to plant and then to harvest, but there is something unexpected in the season for plucking up. Of course there is a time to love, but do we ever admit a time to hate? We emphasize the time for peacemaking, but hesitate to say there is a time for war. Christians tend to be suspicious of what seems to be cynicism on the part of the author who begins his book, "Vanity of vanities. All is Vanity."

But remember that Ecclesiastes says that everything has its season. When out of season, these things are inappropriate. How hurtful it is to laugh when you should be weeping, to mourn when you should be dancing! By the same token, sometimes it is inappropriate to hold on to life that should be released. Sometimes only war makes sense in a season of violence. The huge moral problem is to discover the appropriate response for the season. Surely we ought to arrange our lives as much as possible so that no season for war ever arises, that hate is never appropriate, that no mourning is called for, nor weeping. Would we not be blessed if there were never seasons for killing and dying?

A certain strain of Christian piety supposes that God will sometime arrange it that no seasons for death or weeping would ever exist. This is the vision of the book of Revelation, which says that God "will wipe every tear from their eyes. Death will be no more; mourning and crying and pain will be no more, for the first things have passed away." God says, "See, I am making all things new." This strain of Christian piety, which stresses the destruction of the created world with an extreme nonnatural makeover, is dominant in the book of Revelation. The overall plot of that book is the final battle between God's forces and those of Satan, resulting in the destruction of most of creation, with stars falling and the earth going up in smoke. Nearly all God's creatures are lost except for 144,000 saints, and the new Jerusalem comes down out of heaven with only straight edges and polished stone. Natural rhythms such as night and day are dismissed in favor of the steady light of God's glory.

Piety of this sort stands in contrast with the piety of the incarnation that says that God comes into the created natural world that we have to redeem it. According to incarnational piety, God does not have to make "all things new," but is able to exist in the original creation that God saw to be good, according to Genesis 1. Last week we reflected on the incarnational piety of John's Gospel that says that the divine Word, in which the original creation is made, itself becomes incarnate in Jesus so as to redeem the world from the darkness into which it had fallen. All things do not have to be made new, only lighted up, perfected and redeemed.

This week, I want to affirm that incarnational piety and therefore need to take very seriously the vision of Ecclesiastes. For that text, attributed to Solomon although surely of much later composition, is extremely attentive to the realities of life, the bad parts as well as the good, the need for compromise as well as the need for celebration. Underlying the metaphor of the seasons is a recognition of the cyclic processes of nature: emergence in the spring, growth in the summer, harvest in the fall, and hunkering down as if in tombs through the winter, waiting for the next cycle. The point of saying everything is vain is not to depreciate the pleasures and achievements of life. In fact, the text says to pay attention to the work that you have to do. The point rather is that nothing lasts beyond its season. Kings can build empires, but they too will die like the paupers, and their empires will crumble in time. Everything has its season, and nothing outlasts its season. To think we will outwit the way creation works and establish something that will stand forever, something like the new Jerusalem in Revelation, is vanity.

Incarnational piety holds that God redeems the time, the season that we have. To redeem us, God does not have to create a new time, something beyond seasons. With this in mind, think about our gospel text this morning, from Matthew. At first glance, it looks more like the book of Revelation than Ecclesiastes. Jesus says there will be a time of judgment when the Son of Man will separate the sheep from the goats, rewarding the good and punishing the wicked, sending the righteous to eternal life and the wicked to the eternal punishment prepared for the devil and his followers. On second glance, notice that Jesus's conception of judgment says nothing about making all things new. In fact, the eternity of life and the eternity of punishment are elements of the original creation. Jesus had a larger view than we do of what the original creation consists of, including heavenly and devilish realms. But it is all there from the beginning, and the judge places people according to what they do within their own seasons of life.

The remarkable part of Jesus's message here is that our judgment depends on what we do *to him* as the incarnation of God within our few seasons. The righteous are those who gave him food when he was hungry, drink when thirsty, welcome when a stranger, clothing when he was naked, and companionship when he was imprisoned. The disciples were dumbfounded to hear this, because they never did anything like that for Jesus. If anything, he took care of them. You know his profound response. "Truly I tell you, just as you did it to one of the least of these who are members of my family, you did it to me." And we know that by his "family" he referred to all people, especially those in need.

Matthew's text rubs it in, twice. "Then he will say to those at his left hand, 'You that are accursed, depart from me into the eternal fire prepared for the devil and his angels; for I was hungry and you gave me no food, I was thirsty and you gave me nothing to drink, I was a stranger and you did not welcome me, naked and you did not give me clothing, sick and in prison and you did not visit me." Those poor souls were shocked! "Lord, when was it that we saw you hungry or thirsty or a stranger or naked or sick or in prison and did not take care of you?" Surely, if those disciples who loved Jesus had seen him in distress, they would have jumped to his care, as they tried to fight off the people who came to arrest him after the Last Supper. Jesus answered, "Truly I tell you, just as you did not do it to one of the least of these, you did not do it to me." This moral applies to us, who purport to love Jesus.

Now you see the downside of an incarnational religion. Any time we fail to help our neighbors, abuse our environment, or lack compassion for any part of creation, we are failing God who is present here. The false attractiveness of the "all things new" piety is that it puts off all the important stuff until later battles. For all the tantalizing excitement of getting on Jesus's side to fight in the apocalypse against Satan who must be destroyed, that "all things new" piety actually legitimates postponement of both effort and judgment. Incarnational Christianity says that what we do now is what counts.

I don't know what you believe about future judgment. Jesus used that imagery as a literary figure, and we do not know his literal beliefs. But whenever judgment occurs, it occurs about what we do in our season. Have we fed the hungry? Often the churches have been magnificent in this regard. But as a nation we recently have made more people hungry by our wars and economics than we have fed. Have we given drink to the thirsty? If that means "thirsty for knowledge" as Jesus sometimes used the image, as a nation we have been very selective, educating some to a high degree and pushing the poor farther and farther down. Have we welcomed strangers? Some of us have been heroically inclusive in our fellowship, while others of us have pushed away the poor, the minorities, the gays, the Muslims and others who seem strangers to us. Sometimes we have clothed the naked, and other times have made them naked. Few of us have visited those in prison with the love and mercy due to children of God.

Is it not a shock, however, to think that whatever our record, that is the record of our love of God, in our neighbor? None of us has fed every hungry person we could, every thirsty person, befriended every stranger, clothed every ragamuffin, or engaged every prisoner. Jesus's speech is an extraordinary demand for perfection, one we cannot possibly meet. In this sense, even the best among us are with the goats rather than the sheep.

The upside of Christian incarnationalism is that God is right here with us not only to judge but to love and heal with mercy. Jesus is present not only in the hungry, poor, and downtrodden, but also in those who teach us that we can still go on loving Jesus, despite the fact we fail him in many ways. We can still do what we can for the hungry and poor. We can still give ourselves to the causes of peace and justice despite continuing lack of success. We have salvation because God has come to us with the power to enable us to live in the face of judgment and still be God's people. We do not have to wait until God makes all things new, and we do have to love the old world God has created. We can love in the lives we have. That is the way God loves, incarnate in the lives we have in the world in which we are created.

When we contemplate the turning of the New Year, we should see it as our season, with the particular tasks given us, the particular enjoyments, the particular trials, and the particular ways of participating in the Creator who created very much more than appears this season. For the most of us who are comfortable with our season, this is an easy lesson. For those of us who suffer hell this season, the lesson is bitter. Nevertheless, even this bitterness is sweeter than the false lesson that the world in which we live is a bad creation that must be replaced by another. The Creator of a bad creation, who has to destroy the most of it to bring about an improvement, is a sorry Creator. That is a God conceived to be too small to be worthy of our efforts at righteousness, of our deferential respect of the divine works, of our faith in salvation, of our hope for resting in Glory, and of our love that learns to love our enemies and all those sinners. I pray that in reflecting on this day, you find the immense, eternal God, not elsewhere, but here in the point of this season. Amen.

17

God Calls[1]

1 Samuel 3:1–10; 1 Corinthians 6:11–20; John 1:41–51

The idea that God calls us to do something is unsettling. Most often the phrase is used by people who worry that they are being called to ministry. The metaphor of calling in this circumstance is ancient. The Latin-derived word "vocation" means a calling. We all want to have a calling. But we are nervous when we think it might be God who calls us to do something, especially to minister. I mean "ministry" here in the broad sense that Protestants use in referring to the priesthood of all believers. Next Sunday I'll talk about ordained ministry.

The story of Eli and Samuel is particularly instructive here. Eli was the judge of Israel who, according to those times, ruled Israel as the viceroy of God. God was the official King of Israel. Eli's job mainly had to do with judging legal cases and maintaining the ark of the covenant, which was the Israelite talisman for God. Although the text mentions the ark being in the temple, in fact this was long before Solomon built the first temple. Eli made his home base at the town of Shiloh, and the ark was housed in a tent. As judge, Eli also mustered the troops when Israel went to war, but by the time of our story he was very old. Eli's sons, Hophni and Phineas, were presumed to be his heirs, and they did accompany the ark into battle. But they were corrupt and not at all respected. Samuel was raised in Eli's house, with Eli treating him like a son; later he did become Eli's heir as judge of Israel.

1. Preached January 15, 2006, the second Sunday after Epiphany.

In our text, Samuel is about twelve years old, according to ancient commentaries, and is sleeping by the ark when he hears a voice. He thinks it is Eli, but in fact it is God. Eli figures out who it is, and he sends Samuel back to await God. God comes into Samuel's room in person and stands by him, calling his name. Samuel answers with the classic expression of a prophet's obedience: "Speak, for your servant is listening."

Would it not be great piety on our part always to be attentive to God, saying in effect, "Speak, for your servant is listening"? But, alas, we rarely have such extraordinary epiphanies. In fact, when we think about Samuel's story with our modern understanding of the dynamics of the psyche, we are a bit suspicious about voices that come to us when we are asleep. The fact that God's voice sounded so much like Eli's makes us suspect a bit of projection on Samuel's part. Then the message God goes on to give to Samuel, which we did not read, is a nasty bit of retribution against Eli for not controlling the actions of his sons. Wouldn't we suspect a little bit of oedipal byplay here on Samuel's part, unconsciously willing Eli's natural sons out of the way so that he himself could supplant Eli? None of this takes away from the true piety of Samuel's obedience. But it does force the question of how we know when God is calling, and what God is calling us to do.

Perhaps we can find help from John's version of how Jesus called his disciples. Matthew, Mark, and Luke, you remember, tell the fetching story of Jesus calling Peter, Andrew, James, and John by the Sea of Galilee where they were working as fishermen; Jesus tells them he will make them "fishers of men." That's in our text for next week. John's version is very different, and I'll begin by recounting events that lead up to our text for today. When Jesus goes to be baptized by John the Baptist, John does not know him until the actual baptism, and he sees the Holy Spirit descend on Jesus. According to the other evangelists, you know, John the Baptist and Jesus are second cousins. John the Baptist already has a number of disciples of his own. The day after Jesus was baptized, while Jesus was still with the crowd, John points out Jesus to two of them, saying "Look, here is the Lamb of God." One of those disciples of John the Baptist was Andrew. We don't know who the other was, but it might have been the one who became Jesus's Beloved Disciple, who is present throughout John's Gospel but never named. Those two disciples of the Baptist follow after Jesus—that is, they stalk him. He turns and asked them, "What are you looking for?" They respond by asking him where he is staying, and he takes them to his room. The evangelist remarks that this occurs at about four in the afternoon. None of the other evangelists records anything like this much detail of personal interaction. We don't know what happens late that afternoon, but by the end of it Andrew and his friend become disciples of Jesus, leaving John the Baptist. Andrew dashes out and finds his brother Simon, who apparently also has been with John the Baptist as a disciple. Andrew tells him, "We have found the Messiah." When Andrew brings Simon to Jesus, Jesus calls him by name, "Simon son of John," and renames him Cephas, or Peter.

Our text picks up the next day when Jesus heads north to Galilee with his three new disciples, Peter, Andrew, and the unnamed one. They go to Bethsaida, Peter and Andrew's hometown, where Jesus finds Philip and says to him, "Follow me." Philip accepts the invitation, apparently, perhaps because he was a friend of Andrew and Simon Peter. Philip goes to his friend Nathanael, who lives in Cana, and says, "We have found him about whom Moses in the law and also the prophets wrote, Jesus son of Joseph from Nazareth." This is the only time in the New Testament when Jesus is referred to with the title Jesus son of Joseph. Our text today, you notice, also calls him Son of God and Son of Man. Cana was near Nazareth, and Nathanael perhaps knew Joseph and his family. (Parenthetically, you remember that the very next day Mary will take Jesus and his disciples to a wedding in Cana where he makes a name for himself as a winemaker.) Nathanael snorts, "Can anything good come out of Nazareth?" So when Philip brings Nathanael to Jesus, Jesus has a hard sell. He tells Nathanael that he, Nathanael, is "an Israelite in whom there is no deceit." This flattery works. Nathanael says, proudly we might imagine, "Where did you get to know me?" Of course Jesus might have known him from the neighborhood, but what he says is about the character of Nathanael's heart. Jesus responds with a bit of clairvoyance about where Nathanael was sitting before Philip called him. Nathanael is completely won over and responds with the enthusiastic confession of discipleship: "Rabbi, you are the Son of God! You are the King of Israel!" Jesus then brings him down hard, chiding him for believing because of the fig tree vision, and saying that he will see much greater things than this, "heaven opened and the angels of God ascending and descending upon the Son of Man."

Now there is a lot of symbolic stuff going on in the text, as happens throughout John; nothing ever means only one thing. For instance, the image of angels ascending and descending is a reference to Jacob's vision back in Genesis, and Jacob was a notoriously deceitful man, quite the opposite of Nathanael. But I want to call attention to the detailed web of personal interactions involved in the calling of these disciples. These people knew one another. They had a history together. They had a common background of knowing the Hebrew Scriptures that formed their expectations. We know from the rest of the Gospel that the disciples required a long time fully to understand their discipleship, and the true identity of Jesus. But for them it was all very concrete, and the quality of the calling proved itself in the end.

I suggest that God calls us in concrete, testable ways as well. Few people hear God's voice, as Samuel thought he did, and the first thing to think when a person hears a divine voice is that the person is delusional; hearing voices is a well-documented symptom of mental illness, whatever else might cause it. At any rate, as is said with the spirits, we have to test them, for not every spirit is the Holy Spirit. The same is true with the promptings of spirit that we think might be God calling us to some special task or vocation. They need to be tested for their clarity and veracity.

The first test comes as we deepen ourselves consciously into an understanding of the shared religious culture that provides our expectations for God's work. We are not in the same position as the people in John's text, because we come after the Christ, and carry on his ministry in our time that he was only slowly working out with his disciples. We don't feel the same urgency to the question of whether Jesus was the messiah because our tradition has gone on to define messiahship in far more complicated ways than anyone thought in the first century. Rather our urgency is with being contemporary disciples, with deepening our own spiritual lives, with learning to live with kindness for all, with finding justice in a world of economic competition and blind forces of investment, with being peacemakers in a world where even Christians pride themselves on fighting wars against terrorism and Evil Axis nations. There also is a need to carry the call of God across the world. Our urgency has to do with finding out what each of us in particular can do about these things. To do this, we need a profound Christian understanding of our situation, both as a community and as individuals. The church can help here, as the worship life in Jesus's time provided widespread scriptural literacy. But each of us needs to ponder over a lifetime what the Christian needs are that face us. An authentic call from God is to serve needs such as these.

The second test is finding and assessing the particular pointers that are directed at us, and usually this means particular people. The church needs ordained ministers, but not everyone would be good at that. Jesus's ministry needs those who can nourish the spirit, their own and the souls of others; not everyone would be good at that. Jesus's ministry needs peacemakers; but not everyone has the skill to be a diplomat. Jesus's ministry needs prophets and producers of justice, and this sometimes requires martyrdom; this is not for everyone. Jesus's ministries need money, and sometimes people need to give more, to devote themselves to amassing wealth and giving it to charitable causes; but not everyone has this calling. Chances are, someone around you will suggest that you might fulfill this or that need. Chances are, the people around you will not suggest that you take up a calling to which you obviously are not fitted.

Sad to say, however, this neat fit of God's needs with our own talent areas hardly ever happens. The crises of our time are not relevant only for the few with the talents to address them. They become crises for all of us, and many have to respond. When your neighbor is suffering, you are called to help even if you are clumsy and have a terrible bedside manner. In fact, the trajectories of our careers in Christian service that we project in our youth hardly ever turn out to be what happens. Accidents of fate demand responses from us that are not in our plans at all, and we end up doing jobs that others could do far better just because we are the ones on hand. Isn't it one of the pleasant ironies of the Christian life that our careers are formed not so much by what we intend them to be but rather by what needs to be done when our hand is on the plow? This is one of the deepest meanings of providence.

The discernment of God's call thus triangulates on our cumulative life decisions. The first angle is to understand what Christian needs exist in our world, nation, society, town, neighborhood, family, and circle of activities. This requires theological understanding. The second angle is to understand ourselves, our talents, resources, and interests. Whatever we do to respond to God's call has to be true to ourselves. The third angle is to let the needs of ministry, sometimes ordained but far more generally the ministry of each of Jesus's disciples, shape how we grow by engaging those needs with our talents. God's call, you see, is not just to get things done that need to be done in order to carry out the ministry begun by Jesus. God's call also creates us, makes us who we should be before God. In this sense, every one of us should be hearing God call our name. Discerning God's call is how we become who we should be.

And so, my friends, perhaps this is a time when some of you are called into ordained ministry: obedience to that call will make you God's person. Perhaps this is a time when some of you are called to be teachers, or social workers, or nurses, or physicians, or scientists, or singers, or poets: obedience to that call will make you God's person. Perhaps this is a time when some of you are called to produce and acquire wealth so that it might be put to godly use: obedience to that call will make you God's person. Perhaps this is a time when some of you are called to testify for Christ's ministry at your job, in your neighborhood, in your family: obedience to that call will make you God's person. Perhaps this is a time when you are called to sacrifice something important for the sake of the gospel: Jesus shows that this makes you God's person.

The real test of a call from God, which quickly shows up the false callings and over time confirms and blesses the true ones, is how the call contributes to a community of loving friends. John's Gospel is all about this. The story of Jesus gathering his first disciples shows him beginning a community of friends. The call in the other Gospels to become "fishers of men" sounds a little like a CEO organizing his workers. In John's version, which I like best, Jesus starts knitting them into a community of friends. John's Gospel ends with Jesus cooking breakfast for his disciples and sending them on to take care of one another. He heals Peter's broken heart of denial, and claims his special relationship with the Beloved Disciple. I would hope that our sense of ministry, individually and collectively, might have this intimacy that purifies our callings and blesses us in them, even when they are not successful in worldly ways. Jesus assured his friends at the end that he had overcome the world. That is the way God calls. Amen.

18

Call to Ministry[1]

Jonah 3:1–5, 10; 1 Corinthians 7:21–31; Mark 1:11–20

Our texts from Jonah and Mark illustrate very different responses to the call to ministry. Jonah first of all did not want to go to Nineveh to preach repentance. You know the more famous story about how he tried to flee by boat but was thrown overboard by the crew when they thought a perfect storm was God's punishment of Jonah for his flight. He was rescued by the great fish and reluctantly went to Nineveh. His preaching was spectacularly successful, however, and everyone repented, from the king to the peasants, and even the animals. Jonah, however, was furious, because he wanted the Ninevites destroyed; he did not want them to repent. After our text for today, God had to teach Jonah a lesson about why mercy is a good thing.

Mark's story is just the opposite. Simon and Andrew, James and John, left their boats where they were, dropping everything to follow Jesus. They were like enthusiastic puppy dogs. James and John were probably teenagers, because they had their mother speak for them when later they wanted Jesus to make them his chief staff members. Unlike Jonah's successful evangelism, Jesus's disciples nearly all ended up as martyrs. The Bible does not record Zebedee's attitude when his two sons left him, and the work, in the fishing boat with the hired hands to follow their new guru.

---

1. Preached January 22, 2006, the third Sunday after Epiphany.

Nurture in Time and Eternity

Today I do not want to dwell on the sense of called ministry that was taking shape in the ancient Christian world, although that is a fascinating topic. I want rather to lift up some of the issues of ministry today. My reflections are much shaped by years of my own ministry, forty-two as an ordained deacon in the Methodist Church and thirty nine as an elder. For fifteen years I was dean of the Boston University School of Theology, which educates people for ordained ministry, and during that time I served on a nearly infinite number of denominational committees that defined various elements of ministry. The Methodist Church in which I was ordained, now the United Methodist Church, represents the Roman Catholic–Anglican tradition of ministry, which is somewhat different from conceptions of ministry in free-church Protestant traditions. Most basic issues are the same, however.

In our tradition, two orders of ordination exist, deacons and elders. You will remember from the book of Acts of the Apostles that in the earliest days after Jesus's ascension, his own disciples, the apostles, led the growing Christian community, teaching and healing, and deciding directions for development. These are the people whose office eventually came to be called elders, although the New Testament is not consistent with regard to titles. Early on in the church, however, a dispute arose between widows who spoke Greek and widows who spoke Aramaic, concerning who was getting the most help from the community. Doesn't that kind of thing sound familiar? So the apostles appointed several people, among them Stephen, to be deacons, that is "servers," whose job was to "wait on tables." "Waiting on tables" probably meant community management and service of all sorts, but particularly financial management. The deacons would take care of the community while the apostles or elders attended to "more important things." Stephen, you remember, did not limit himself to managing the day-to-day life of the community but went to the temple to teach in public, just as Peter and John did. He got himself in trouble with the authorities, and was stoned to death for it. To this day, many deacons think they really ought to be elders, though without the educational requirements, and with disastrous results. But I'll not burden you further with church politics!

In our time, ordained ministry means leadership in the church for which there are both educational and spiritual requirements. In Protestant denominations, all laypeople are regarded as having ministries, a doctrine Luther called the priesthood of all believers. But not all laypeople are held responsible as leaders who are certified because they have fulfilled requirements. In fact, precisely because all people are regarded as ministers, and not all people are capable of fulfilling educational and spiritual requirements, the church expressly limits leadership roles so that all people can participate somewhere in corporate ministry. Of course, some laypeople are far better in leadership roles than some ministers, but even when they are better, they are not accountable to the discipline of the church as ordained people are.

Ordained deacons lead in the ministries of service. All Christians are supposed to serve in one capacity or another, and for this ordained deacons provide specialized leadership. Sometimes this means service within congregations, such as in religious education, music, or liturgical leadership. Often it means Christian service in the world, in health care, for instance, or social justice movements. When I was a young man, everyone who wanted to be ordained an elder had to be ordained a deacon first, because leadership in ministries of service was taken to be basic to all other forms of ordained ministerial leadership. Now in the United Methodist Church, deacons and elders are separate orders of ministry. I suspect, however that few elders can be successful with their specific ministries of leadership without also attending to leadership in service.

The ancestor denominations of most contemporary mainline American Protestant churches now were powerfully affected by the formation of the American democracy in the late eighteenth and early nineteenth centuries. For many congregations the heritage of that democratic ethos is that the members take on the identity of a kind of legislature which, through various committees, determines what the congregation's ministries should be. Then they conceive of the ordained ministers as hired hands to carry out the ministries decided upon. This has sometimes had three disastrous effects. First, the lay members of the congregation are removed from the actual ministries of service in which their Christian life consists, leaving that to the ministers. Second, the ordained ministers who are trained and vetted by their peers are given nearly impotent leadership roles within the congregation, thus weakening the expertise needed in a complex world. And third, the people attracted into ordained ministry of the hired-hand sort tend to be followers who want to be told what to do; they conceive their ministries as performing Christian exercises as defined by their congregation and culture rather than as leading in the formation of those ministries. The Boston University School of Theology has been assiduous in pursuing leadership types rather than "servant ministers," as the recent jargon calls it, but it has had to row hard against the cultural tide.

In our tradition, the ministries of elders are defined by three notions, Word, Order, and Sacrament.

The ministry of the Word, of course, means preaching, primarily but not exclusively pulpit preaching. All Christians share the ministry of the Word, usually not in pulpits but surely in families, at work, among friends, and in participation in Christian communities. But ordained elders have the leadership in discerning what that Word is. To understand the force of this, let me call your attention to a distinction between two kinds of expressions of the Word. One is that in which you believe and say things because that is what acculturated people in our community believe and say. Such belief and speech performs the act of affirming solidarity and inculcating a culture. You do not have to think very hard to perform the Christian Word in most circumstances. You just say what Christians say in those circumstances. The other kind of expression of the Word is tied to genuine inquiry when you have to ask, not what do we usually say, but what should we say. Is it true? Discerning the true Word of God for our situation is extremely complicated and difficult. It requires being able to see things in a fresh light and to have the ego strength to admit that what we have "usually said" might be mistaken. For years the Christian Word was that women ought to keep silent in church and to play subordinate and merely domestic roles; that Word was wrong. For years, the Christian Word was that slavery was inevitable and that Africans and some others deserved to be slaves; that Word was wrong. Many people today, including the official voices of the United Methodist Church to which I belong, say that the practice of homosexuality is incompatible with the Christian gospel; having examined every argument I can find, I have to say that so-called Word is wrong. Preaching the Word of God should always be prophetic, that is, willing to ask whether the words we so easily perform are really true. The leadership in the Word of God that comes from inquiry rather than custom is intellectually difficult, emotionally tense, and spiritually humbling. But would you not rather have a preacher who wrestles with the Word than one who merely rehearses Christian things, especially these days when yesterday's Christian commonsense turns out to be today's bigotry?

Elders' ministries of Order have to do with acquiring, collecting, and deploying the wisdom to make good decisions about the shape and future of Christian life, especially the life of Christian communities as they relate

Call to Ministry

to the larger world. This leadership ministry is ill served by the supposition that decision-making for Christian life is sheerly democratic, however important it is to hear every voice and include everyone in the process. The appeal of democracy in all walks of life comes from the very profound truth that each of us is responsible for what we do and cannot excuse our mistakes by palming off responsibility on some authority. Nevertheless, we cannot assume that merely by voting we are exercising our responsibility, for the outcome of a majority vote might be an atrocious decision to which we would have to defer as an authority. Ordained elders are also ill served by supposing that leadership should be hierarchical, with decisions coming down from themselves at the top (or from bishops in those denominations with an episcopacy). Rather, elders are responsible for developing not only the collective wisdom to make good decisions but also for developing the leadership skills to operate within a large community of people, all of whom have a stake and should be involved in ways that respect their personal responsibility. Such leadership requires energy and intelligence, as well as the people skills we sometimes see in charlatans who have no real wisdom.

Elders' ministries of Sacraments relate to baptism and the Eucharist, for most Protestant denominations. A certain amount of expertise is required to administer the sacraments, and good theology is required to explain them. Expertise and theology are not what make the sacraments the special ministry of elders, however. Our sacristan, Mr. Ames, a layman, is more expert and theologically acute on sacramental matters than most ordained elders, I wager. The reason the ministry of sacraments is especially assigned to elders is because of their representative status. An elder represents the whole church, through the whole of its history. An elder does not act on his or her own behalf or on that of the congregation only, but on behalf of the whole body of Christ. To be baptized and to participate in communion is to be a member of the church universal, however that church is fractured in practice. Because of the processes of ordination, elders are given the status of being tested and approved representatives of the whole church. That representative function also adds a dimension of authority to elders' ministries of Word and Order.

I have spelled out these complicated issues defining ordained ministry because they are important for everyone to understand who is interested in the Christian life. I apologize for the lecture style of this sermon so far. You deserve more juice. Here it is. Just as Jesus called people to ministry who became deacons and elders, so his representatives now call some of you to ordained ministry. I have sketched something of what this calling means: that you would be designated representatives of the whole church, which is Christ's body, exercising leadership in the Service by which God brings redemption to the world, in the articulation of the Word by which we understand the presence and guidance of God, in the Ordering of the community's life, and in the administration of Sacraments by which the Church hosts God in its midst and hosts the people in God's presence. These ministries of ordained people can all be dumbed down. Ordained ministers can be turned into hired hands. But I do not call any of you to dumbed-down servant ministries. I call you, as Jesus did Simon and Andrew, James and John, to ministries where your leadership in Service, where your intellect in expressing the Word, your skills in wise Ordering of the Church, and your holiness as representative administrators of the Sacraments will be worthy of the God you represent. If you heed that call, despite your personal failings, misgivings, and pains, you might just save Nineveh: God does that sometimes. Amen.

19

Authority Now and in the Old Times[1]

Deuteronomy 18:11–20; 1 Corinthians 8:1–13; Mark 1:21–28

The problem of authority in religion vexes us today as it has throughout history. One of the ongoing battles of the American culture wars is the dispute over the authority of Scripture. Fundamentalists say that the scriptures are literally true. More moderate evangelicals say it is sometimes hard to determine what the Scriptures say, but when you do determine that, it is absolutely binding because its truth is divinely inspired. Neo-orthodox theologians such as Karl Barth say that the Scriptures themselves are not inspired but that they are witnesses to events that are divinely inspired, or are God-in-action. Theologians such as Paul Tillich say the real authority is the depth dimension of human experience, and that this allows us to interpret the religious meaning of Scriptures. Eastern Orthodox theologians tend to say that the Scriptures are primary in a long tradition, which, as embodied in church councils, is authoritative, including its interpretation of Scripture. Roman Catholics theologians say much the same thing but add that the pope is the authoritative arbiter of competing elements in the tradition when he speaks ex cathedra. One dimension of the Protestant Reformation stresses the authority of individual responsibility so much that each person is his or her own authority, even in the interpretation of Scripture. Many Americans like to think there is no authority at all, that all truth is relative,

---

1. Preached January 29, 2006, the fourth Sunday after Epiphany.

and that each person can decide what to believe and do on the basis of will, or whim.

If you think this is a confusing situation with regard to authority, things were no better in the ancient world. Consider our three texts.

In the Deuteronomy text, just before Moses died and the people entered into the promised land, he was exhorting them with the news that the Lord would raise up a prophet like himself after his demise. Look closely at the reason the text gives for why there have to be prophets. On Sinai or Horeb, God himself (yes, he was male) came close and almost killed the people with his holiness. So Moses as prophet was a safe substitute for God, speaking for God without threatening the people with God's own presence. He also said the people should obey his successor, because he too would speak for God. In point of fact, no prophet ever arose in Israel as great as Moses, who was a friend of God. Moses could get close without being consumed. Joshua, his immediate successor, was an effective military leader, but no profound friend of God or spiritual guide. Elijah was a fearsome agent of Yahweh's powers, blasting the priests of Baal and rallying the people; he heard the still, small voice. But he was no friend of God who liberated the people of Israel to the extent Moses had. Christians, of course, like to think of Jesus as the successor prophet to Moses. The name "Jesus" is the Aramaic version of "Joshua," who was the historical successor to Moses as the leader of the people, a point not lost on his first-century comrades. But Jesus, however powerful and even divine, was not a prophet like Moses. Nowhere does the New Testament record a conversation between God the Father and Jesus, except from Jesus's side; and Jesus did not win a war of liberation. No Jew would say that Jesus was Moses's successor except in small ways. Moses, at least in the biblical tradition, delivered God's Word as the authoritative Torah, the Pentateuch, the Law. Jesus left only some sermons, parables, and other sayings. Jesus himself believed that Moses had given the authoritative law.

Mark's Gospel text about Jesus says that Jesus taught as a person with authority, not as the traditional teachers of Israel. The traditional teachers had to cite the authority of Moses and the other Scriptures. Jesus just taught as he thought, although we know from other passages that he also sometimes cited Scripture. The drama in our text comes from the presence of a man in the synagogue with an unclean spirit. The spirit was a demon, as they conceived it in those days, that made him crazy. That the demon was unclean meant that it rendered the man unworthy to be in the presence of God, as Leviticus and Numbers described ritual uncleanness and what can be done about that. Now the demon named Jesus as the Holy One of God, which we might think was a wise and true thing to say. But Jesus commanded the demon to be silent, and to leave the man, which is what happened. From this the rest of the people concluded that Jesus was authoritative not only because he spoke without footnotes but because he had powers to cast out demons. The ancient world took such exorcisms very seriously. We know that the religious meaning of casting the unclean spirit out of the man was that the man was allowed to approach God again, a far more profound and general point that Christians make about Jesus. The book of Hebrews says that Jesus leads us all into God's presence in the heavenly temple. Jesus has the capacity to make *us* friends of God. Nevertheless, when we think about authority, it does not cut much ice with us when a person speaks his or her own mind with originality, or even when a person does what we see as magic. You cannot believe everything proclaimed with originality, nor can you be overly swayed by unusual powers. As the great early American theologian Jonathan Edwards said, Satan can counterfeit anything in experience.

So let us look at Paul's more complex case. Paul never claimed to be a prophet, only a teacher. Several times he drew distinctions between what he thought was revealed by Jesus and what he figured out on his own that he hoped was an extension of Jesus's teachings. In our text he was dealing with the following problematic situation. In Corinth, just about all the meat for eating was to be bought at temples of various sorts where it had been ritually slaughtered, as in the kosher preparation of meat. Many religions had temples in town, with many gods served by ritual sacrifices that produced meat for the temple market. That was the way the butcher business was run in those days. Paul noted a class distinction within his Corinthian congregation. On the one hand were the sophisticated, literate folks who would read his letters. He and they knew that there is only one God, whom they knew as the God of Israel, the Father of Jesus Christ. All the rest are either misunderstood versions of the one God or are merely idols, statues. So it was fine with the sophisticated community to get its meat from any of the temple butcher shops because there was nothing there to be afraid of. On the other hand were the unsophisticated and superstitious people who had joined the Christian movement but were convinced that there were competing gods who had to be avoided. For them, eating meat sacrificed to idols was idolatry.

Had we twenty-first-century people been in ancient Corinth, we would have educated the superstitious people and brought them out of their cultural ignorance. It is second nature to us to believe that part of the Christian life is education. The Methodist tradition of this University reflects John Wesley's assumption that educational institutions for the improvement of the lower classes are properly religious institutions. But Wesley was one of the first to believe in religious social transformation. Paul, like nearly everyone else in the ancient world, thought that social classes were fixed categories. So the superstitious Corinthians either had to be vegetarians or fall from their Christian faith by what they had to conceive as idolatry. Paul advised the sophisticated Christians, who could eat meat without threatening their faith, to refrain nevertheless so as not to tempt their tender neighbors.

What kind of authority did Paul have in this advice to the Corinthians? He did not claim to have gotten it through a direct revelation from God, as he did in some other matters. Nor did he claim that he was making his own inferences from what Jesus said about analogous things, as he sometimes did in sexual matters. Rather, his authority came from his being an arbiter of what is good for the community. He argued that the sophisticated people should put up with restrictions on their liberty to eat meat, and the pleasure that goes with it, in order not to sow confusion and temptation to others in the community. While we may lament the patronizing attitude this expresses toward the unsophisticated, we can note with approval that Paul was sustaining a very mixed community.

The people respected his authority, or he at least hoped they would, because he appealed to the larger value of the faithful community. His argument about the issue at hand was pragmatic. He said there was absolutely no religious significance in whether you eat meat or not. But the dilemma lay in whether some people would be tempted to betray what they thought was required for their faith, and this affected the whole community.

Authority in our day is legitimate when it is more like Paul's than like that ascribed to Moses or to Jesus in these texts. Moses and Jesus were charismatic authorities, commanding because they expressed the powers of their relation to God. But we know that charismatic authority can be completely irresponsible, as it was in Hitler's case. We know how the media can be used to deceive and make people look godly when they are only charlatans. Of course, it is difficult to be inspired to do difficult things that require sacrifice, without charismatic leadership. Charismatic leaders are important and perhaps even necessary, in religion and politics. But charisma should not convey authority. We should be suspicious of that. Rather we should look for the authority that comes from being expertly faithful to the good of the community. For religious communities, that expert faithfulness to the good always includes the capacity to relate the religious ground of that community to the circumstances at hand, as Paul did with the Corinthian vegetarians.

Expertise is an important part of authority, but not a sufficient condition. Paul knew about how some people eating meat in the congregation would put terrific psychological pressures on people who think they have to abstain from meat because to eat would betray their faith. He said that the liberty to eat meat was not as important as sustaining the superstitious people in the community of faith. Paul was an expert in the charity and forbearance required for life in Christian community. Our own issues for Christian life are just as complex as his, and expertise both in spiritual matters and social matters for churches is more detailed and scientific now than in his time. Our authoritative leaders need to have that expertise, or our religious life will be like Saint Francis's when he called all the people to gather in the church to pray about the plague, thereby infecting nearly everyone.

But expertise by itself is not enough for religious authority in our time. We also need the recognized wisdom to discern the good for the community. Wisdom comes from experience, but also from a readiness to learn, humility, practice in the exercise of authority where mistakes are not disastrous, and from a deeply chastened religious sensibility. Religious authority now as much as ever, perhaps more than ever, requires deep spirituality, long experience with the dark night of the soul and with the bliss of God's loveliness.

As we all know, not a few people believe they themselves have the requisites for authority, the expertise, the experience, the spiritual qualifications. But authority is bestowed by those who respect it, not by those who claim it. Religious institutions seek to vet claims to authority by various requirements and trials, including processes that allow the community to approve or disapprove those to whom they would grant institutional authority. My discussion of ordained ministry last week touched on that. But alas we know that institutions can promote to official authoritative positions people who lack the expertise, the experience, and the spiritual substance for true authority. Furthermore, authority rather than mere law enforcement is needed precisely at the point where new circumstances require institutions to change and where the old tests might have become irrelevant.

Therefore, Beloved, I am sad to say that the responsibility for cultivating and identifying religious authorities lies with us who need authorities to respect. To some degree we can count on professional peer evaluation and certification. Nevertheless we need to be skeptical both of charismatic charlatans and institutional bureaucrats defined by faithfulness to the status quo. We cannot do without authorities, nor each be our own authority, because we live together in communities that need authoritative leadership. So we need to cultivate and assess authorities ourselves. This imposes a burden of expertise on all of us, and a responsibility to discern our own as well as other people's depth of experience and spiritual substance. All of this is to say that part of our calling as Christians is to create a community that understands and creates the authorities it needs, and that knows how to respect and embrace that authority critically. Although we might think this is merely a political necessity for community life, it is in fact a matter of divine call. For, the authorities we respect and should respect in religion are those who speak for God in matters great and small. To be sure, we all are responsible in the end for our own behavior and beliefs, and cannot pass that responsibility off to others. Nevertheless, we have learned enough humility about ourselves to know that we ourselves are often not the authorities we need, even for ourselves. Are we not often charlatans to ourselves? Do we not often think we have the requisite expertise when we do not? Do we not often think we have experience when it turns out we missed what was before our face? Do we not know that the spirit in our lives is sometimes not the Holy One? Our personal, as well as corporate, responsibility is to find and follow those who, like Moses and Jesus, and Paul too, genuinely speak for God. Or to say this another way, we need to find friends of God who can lead us to become friends of God. Amen.

20

Healing, Praying, Preaching[1]

Isaiah 40:21–31; 1 Corinthians 9:11–23; Mark 1:21–39

We are about to celebrate the Eucharist, which in various symbolic ways is a participation in Jesus Christ. Some of these symbols are deeply mysterious. But others are fairly plain. Who is the Jesus in whom we participate? According to our gospel this morning, Jesus was a healer, a prayer, and a preacher. When we participate in Jesus, taking in and taking on the flesh and blood of Christ, we become healers, prayers, and preachers. Let's think about this for a bit, and I want to do so in reverse order of those ministries.

What did Jesus *preach*? It certainly was not himself, except on rare occasions, mentioned mainly in the Gospel of John. The Christian preaching tradition has a long history of preaching a lot about Jesus as a divine member of the holy family, come to earth to redeem humankind from its merited consignment to the devil. But Jesus himself knew nothing about that. Rather, the usual subject of his preaching was the kingdom of God: we are in that kingdom and are usually unaware of that. If we were to become aware, we would know we were under judgment, as John the Baptist had said. We would know that the kingdom's content is near-infinite demands of justice and mercy, served up with the force of cosmic love. Jesus's sermons were about waking up to this fact and amending our lives in accord with the sudden discovery that the worldly values of our ordinary politics

---

1. Preached February 5, 2006, the fifth Sunday after Epiphany.

are only abstract and often misleading parts of God's cosmic kingdom. The proper way to address all this, preached Jesus, is to become lovers of everyone, beginning with the formation of small communities of friends. The shock of his "good news" was that everyone, every kind of person, should be included in such communities, including women (who in his time were relegated to the kitchen), poor people oppressors, Gentiles, and even enemies. Jesus's preaching amounted to proclaiming that a new and holy life is possible when we recognize that we live in God's world, not just in the plain old world we see day to day.

Now the language of Jesus's preachment is problematic for us. Hardly anyone lives in kingdoms any more. Even the nations with monarchs also have parliaments that usually are more powerful than kings. We do not acknowledge lords, and we do not own vassals. So when we preach the kingdom of God in Jesus's name, we use the notion with much greater metaphoric distance than that language would have been heard to have in Jesus's time. Post-Enlightenment culture puts a far higher premium on universal personal responsibility than did folk religion in antiquity, and we would think it a fault merely to do what some king tells you to do. Furthermore, we know the cosmos to be so vast in extent that the idea of God functioning as a king over human affairs on planet Earth is ludicrous when we think about it. So what does the central metaphor of Jesus's preaching mean in our time, as we discern its significance as the word of God? I believe it means two things.

First it means that God has created a cosmos that has moral standards within it for creatures such as human beings, who are capable of moral behavior. The content of those standards can be discerned, among other places, in the specific preaching of Jesus, in sermons such as the Sermon on the Mount and in many parables. One of the deepest and most difficult parts of being Jesus's preachers today is discerning just how those standards apply in our current situation. In a nation that puts economic greed before justice, the enforcement of alleged national interest through military invasion before peace, the manipulation of information to support ideologies before the uncovering of truth, and self-deluded self-righteousness before love of enemies, a desperate people calls out for prophetic preaching.

Second, Jesus's metaphor of the kingdom of God means for us that we stand under judgment for how we live in the world with moral standards. Our identity before God does not consist in our power or wealth as the world's kingdoms measure it, but in how we affect the world for better or worse in the ways Jesus described as matters of righteousness. This part of preaching leads us to confession and repentance, and another part of Jesus's preaching shows us God's mercy and love that saves us from ourselves. As a preacher, Jesus pointed to how we should live in the world before God, and who we are before God. Jesus's preaching gives us a vision of God incarnate. We need continually to update that preaching for our time.

Jesus also was a prayer. Our text says he went out before dawn to pray in a secluded place, and other texts also describe his efforts to find solitude for prayer, which were often frustrated, as here, by people wanting him to help them. Ironically, in the garden of Gethsemane, when he did want friends to pray with him, they went to sleep on him, and he sweated blood in unwanted solitude. Jesus's prayer life was the center of his ministry, and he taught its importance and techniques to his friends. The Lord's Prayer is one of the most remembered prayers in the world. Now I have to say that Dean Olson, our liturgist, is deeply disappointed that there are no records of Jesus leading any Jewish liturgies, except by attendance and preaching. But nearly all Christian liturgies are about Jesus, inspired by him, and organized to lead us to participate in his prayer life; the early Christians made his last supper into the liturgy that we are about to celebrate.

We have a special way of participating in Jesus's life as a prayer. In our prayers we can imagine Jesus to be with us, to know us, to be our comfort in the dark valleys of our lives, to be our friend in life's mountain-peak experiences, and to be our companion in the daily round of ordinary life. Imagining Jesus to know our own hearts fully, we can admit to them ourselves. Imagining Jesus to judge our hearts exactly, we can make confession. Imagining Jesus to love our hearts despite it all, we can love ourselves and one another, despite it all. The spiritual life of prayer leads us, layer by layer, to greater self-knowledge, judgment, and unconditional love. Our Christian traditions in thousands of ways make Jesus accessible to the imaginative power of our spirits.

Jesus, finally, was a healer. The cognates for "healing" in Greek and Latin as well as English have to do with wholeness and salvation. Jesus's healings had to do with making people whole. Some people are not whole because they are alienated from society; so Jesus healed lepers who had been ostracized. Some people are not whole because they cannot relate to their world; so Jesus healed blind people. Some people are not whole because their own personalities war against themselves; so Jesus healed people possessed by demons, as they thought in those days. All of these conditions, and others that Jesus healed, make those who suffer them unclean and therefore unready to meet God, according to the ancient Israelite religion. So the bottom line of salvation or healing is the wholeness that consists in being at one with God, not alienated; engaged with God, not distant; centered before God, not in self-contradiction.

What does this wholeness or salvation mean in our time? The most influential philosophical tradition in the West, stemming from Aristotle, says that wholeness or salvation means completeness, achieving a kind of total fulfillment; the root meaning of "perfection" means being complete. But this cannot be what Christian wholeness or salvation means, however fortunate such total fulfillment might be. For, the condition of human existence necessarily is fragmentation and ambiguity, not completeness. Look at Jesus: he treated many but not all sick people, he had disciples who could not fully understand his teachings, he attempted vainly to purify the Judaism of his time, he never got around to having a family, and he died too young. He was executed for no crime that he committed. He was an accidental victim in the politics of an imperial power trying to keep the peace in a subjugated people with a puppet government: think of the innocents of Baghdad. Pontius Pilate knew Jesus's death was undeserved "collateral damage." The lives of all of us are fragmentary that way. Salvation or wholeness means living with that fragmentariness and ambiguity without losing the capacity to love ourselves, one another, and our Creator who gives us this fragmentary and ambiguous world. With such love, we can accomplish amazing things, perhaps even make our world a bit like the kingdom of God.

I invite you to come to this Eucharist to participate in this healer, prayer, and preacher, Jesus. When you consume the elements, you put a little bit of this Jesus into you with the power to heal you, to lead you to God in prayer, and to open your mind to a vision of God's holiness. That little bit will grow into great powers. When you consume the elements, you also put yourself into Jesus in his larger identity as the heart and mind of the church. You will take up his ministry of healing others, his practices of leading people in prayer, his preaching of the kingdom of God. That you become part of the living Christ is perhaps more important than that the healing, praying, preaching Jesus becomes part of you. For the full significance of Jesus is that he places us within the divine life, judged, but also loved and at home. Jesus makes us clean, and presents us to God. We become God's story, then, not our own story.

Healing, Praying, Preaching

If you would be healed, come to this table. If you would come to God in prayer, come to this table. If you would know the truth and speak it, come to this table. If you would love your neighbors by healing them, come to this table. If you would love your neighbors by leading them to God in prayer, come to this table. If you would enlighten them with God's truth, even a little bit, come to this table. If you would love God with all alienation healed, come to this table. If you would love God with a spiritual union in prayer, come to this table. If you would love God in vision and truth, come to this table. It has been set for us from the beginning. Amen.

21

Witness[1]

2 Kings 5:1–14; 1 Corinthians 9:21–27; Mark 1:1–45

How hard it is to tell the truth, to bear true witness! Bearing true witness is not just saying true things. It is communicating the truth, making the truth believable. Sometimes bearing false witness is an attempt to deceive people, but other times it is a failure to understand and bear true witness. Think of the bizarre story of Elisha healing Naaman the leper. I should tell you that the pious Christians who constructed the lectionary included only the first fourteen verses of this text, believing, I suppose, that Elisha's transferring of Naaman's leprosy to his own servant, as related in the remainder of the chapter, is not morally uplifting. Elisha was not a nice man, however. When some small boys called him "Baldhead," he summoned two she-bears to maul forty-two of them; I'll bet that story was not discussed in your Sunday school class, so you should look up 2 Kings 2:21–24.

Naaman was the general for the king of Aram, who was a neighbor and generally an enemy of Israel. Naaman had engineered an Aramean victory over the Israelites, and our text says it was Yahweh who gave Naaman that victory. So the Israelite claim that God was on their side was a false witness in this instance. Naaman, in contrast to Elisha, must have been a nice man because one of the Israelite girls he had captured and turned into a slave in his own household urged him to go to Elisha to be cured of his

---

1. Preached February 12, 2006, the sixth Sunday after Epiphany.

leprosy. The slave gave a true witness to Elisha's power. The king of Aram was supportive of this and gave Naaman a letter of introduction to the king of Israel, asking him to facilitate the cure; this was a true and good intent. But the king of Israel misconstrued the letter as a false witness, thinking it a trick to give the Arameans a cause to invade again. Saddam Hussein must have felt like the king of Israel when the American government talked about Iraqi weapons of mass destruction. When Elisha heard of his king's distress, he sent word for Naaman to visit him, which is what happened.

Elisha did not go out of his house to greet Naaman, however. He sent a servant, perhaps Gehazi, to tell him to wash seven times in the Jordan and he would be clean. That was a true witness, but Naaman heard it as false. Naaman was probably offended by the lack of courtesy, and he thought that bathing in the rivers of his own country would have been just as effective as the Jordan. Leaving in a rage, Naaman was turned back by his own servants' argument that he would have been willing to do something difficult if Elisha had told him to, so why not just try this easy thing? He did and was cured, now believing Elisha's true if discourteous witness. He returned to Elisha to pay him, but Elisha refused pay; Naaman affirmed his service to Yahweh and asked for two mule-loads of earth to take back to his own land so that he could worship Yahweh on Yahweh's own land. He said he would worship only Yahweh, with the exception of his official duties escorting the king of Aram to worship the god of Aram. Naaman's act of piety in thanks to Yahweh for his cure was an extraordinary true witness.

Elisha's servant, Gehazi, however, saw an opportunity for graft and with a lie, a false witness, put the touch on Naaman for booty shortly after he had left Elisha's house. Naaman was told the request came from Elisha and he obliged. Gehazi put the booty in his own quarters. Elisha caught him, and Gehazi lied to Elisha about where he had been. But Elisha was an accomplished clairvoyant and had seen Gehazi misrepresent Elisha's wishes for a reward; Elisha's extrasensory perception was a remarkable true witness. So he punished Gehazi's false witness by covering him with leprosy. Perhaps that was a bit harsh by our standards, or cruel and unusual punishment, but we have a fairly stiff alternative in mind for the crooks in big business. The moral of the story is threefold: do not bear false witness, do bear true witness, and sometimes it is hard to know what to believe.

This colorful story was paired with the gospel in the lectionary because both deal with healing leprosy; I'm sure that Mark had in mind to compare Jesus as a prophet to Elisha's healing power in the way he told the story. The witness in Mark's story was the leper who came to Jesus, proclaiming Jesus's power to heal him if he chose to do so. That was a true witness and Jesus verified it. He reached and touched the leper—not many others would have done that. Then he said he chose to heal him, and did so. After the healing Jesus gave the man a stern warning not to witness to how he was healed. Instead, the man should only go to the temple to be ritually cleaned and approved by the priest. What was that all about? Some people say Jesus did not want to become known as a miracle worker, because all the lepers would come to him. Jesus obviously did not spend his time healing everyone who came to him, and did not think of his ministry as a medical one in our sense of that term. But why would he not want the healed leper to witness to his powers? In other places his healing power is construed as testimony to his spiritual power and the truth of his message. Why not here? Was he trying to disguise his real identity this early in his ministry? We do not know.

At any rate, the leper gave true testimony about Jesus, according to the story, and spread that word effectively. As a result, Jesus could not go into populated areas, and the people sought him out in the countryside. We know the end of the story, of course. The people abandoned Jesus, and Jesus had no magical powers to cure the sickness in the religious and political leaders about whom he was concerned. Of all the Gospels, Mark's is the most ambiguous. You remember it ends with the women terrified, gazing at the empty tomb. No resurrection appearances, just terror. The last line of the Gospel is, "and they said nothing to anyone, for they were afraid."

Now I ask you, what is our witness about Jesus today? How can we give true witness rather than false witness? It would be false witness, I fear, to represent the Gospels and other writings of the New Testament as giving literal histories of Jesus. The New Testament writers were themselves witnessing to what Jesus meant to them, and their witness is that he is Messiah and Savior of the world—not just of Israel but of the world. Of course, there was a historical Jesus and he did the things that got him remembered and interpreted in the New Testament way. But the biblical writings are not histories in our sense, and they fall into contradiction and implausibility if read as histories. There was an important theological movement of the nineteenth and twentieth centuries that attempted to identify what can be known with critical certainty about the historical Jesus, and then to draw religiously significant meaning from that historical knowledge. That movement was a bust. Moreover, it bracketed out of consideration all the attempts in the New Testament to say what Jesus meant religiously, precisely because those things were interpretations, not historical reporting. So the movement obscured the Bible's religious testimony.

The Jesus that is real to us is the remembered Jesus, the literary Jesus, the Jesus remembered in the New Testament and then in subsequent theological writings. We also have the liturgical Jesus, the Jesus remembered in our rites and music. The remembered Jesus is the one that is real to us, and effective, the Jesus we can touch. So who is this remembered Jesus to whom we witness?

First, Jesus is indeed a healer. We do not have to believe in the healing miracles of the Bible to make this point. I recommend strongly that we think of those miracles, such as the one in our gospel today, as symbols of something else, however credible they were to people in the first century who believed that magic is a common event. But I have seen the remembered Jesus heal. I have known people whose lives were so broken, so confused, so addicted to destruction, so self-destructive, that they had no hope for being decent persons. Then someone told them about Jesus, they remembered Jesus of the Bible, who loves even them. And their lives were transformed. They clung to that literary Jesus, that liturgical Jesus of some worshiping community, and were healed. Their theology might not have been sophisticated at first, but Jesus saved them and they were healed. The Jesus I remember says that anyone can come to him and have their souls made whole. I've seen that work, and witness to those miracles.

I've seen communities, families, and even church congregations, that were filled with hate, recrimination, lust for vengeance, and an infinite round of resentment. We all know about the round of hatred in Northern Ireland and the Middle East. We've also all known smaller communities like that up close. But have you ever seen such a wrangle of wretched hate brought up short by the memory of Jesus and his love, by the hearing of his call to love our enemies, by his proclamation that even God is merciful and forgiving, by his willingness to sacrifice his work and friends and his whole life for the sake of reconciliation? I've seen that happen, and the community slowly deconstructs its hate and recrimination, its lust for vengeance and resentment; it learns to forgive, and to practice love. That is Jesus healing now, and we have seen it and touched it. The master witness to this kind of healing in our time was Martin Luther King Jr., who made aggressive pacifism a powerful instrument of justice in the name of love. We too can witness to this healing, for we have seen it.

Nurture in Time and Eternity

Jesus is not only a healer, but a preacher who himself witnesses to God's justice and mercy. Through sermons and parables recorded in the New Testament, and then through two thousand years of interpretations of Jesus, we have his word that every creature in the world is God's creature. God is equally close to them all. Justice consists in treating every creature as beloved of God, without favoritism. Our ethical principles for relating to one another attempt to express this. The norms for international politics demand this. Our environmental concerns should be guided by this word about God as creator and lover of all. That we are personally sinners, wicked as a nation, and abusive to our environment is itself the judgment upon us, however balanced that is with some virtue, kindness, and care. We cannot bear false witness about ourselves to God: that is metaphysically impossible. More powerful than judgment, however, is God's redeeming mercy that Jesus preached. Indeed, Jesus said, and we have seen it proved again and again, that even sinners are loved and can be healed by that love, even rogue nations can repent, make amends, and return to justice, even abused ecologies can recover. The wild fecundity of God, who with abandon sends rain and sun on the just and unjust alike, blows through the world with a cosmically vast power making things new. We have seen all this, we have touched it, and we can understand it to witness for it.

Jesus is not only a healer and a preacher, but, as I said last week, Jesus is among us as a prayer, a spiritual force who brings us to God as he himself was in love with God. We don't witness only to Jesus teaching people to pray, or to the prayers inspired by him throughout the life of the church, although those things are important. It is more important to witness to the mystery of God that Jesus shows us. Jesus reflects in our midst the ambiguous, uncanny, undomesticated, larger-than-life wildness of God. Jesus points to the Abyss of creation, the nothing from which we come. Jesus is the Light of God in which all things might be understood. Jesus is the Fire of the Spirit that can cleanse us and make us God's hands. Jesus is the Deep River of our spiritual lives, the divine flood that carries us to the unimaginable God. What a blessing it is that the Bible is not a straightforward history of the man Jesus! At an important level Jesus cannot be comprehended, and we must comprehend that.

When we remember this wild Jesus we are brought closer to the wild God. Jesus is remembered not only as a man but as a mysterious wonder worker, a preacher whose text came from heaven, the incarnation of the divine Word itself, the Cosmic Christ embracing the Big Bang and the Final Dissipation as Alpha and Omega, all glorious, the King of the Universe whom you can sense sitting beside you on the pew, in the poor man, the suffering woman, the starving child. Jesus is all these images remembered together who shocks us out of our ordinary sleepwalking and lets us know we are in God's world. The remembered Jesus is here and now, incised in the carvings and windows of this church, in all the images that wake us from sleep. Jesus is the cosmic witness to God.

In our time, we are the witnesses to Jesus, just like the healed leper. Our witness is not to something in the long past but to something we have seen and touched. We have seen the remembered Jesus heal persons and communities. We need to testify to this, especially in light of all the people and groups who have not been healed. The teachings of Jesus have seared our consciences, opening our hearts to know we are under judgment, but also in the thrall of cosmic mercy. Everyone here has experienced this in one way or another. The remembered Jesus, whose images are so fantastic, so exaggerated, so profound, wakes us to the wildness of God and the reality of our situation as creatures. The moments of this awakening are bliss, heavenly vision, the ultimate witness. O Lord, we are infinitely grateful to be your witnesses, testifying to what we have seen and touched. Amen.

22

Transformation to See God[1]

2 Kings 2:1–12; 2 Corinthians 4:1–6; Mark 9:1–9

In the story of the Transfiguration, as related in Mark, with similar accounts in Matthew and Luke, Jesus is revealed to his disciples Peter, James, and John as in a heavenly state with Moses and Elijah. Many people in antiquity believed that the natural universe is composed of a stack of levels of physical planes, with different properties and natural laws obtaining on each level. The earth is somewhere near the middle with a series of heavens above and hells below. Aristotle, for instance, believed that in the earth's plane below the orbit of the moon things naturally travel in straight lines unless deflected whereas the moon and higher "heavenly bodies" travel in circles; the moon itself keeps the same face toward the earth whereas Aristotle thought that the higher stars spin as well as move circularly. In the popular imagination, beings whose natural properties fit some heavenly or hellish level sometimes cross boundaries and come to earth as angels or evil spirits, and behave in ways appropriate to their native level that look weird or miraculous according to the causal patterns of the earthly level. Paul imagined that God dwells in the highest level, or even beyond that insofar as God is creator of all the heavens and the earth. Paul thought that Jesus's natural place was at the highest heaven with God, but that he had descended to the earthly level, taking on human form, even that of a lowly slave. Jesus did not keep his heavenly form, as angels did when they

---

1. Preached February 26, 2006, Transfiguration Sunday.

Transformation to See God

miraculously appeared on earth, but really took on the natural properties of a human being. Paul also imagined that Jesus would draw saved human beings up to some high heavenly level with God, and the human beings in this journey would take on the natural properties of that heavenly level, which include immortality. That is, we shall be transformed from a human mode of existence to a heavenly mode, with physical properties appropriate for that higher level. Because several levels of heaven exist, each with its own properties, we can reconcile seemingly contradictory stories. For instance, when talking with the Sadducees about whose wife in heaven the woman would be who had married all of seven brothers, Jesus said she would be sexless, like angels. But in speaking of the conversation between Abraham with Lazarus in some heaven and the greedy rich man in some hell, they characters retained very much of their earthly identity. In the story of the Transfiguration, our gospel for today, Moses, Elijah, and Jesus are all recognizable, as if they have taken on the properties of a heaven very close to earth with only an unearthly iridescence and an immortality for human life so that Moses and Elijah could converse with Jesus.

The spiritual point of the Transfiguration scene, of course, is not about heavenly and earthly geography at all. It is rather about how we can see God in Jesus. And the precise moral is that Peter, James, and John missed the point. They misunderstood what they saw, and Jesus told them not to talk about it until after the crucifixion and resurrection when they might understand. This is to say, the disciples would have to be transformed before they could see God.

In our day we have a vastly different cosmic geography from that of the ancient world. The heart of the difference is that we think the same physical laws apply throughout the whole cosmos, not different laws for different levels. The laws of motion, say, for the propagation of light, are the same here as on the moon, on Mars, on Alpha Centauri, in the farthest galaxy, and all in between. Therefore "nature" embraces everything with which we are causally connected with the same causal laws. The unearthly properties and causal patterns the ancients attributed to the levels of angels and devils, and to which human beings might aspire in attaining closer proximity to God in salvation, we moderns call "supernatural." In the ancient world, all the levels were natural, and all equally part of creation; nothing was supernatural. In the modern world we imagine a huge distinction between the natural and supernatural, and many people do not believe in the supernatural. In the ancient world, Jacob's Ladder, on which angels and human beings ascended and descended, was a powerful and innocent metaphor for moving through the levels of cosmic existence. So was the image of the chariot that carried Elijah off to heaven, in today's Hebrew Bible text. For us, those metaphors are at best broken symbols because we know that when you go very high the air thins and disappears and you get to outer space, not heaven.

So how do *we* see God? To put the point a slightly different way, with what images or concepts can we engage God experientially? Without some images or identifying concepts we cannot discriminate God at all within our experience. Yet we long for God. Like Jesus and his friends, our hearts are not at rest until they rest in God. Let me suggest two classical answers to the question: like the ancients, we see God as the creator of our cosmos, God in nature. Like the ancient Christians, we see God in Christ.

The ancients, not only the Jews and Christians, understood God as creator of the cosmos, which they imagined as a stack of planes of different natural worlds. For us, the cosmos is a natural causal unity, most likely beginning some billions of years ago with the Big Bang and perhaps ending some billions of years hence with a final dissipation of energy in which nothing is close enough to anything else to exert or receive influence. Whatever turns out to be the best hypothesis, its image of the cosmos is vastly different from that of the first century, astonishingly larger and older, even different in the conception of space and time. Where is God in that?

God is the creator of the world we are coming to know better and better. God is the creator of time and space, since time and space are functions of matter or energy in motion. Although some of the great ancient philosophers had ideas that are remarkably modern in this respect, most ancients imagined God to be contained within time and space, at the top of the spatiotemporal plenum. We, by contrast, have to imagine God as creating both time and space. God's creative act is not in time. It does not have a date. All dates are its products. God's creative act is not within space. It does not have a place. God does not exist somewhere, alongside the cosmos or anywhere else. God's creative act is eternal, not temporal with regard to time, and it is immense, immeasurable, not spatially locatable. Can you imagine that? Can you get your mind around the eternity and immensity of God who is nowhere and at no time, not even now? Our contemporary spirituality needs to see through the imagination of contemporary physics, just as the ancient spirituality saw God through the terms of their physical imagination of the multilayered universe.

Transformation to See God

One implication of our imagination of God as the creator of the whole space-time cosmos is that God cannot be separate from the cosmos, not in another distant place or in some precreation or postapocalyptic time. Rather, God is the immediate source of everything within this world, not separate, but interior, our inmost essence. We are the products of God's singular creative act, the end-products, the light from the divine fire, the water from the divine fountain, the dance of the dancer. As Augustine said, God is closer to us than we are to ourselves. We can see God in a snowflake, in a biological ecosystem that displays the intricacies of the interrelations of things in God's creation, in the grinding of tectonic plates floating on the earth's molten core, in the blasts of supernovas, the births and deaths of stars. God is the intimate creator in all those things, and when they pay no heed to the needs of the human scale, overwhelming civilizations with blind destructive forces, God is intimate to that too.

Perhaps the most awesome result of finding God the creator in the cosmos is sensing God's intimate presence within our own hearts and relations. How are we free in our greatest achievements and deepest sins, if God is our inmost self and the ground of our every relation with others? The advantage of the ancient image of God as a being separate from us in a very high place was that people could imagine the problem of freedom relative to God on the analogy of freedom relative to other people. Many people today insist on keeping that ancient image of God as just another being, however exalted, in our space-time world, precisely because it facilitates thinking of God as another being with whom we negotiate our freedom and destiny. If we wish to see God through the cosmos as we know it, then we must come to terms with an intimacy with God that far surpasses the ancient images of God as king whom we petition for benefits. If we would see God ourselves, and not just repeat what the ancients said they saw, we must engage God as far more transcendent, beyond space and time, and yet far more intimate, not separate at all from us God's creatures. Furthermore, that engagement of God is to love God. Can we love the God of cosmic blasts, minute attractions, the intimate springs of our souls, who is nowhere and no-when? The love of God is no easy matter, yet I tell you it is bliss.

I invite you to such a spiritual life with the imagination of our time. It is what the ancients pursued with the imagination of their time, which is why I say this spiritual quest for God is classical.

The other classical answer to the question of how to see God is that we should look for God in Christ. But it is hard to see Christ today. Jesus said that we are to be peacemakers, and yet for nearly two thousand years we have reconciled Christianity with wars of conquest and domination. I'm pleased to say that the great majority of Christian denominations condemned the war in Iraq from the beginning; but I fear that the majority of American Christians voted for the war, or at least for the administration that sought the war. How have we filtered our image of Jesus so as to reconcile him with Christian-sponsored belligerence?

Jesus said that we are to pursue justice, and yet for nearly two thousand years we have acquiesced in devastating injustice. To be sure, we have come to understand that injustice is not only in the will of the powerful and greedy but also in the institutions of society. In Jesus's time people thought slavery was natural, that women should be dominated by men, and that the poor will always be with us. Jesus preached values that criticize these injustices, but only now do we understand how the injustices are built in to social systems that ought to be changed. Christians in our time can no longer acquiesce in injustices such as these. We need to be able to see Christ as preaching freedom of the oppressed, equality for all people, care for the poor who suffer from economic relations, and dignity for the entirety of God's creation. Until we can imagine Jesus in these late-modern terms, we cannot see Jesus, or God in Christ.

Jesus said we should love, extending that love to people our culture forbids us to touch, to people of different social classes, even to our enemies. His table fellowship embodied this teaching, and he said love is the way we connect to God. We can see God in Christ when we see Jesus teaching us to be lovers. Nevertheless, we have blocked this vision of God in Christ by filtering it through cultural definitions of who is lovable. Of course, we cannot live without cultures that define who is with us and who is outside the cultural group. Yet a Christian culture should be explicit that everyone is inside the divine culture, however bizarre they might be in their taste in food, clothing, and friends. In a profound sense, Jesus was anticultural in his critiques of the boundaries of cultures. The problem with cultures is that they make us think that their conventions are intuitions into reality. In the culture of my grade school in St. Louis, my friends just saw that African Americans were of lesser human standing, no one to share a toilet or water fountain with; my father taught me that culture was wrong. Think of the bigotries we still entertain, even in liberal Boston, against those whom our culture defines as different from some human norm. How can we see Jesus's gospel as relativizing even our own cultures?

Transformation to See God

We find it hard to see God in Christ because we have accommodated our visions of Jesus to our war making, our injustice, and our cultural denials of love's scope. Surely other reasons exist as well for why it is so hard for us to see Jesus in our current lives. To surmount this difficulty we do not need to learn more about Jesus as much as we need to transform ourselves so as to accept the Christ who is so plain before our faces. To learn enough about our natural world to understand how God can be creator of it is hard enough. We need to remake ourselves so that we can see Jesus who reveals God to us.

So we return to the Transfiguration. Do not get hung up on the image of Jesus taking on the visage of some heavenly, unearthly, apparition. Think of him rather as displaying with a dazzling brightness no bleach can reproduce the truth about peace, justice and love, and how we distort all that, and how our true home is to live in a clearly confessed and redeemed faith that grasps that. But we do not understand this any better than his disciples who thought they should build little houses. We need to be transformed in order to get the point, just as Jesus's disciples did. We need to understand our cosmos to see God as its creator. The disciples' transformation came when they learned to love Jesus, lost him to the cross, and found him again. I fear that we Christians who think we love Jesus and still are bellicose, unjust, and bigoted about who is lovely need to lose Jesus. Such Christian culture needs to collapse and the raw hunger for God needs to be felt again. Perhaps then we can be changed so as to see God revealed in Jesus who says to love both God and neighbor. Amen.

23

Hypocrisy and Piety[1]

Joel 2:1–2, 11–17; 2 Corinthians 5:20b–6:10; Matthew 6:1–6, 11–21

So far as I can tell, the only sense of humor exhibited by the people who assembled our lectionary readings is the assignment of Jesus's remarks condemning public displays of piety to Ash Wednesday, the day when most of us are going to display the ashes of penance on our foreheads. Jesus says explicitly to wash your face so that others will not see your pious practice, which is for the sight of God alone. How can we take this text seriously, given what we are about to do?

Ash Wednesday, of course, introduces the season of Lent, in which we systematically, for a set period of forty days plus Sundays, come to terms with our sins, individual and corporate. Coming to terms with sins first means identifying them. Then it means acknowledging them as our own, taking responsibility for them. Finally it means doing something about them, making amends where we can, discontinuing sinful behavior, and altering sinful conditions and institutions. All this counts as Lenten penance. We undertake Lenten penance, not because we win salvation by it, but as a response to God's gracious salvation that allows us to become holy through penance in the first place. Additionally, Lenten penance prepares us to participate in Christ's passion, his crucifixion, resurrection, and ascension, as that is celebrated in Holy Week which concludes the Lenten season.

1. Preached March 1, 2006, Ash Wednesday.

Hypocrisy and Piety

Now Jesus was suspicious of this high-powered organized, indeed ritualized, piety because it was so susceptible to hypocrisy. He thought that conspicuous displays of self-discipline and charity can be ruined in their true intent by being used to persuade others that we are better than we are. If we practice pious acts, or dress in special ways, or beat ourselves up in front of others so that they will think us especially religious, then that skewed motive takes away the real religious value of what we do. Jesus was particularly concerned about hypocrisy, more than any other sin, perhaps. The reason, I believe, is that hypocrisy substitutes a lie for honesty, a lie disguised as pious honesty. Honesty is made to undermine itself. Without honesty there can be no true love. Without honesty, people cannot present themselves to God except as condemned already. Jesus was concerned that the practices of Judaism in his time were hypocritical and therefore self-defeating.

Today we need not be concerned about hypocrisy in Second Temple Judaism, which might not have been as universal as Jesus sometimes suggested. Rather, we need to be concerned about hypocrisy in our own Lenten penance. The danger is not that we will fool others. People in our time, perhaps because of Jesus's teaching, are highly attuned to pick up on hypocrisy. The danger is that we will try to fool ourselves. That sounds like a contradiction, does it not? How can we lie to ourselves? It's easy: we deny our real motives.

Would it not be easy to wear the ashes of penance today in the ostensible conviction that we are going to come to terms with our sins when in fact it is a cover for our real intent of maintaining things as they are? We can be firmly convinced this morning that we shall be honest about our sins, but have all the defense mechanisms in place to prevent our discovering the ones that lie below the surface. The thing about penance is that it is a process, one that takes time, and one that turns up new and worse material along the way. You might think you suffer from the sin of sloth or laziness, when in fact you might be in flight from life itself, from the life God has given you. You might think you suffer from the sin of selfishness and greed, when in fact you might be in despair because you think your life is meaningless unless you own or control something. You might think you suffer from the sin of hatred and anger toward others, when in fact you might hate yourself, God's own precious gift. You cannot love others if you hate yourself. So Jesus warns us that we should beware of hypocrisy in our

Lenten journey when we beat ourselves up about the surface sins in order to hide from ourselves the deeper ones that have to do with rejecting God's gracious creation. True piety requires an honesty that we can acquire only with great difficulty as we open ourselves to God.

This focus on personal piety was not at the center of Jesus's attention. He was more concerned about the hypocrisy that affected the people as a whole. Many of our nation's Christian leaders tell us, and themselves, and possibly believe, that the way to peace is through making war. What a disastrous self-deception that has been! Is the real unacknowledged motive a misplaced pride in power or greed for oil or desire to impose an American will? Many of our nation's Christian leaders tell us, and themselves, and possibly believe, that the way to economic justice is to enrich the rich more and more so that they will spend their money on things that benefit the poor. What a disastrous self-deception that has been! Is the real unacknowledged motive a desire to be admired and accepted by the rich and powerful? Many of our nation's Christian leaders tell us, and themselves, and possibly believe, that our freedoms should be curtailed, including the freedom of information, because that will limit the freedom of terrorists to do bad things. But then the terrorists will have won without the necessity of bombs. Our nation's self-understanding as a bastion of peace, justice, and democratic freedom has been turned to a hypocritical cover for the sins of empire and oligarchy. Can we enter the season of Lenten penance warned about the need not to be fooled by this hypocrisy?

I invite you to wear the ashes of penance as a sign of vigilance against the hypocrisy of pious self-righteousness that prevents true penance. Let this be a badge of courage to face the humiliating revelations that our virtues might in fact cover faults, and that the little sins we acknowledge might open as windows onto our true condition. This badge also signifies, always remember, that no matter how bad we find ourselves to be, God redeems and loves us. Amen.

24

Baptism[1]

Genesis 9:1–17; 1 Peter 3:11–22; Mark 1:1–15

The Eucharist, which we are about to celebrate today, is a common theme in Christian thinking, probably because we do it so frequently. Baptism, the other great sacrament for Protestants, is commonly regarded as an adoption ceremony for people entering into the Christian family, something that happens once for each of us, and that we think about mainly in reference to the children and new members in our midst. Lent is a time of preparation for baptism which we celebrate at the Easter Vigil service during Holy Week. We have classes going on now to guide that preparation.

Baptism is a deeply paradoxical practice within Christianity, however. On the one hand it marks the acceptance of an individual into the Christian family, with a commitment on the part of the community to support the individual's progress in the Christian life, and an implied commitment that the individual will take responsibility for his or her Christian life at the various stages of development. On the other hand, the Christian life into which the individual is baptized rejects the distinction between insiders and outsiders, although this is a controversial point on which the church has been ambivalent. To put the point at its most paradoxical, the Christian life into which we are baptized is devoted to people who are outside that fold, and the internal discipline of the Christian life aims to perfect our hospitality for all people.

---

1. Preached March 5, 2006, the first Sunday in Lent.

Nurture in Time and Eternity

Let me raise up for you, if I might, the views of some Christians who make a sharply significant distinction between who is in the church and who is out, and for whom baptism marks that distinction. The New Testament was clearly enthusiastic about Christian baptism because it signaled a commitment to the new movement that offered authentic new life and salvation to Gentiles as well as Jews. For the author of Colossians, baptism is a symbol of our participation in the life of Christ, dying with him in a spiritual sense and already being raised with him while remaining in this life. The New Testament is not definite, however, about baptism being necessary for salvation. Jesus clearly did not believe that because he honored faithful Jews and, more interestingly, faithful Romans, Samaritans, and Canaanites. Jesus himself was baptized to show his support for John the Baptist's renewal movement within Judaism. Paul agreed with Jesus's stance about salvation for Jews, and was concerned that the salvation God offered through Jews be understood to apply to all kinds of Gentiles because of the sacrifice of Jesus. Nevertheless, as the early Christian movement began to institutionalize itself in the first century, first as a distinct practice within Second Temple Judaism and then as a distinct religion apart from Judaism, it became conscious of its boundaries relative to wider cultures and other religions. From the earliest times a tension has existed between those who see the Christian movement as a vehicle of grace for saving the whole creation and those who see it as a special island in the midst of a sea of corruption, a ship for protecting its passengers from storms, an exclusive vehicle for saving Christians alone. Some contemporary Christians such as Stanley Hauerwas like to think of the baptized faithful as "resident aliens" in this world, testifying to the spiritual and moral truth but essentially living in opposition to the world. Many Christian denominations today require that one be baptized before being allowed to participate in the Eucharist.

The Methodist tradition, from which this Chapel takes its form, does not have any such juridical or legal requirements of baptism for taking the Eucharist. Baptism is a means of grace, but not an admission ticket to the church, much less to salvation. How is this so? Remember that our Hebrew Bible text was about Noah. Noah was the father of all subsequent human beings, according to that story, Gentiles as well as Jews, God having wiped out all the other people as well as the animals that were not in the ark. The history of the people of Israel does not begin until Abraham, who appears three chapters later in Genesis. The Noah story, you understand, was an almost-reversal of creation, almost a destruction. In the first chapter of

Genesis, God creates the earth by separating the fresh water of the heavens from the salt water of the sea, with earth in the middle. In the ninth chapter of Genesis God causes Noah's flood by opening the portals of heaven so that salt water and fresh water mingle, making life impossible, as the story goes, save for those in the ark. After the flood, as our text for today says, God makes a new covenant with Noah and his descendents, all the people of the earth, that is, plus all animals, promising never to "cut off all flesh" by a flood. The rainbow is the sign of God's promise not to allow the return of chaos. The moral of this is that even though people sin, God's judgment will not be so severe as to forsake them or the earth. Christians say that the power of God is proactive in salvation.

The importance of the First Epistle of Peter is that it connects Christian baptism with the covenant with Noah, father of Gentiles as well as Jews, not with the covenants with Abraham or Moses, which define Judaism, including Christianity as a form of Second Temple Judaism. The significance of our baptism is that we have been rescued with Noah, not brought into an exclusive club with Abraham and Moses. This point is reinforced with the stories of Jesus's own baptism in all four Gospels. You remember that Genesis tells the beginning of creation in terms of three elements: the chaotic water, roiled up by the divine wind, and given order by the divine voice. The Jordan's water for Jesus is primeval chaos, the divine spirit, or wind—the words for "wind" and "spirit" are the same—shapes Jesus, and the divine word pronounces him the new creation of God. Jesus's baptism did not mean for him that he was entering into a new religion; he was already in his religion and wanted only to purify it. Rather his baptism meant that he attained a new status with God and that everyone else has access to that status too. As Paul said, the promises to the Jews have now been extended to the Gentiles. But the theme of baptism points back to Noah where those promises had already been universal.

So our sacrament of baptism had an ambiguous beginning in New Testament times. The apostles thought they were leading a movement to bring everyone into a relation of reconciliation and holiness before God. Baptism was a rite of entrance into the work of that movement. Only slowly did that movement become institutionalized, so that baptism could be construed as a rite of admission into the institution rather than its work. Now, of course, the Christian movement is one religion among many others, with no others celebrating baptism, though many have rites of cleansing, the basic ritual movement in baptism. I believe that we seriously misunderstand the meaning of the church if we view baptism simply as an admission rite that separates those within the church from those without.

What is the Christian church but those who have become conscious of the gracious healing power of God to effect salvation and who live in response to this, mainly helping others also become conscious of this power? Our rhetoric has to do with proclaiming this message, and living it out, in terms of Jesus and the traditions of the church. Many other people grasp the healing power of God in different terms, and Christians need to be supportive of those different avenues. When Jesus was confronted by the Samaritan woman who said that Jews and Samaritans were not supposed to associate or worship together, he told her that the time was coming when all people will worship God in spirit and in truth. Whether that worship was in the Jerusalem temple of the Jews or on the sacred mountain of Samaria would not be relevant.

Of course, the means we Christian have to advance the work of reconciliation and justice are the symbols and traditions of Christianity, supplemented by the other elements that have been incorporated throughout Christian history, and the new means of grace available today. We do not do this work the way Jews, Buddhists, Hindus, Confucians, Daoists, or Muslims do, although many overlapping practices can bring us into cooperative work.

Nevertheless, to put boundaries around the Christian way of life, distinguishing those who are in from those who are out, is very dangerous. Rather, imagine the Christian life as a large number of concentric circles, with Christian practices scattered on them all, with many practices such as the Eucharist functioning on many circles. Some people might have no tolerance for Christian theology or worship or church organization, but just like the music: Bach is universal. That's fine and saving. Some people might be devout practitioners of some other religious way and merely see certain elements in Christianity as parallel to theirs. That's fine and saving. Some people, including all Christian children, begin on the outer circles with mere glancing acquaintance with the practices, understanding them in simplistic ways, and slowly move toward the more central circles with increasing sophistication. That's fine and saving. Yet other people are deeply devoted to participation in the institutional life of the church, enjoying a rich density of Christian practices, say, as illustrated in the liturgical calendar. That's fine and saving. A few people define their lives by ever-deepening Christian spirituality, maximizing the richness and depths of Christian

Baptism

practices and moving through them to the stage where all those practices can be relativized before the absolute reality of God. The deepest Christians I know believe it is a gracious accident of history that they are Christians instead of something else. Baptism is not one of the more inward of the concentric circles, as you might think, a circle that marks entry to some inner sanctum. It is a trajectory from the outer circles toward the center. If you are moving toward the center, it is time to be baptized.

Now I invite you to the Eucharist, a sacramental rite that has powerful spiritual meaning for those who define their spiritual lives around it. It also has meaning for those for whom it is mainly the regular rite for people who appreciate the Christian mission. It is our invitation of hospitality to any who would taste Christ's way of redemption. To taste Christ's way is to plunge with him beneath the waters of chaos, to feel the vast power of God's spirit that blows with cosmic force, and to be ordered by the divine word that brings us from the depths of the deep to new life. Come to this baptismal feast! Amen.

25

Money[1]

Exodus 20:1–17; 1 Corinthians 1:11–25; John 2:11–22

During Lent, when we worry about putting due proportion in our lives, and try to abstain from excess, of course we should worry about how we stand with regard to money. We know that we should not let making money be the be-all and end-all of life, because where our treasure is, there will our heart be also, as Jesus said. We know from the story of the rich young ruler that those with much money are sometimes fettered by it so that it becomes an unwholesome attachment that prevents the freedom of religion. On the other hand, we know that we should be provident for those in our care and charitable toward the poor, all of which requires money. Moreover, we are enjoined to maximize our God-given talents, which often results in financial prosperity. Poverty we know is a bad thing. It is especially bad because it so often blights the soul. If poverty is bad, prosperity is good. So how should we think about money, when we try to find balance and proportion in life?

The story of Jesus's cleansing of the temple does not provide an easy answer. It is told in all four gospels. In Matthew, Mark, and Luke, the incident is placed at the beginning of the last week of Jesus's life, immediately after he has ridden into Jerusalem in triumph on Palm Sunday. In those gospels, Jesus's driving out of the animals and overturning of the money changers' tables are presented as the trigger that turns the authorities

---

1. Preached March 19, the third Sunday in Lent.

against him so that they decide they have to trap and kill him. In John, however, our gospel for today, the incident is placed at the very beginning of Jesus's ministry, right after he has called the disciples and taken them to the drunken wedding party at Cana.

Let me say a word about the structure of John versus that of the so-called Synoptic Gospels, Matthew, Mark, and Luke. Mark was the first gospel written, probably around the time of the destruction of the temple in 70 of the first century. Both Matthew and Luke know Mark's Gospel, and reproduce many elements of it with their own stresses and variations; this commonality is the reason those gospels are called "synoptic." One of the common elements in the Synoptic Gospels is Mark's dramatic organizing principle. For Mark, after accepting baptism by John in the Jordan, Jesus returned to his home territory in Galilee, north of Jerusalem, and began his preaching and healing ministry. Then he slowly journeyed from Galilee to Jerusalem for his climactic last week, the events of which occupy roughly a third of each of the Synoptic Gospels. All the incidents of Jesus's work and teaching are arranged around the dramatic structure of the journey to Jerusalem. It is possible to read the Synoptic Gospels to say that Jesus's ministry lasted only a single season, aiming at the climactic Passover festival. It is in this context that the story of Jesus cleansing the temple focuses the conflict of his last days, for the Synoptic Gospels. John, by contrast, does not employ the single journey organizing principle but says rather that Jesus went to Jerusalem many times, for a variety of festivals. His ministry might have lasted a number of years. My own suspicion is that John is probably more historical, if only because he does not have such a rigid organizing principle based on the journey. In John's account, the cleansing of the temple brings Jesus to the attention of the authorities at the very beginning of his ministry.

Now what was so outrageous about Jesus's action in the temple? Many things. First, it was violent and upsetting. Imagine all the cattle and sheep running wild through the temple courtyards! (The kids must have loved that!) The money changers must have been panicked by having their coins scattered about. Second, Jesus was accusing the money changers and animal salesmen of desecrating the temple, when in fact they had a legitimate business. The animals, you know, were there in order to be sacrificed. According to the Jewish religion, individuals need to make various sacrifices to atone for sins and to become clean so as to be able to worship in the temple. In older days when the people were farmers, they would supply their own animals. But Jesus lived in an urban age, and at the festivals worshipers came from all over the Diaspora. So hundreds or even thousands of people had to purchase animals to be sacrificed on their behalf so that they would be made eligible to enter the temple for worship. The sacrificial animals had to be purchased with Jewish temple money, and most of the people had Roman money; so there had to be money changers in addition to the farmers selling the animals. How could this be a desecration of the temple when that was the way the very temple system worked?

So, third and most radical, Jesus's action challenged the very system of worship associated with the temple. In many other places, all four gospels depict Jesus as upholding and affirming Jewish practices, while attempting to purify them and eliminate hypocrisy. Jesus did not think of himself as anything other than a good Jew, although his definition of what that means might have differed from many of his peers. He regarded himself as something of a prophet.

How do we reconcile Jesus's apparent self-image as a purifying prophetic Jew with his attack on the temple worship based on sacrificial cleanliness? One historically sensitive answer might be to say that all of the gospels were written after the temple had in fact been destroyed, and that the story of Jesus cleansing the temple was embellished to indicate that Jews should move beyond temple-based worship to synagogue or congregational worship. Thus, whatever Jesus's own motivations for his violence in the temple, the gospel writers used the story to distance the Christian movement from temple Judaism and promote the emerging form of Christian-Jewish congregational life. This is anachronistic, however, and cannot explain Jesus's own motivations. Another answer to the puzzle is suggested by the text itself, namely, that Jesus was "consumed by zeal for God's house," which quotes Psalm 69. The problem with this answer is that God's house, for which Jesus and the author of Psalm 69 had zeal, was the temple with the sacrifice system.

Would it not be tempting to say that Jesus's attack on the temple sacrifice system was just an uncharacteristic bad day for a man who was usually so peaceful, forgiving, and loyal to the truest elements in his tradition? Alas, all the gospels make this episode the pivotal incident that sets Jesus in opposition to the authorities who eventually kill him. So it must be significant.

Perhaps we can get some purchase on understanding this incident by asking what it might mean for us, far removed from Second Temple

Judaism and the cultural and psychological assumptions that killing an animal might make us clean. What can we learn from this text for Lent?

Taking seriously the radical rejection of the heart of his own tradition's religious practice, I think Jesus' act means that we should be prepared to set our religion aside and begin again with God. A crucial part of penance is that we free ourselves from dependence on our religion. Now what a crazy thing this is for me to say! I urge upon you, as a Lenten practice, the freeing of yourself from religious practices of the very sort I am urging upon you. You would think that I had never studied logic! (I did, but did not get good grades.)

Here is the paradox, however, expressed in Jesus's outrageous behavior in the temple. On the one hand, our religious practices are the only things that allow us to engage God and the ultimate conditions of our existence. Without ideas and symbols of God, we cannot think God. Without the emotions of cultivated piety such as love, confession, and forgiveness, we cannot feel God. Without participation in the community of God's people, faulty as that is, we cannot model living with other people as social beings before God. Without the deliberate practices of justice and charity toward all, we cannot be holy before God. Without the patterning of our lives with prayers and gestures of awe and respect, we cannot organize ourselves to live through ordinary affairs as redeemed sinners in search of sanctification. We all know people who think they can get along without cultivating a deliberate pattern for their lives for living in light of ultimate things. They withdraw from organized religion and think it is fine to be "spiritual." When the crises of life descend, however, their thoughts about God are likely to be at the fifth-grade level, unless they have cultivated their theology. Their emotional reception of God is likely to be sappy, unless it has been disciplined through practice. Their love of neighbors is likely to extend only as far as is self-serving, unless they are committed to a religious community or some secular substitute for that. Only in justice and charity are people who distance themselves from deliberate religious practice likely to do as well as devoutly religious people, because those obligations attend everyone in the human condition. In the other issues, facing ultimate matters without organized religious practice is opting for a kind of perpetual immaturity where commitment extends little farther than immediate interests. Serious religious practice is absolutely vital for mature living before God and the ultimate matters of life. So much for why we need religion!

On the other hand, religious practice can become a substitute for God rather than the means of engaging God. We think that if we wrestle with ideas of God, we do not have to use those ideas as names and prayers by which to approach God. We revel in pious feelings and ignore the thousand and one ways that God makes unscheduled demands upon us. We throw ourselves into church activities, with worship services, social gatherings, and good works, including care for the poor and sick, and forget the God for whom we do these things, and the real identities of the other people whom we love and serve. We can devote ourselves to justice and charity like the famous person who loved humanity but hated people. Religion is the most powerful seducer to attachments that turn us away from God. Because religious practices all bear references to ultimate matters, we can become so attached to them that they imprison us. Instead of being windows to God, they become mirrors, so that we see ourselves and our deeds and think ourselves ultimately important. From time to time, we need to take a whip of cords and drive out the beasts of our religious attachments. We need to overturn the tables on which we have carefully sorted the duties of our pieties.

On the one hand, we cannot get along without serious religious practices if we are to live maturely before God. I advocate the Christian practices, recognizing that Roman Catholics, Eastern Orthodox, and low- and high-church Protestants have rather different practices. On the other hand, we ought not become so attached to those practices that they become substitutes for God rather than means to engage God. So we need to free ourselves from dependency on them. We need to see that our religious practices are mere means to the end of living before God. Who are we to say that the practices of Jews and Muslims, Buddhists and Hindus, Daoists and Confucians, are not also windows to the ultimate? Those of us who have chosen the Christian life need to live it fully and passionately, but also with a sense of humor and humility regarding how it can become a damning end in itself.

The Lenten practice I urge upon you today is the discipline of learning to sit easy with religion, wholeheartedly embracing it as the way to live before God, and yet to not get caught by it. Religion is a lot like money. You can't live well without it, but it becomes a deadly snare if you forget its purpose is for something else. Amen.

26

Sickness[1]

Numbers 21:1–9; Ephesians 2:1–16; John 3:11–21

If you have ever wondered about the derivation of the symbol of the snake on the pole that you see on ambulances and medical institutions, now you know. When Moses led the people of Israel through the wilderness, on the forty year journey to the promised land, they groused so much that God sent poisonous snakes to bite them. Many died, and they begged forgiveness and healing from Moses. God said to cast a bronze image of a snake on a pole and hold it up so that whoever looked at it after being bitten by a snake would live. Snake magic was common in Egypt, from which the Israelites had just escaped. Moses, you remember, had been raised as an Egyptian aristocrat by Pharaoh's daughter, and he probably never distinguished clearly between Egyptian magical lore and the new cult of Yahweh he was constructing on the basis of the Mount Sinai covenant instructions. Anyway, the snake lifted up in the wilderness seemed to work. In later generations, however, Moses's snake pole must have become associated with the Gentile rites, since snakes were part of the Canaanite religion. The book of 2 Kings congratulates the good king Hezekiah for breaking Moses's snake pole into pieces as part of his general purification reform.

Nevertheless, John the evangelist refers to that snake pole in our gospel text this morning. "Just as Moses lifted up the serpent in the wilderness, so must the Son of Man be lifted up, that whoever believes in him may have

1. Preached March 26, 2006, the fourth Sunday in Lent.

eternal life." What a remarkable image! Jesus being lifted up in crucifixion is likened to the bronze snake on a pole. As sight of the snake cures snakebite, belief in the crucified Jesus cures the sickness unto death of sin, to use Kierkegaard's phrase. What are we to make of this? What is the sickness, and what is the cure?

Snakebite is not a disease like a cancer or virus, but it is a traumatic intrusion that disrupts the body's processes, causing death in some instances. In biblical times, it was often believed that sickness comes on because one deserves it, that it is punishment or retribution sent from God, which was the case with the Israelites. Even in our time, many people suffering from illness ask "What did I do to deserve this?" If your image of God is small enough, you might think that God runs the world as a just king would a kingdom, rewarding the good and punishing the unjust. Therefore if something bad happens to you, it must be because you deserve it. This was the argument Job's friends gave to him when he said he had done nothing so heinous as to deserve all the suffering God had in fact sent him. It was a pretty bad argument even back then, however, and both Job and God blew it off. We do not believe that sickness indicates a moral judgment of God. Cancers and viruses are parts of nature, and we are learning how to cure them. Snakebite comes from getting too close to snakes, which might be merely accidental or result from the stupidity of wandering into a field filled with snakes. It is extremely important for us to remember that God is the Creator of the whole universe, which includes cancers, viruses, and poisonous snakes, but that the Creator of the universe does not meddle to put snakes in the path of people who complain about food. Coupling a small idea of God with a belief in providence is seriously bad theology. It leads to the inference that, because very good people get cancers, viruses, and snakebite, God must be at moral fault.

When John uses the image of Moses's snake pole, however, he very much wants to transfer from the Moses-account the sense that the sickness Jesus heals is in some sense our fault. What precisely is the sickness unto death of sin? It is some kind of alienation from God that is healed when God sends his Son, not to condemn but to save. We have heard this phrase so many times that we fail to understand its subtlety.

Many people have mistaken this passage to say that we are saved if we merely "believe in" Jesus and that those who do not believe are condemned. From this some draw the inference that only Christians are saved, and that they are saved by their act of belief, just as the Israelites were saved by their

Sickness

act of looking at the snake on a pole. Such exclusivism is wholly at odds with the love attributed to God in this passage, and in so many others in John. Belief by itself hardly makes a person better. Many people who believe in the name of Jesus do so in very superficial senses and are scoundrels, villains, seducers, and fools. What would all the wars among Christians have been about if mere allegiance to the name of Jesus makes you saved?

No, the gospel text says that "this is the judgment, that the light has come into the world, and people loved darkness rather than light because their deeds were evil. For all who do evil hate the light and do not come to the light, so that their deeds may not be exposed. But those who do what is true come to the light, so that it may be clearly seen that their deeds have been done in God." The issue of judgment is not belief but rather whether people deny the light in order to hide their evil deeds. The sickness from which Jesus, lifted up, heals us is the willful cloaking of our selves and society in the darkness of evil, of sin.

Can we get clearer about this dark evil, this sin? The author of Ephesians, likely a student of Paul, follows Paul in the metaphor of sins of the flesh. Speaking of the disobedient ones, the author writes in our text, "All of us once lived among them in the passions of our flesh, following the desires of flesh and senses, and we were by nature children of wrath, like everyone else." I think what he has in mind is a generalization of the swarming siren song of sexual anticipation and excitement. You know how easy it is to become enraptured by the project of sexual pleasure, to enter into a kind of semitrance world where many realms of reality get blocked out, and the whole of one's rational processes are squeezed into acquiring the goal. When your mind is whole, you would never hurt your friends, but you do so when deafened by the siren's song. When your mind is whole, you would never abuse the person for whom you lust, but when tugged by the siren's song, you go for it. When your mind is whole, you would never have unsafe sex, but when the siren blinds, you abandon caution with lies that it will be okay just this once. These are biologically based instincts that sunder wholeness in order to guarantee the statistical victory of procreation for your population, and they are God-given instincts. Now, if any of you are innocent students who are shocked that I am describing something you never heard of, please just forget what I've said and memorize some Bible verses while I go on.

Paul's point has little to do with real sexual passions, but rather with how that kind of captivating, self-chosen, reason-bending blindness is a metaphor for our larger lives. We live in selfishness which, like sexual passion, prevents our hearing the truth, tugs us from our rightful and obligatory connections, and leads us into very dangerous and evil activities. Like the swarming confusions of the flesh of sexual obsession, our ordinary lives are lived in the dark. It's not that our desires are wrong. Within the whole, they are God's gift. But they become obsessions that blind us to the whole. Despite our better judgment, we blinker our reason and plunge into the darkest corners where we hope to get what we want without consequence. Therefore, when the light comes, we blink, cover our eyes, and slink back into the dark.

This is our ontological sickness. Our nation is sick when we gorge on oil greed, when we put profit above the environment, when we cut welfare to support wars whose putative justifications have collapsed. And we ourselves are sick when our grasp of life's wholeness slacks off and we let ourselves fall into the siren songs of our passions.

For John, and for Paul with somewhat different symbols, Jesus is the incarnation of the light of the world. Of course, everyone in their conscience knows about the wrongs that are committed when we are turned swarmy by our passions. The Logos, the Light of the World did not suddenly appear when Jesus was born. The very point of John's Gospel is that the light was here all the time and we block it, we shadow it, we deflect it to misguided zeal.

So Jesus, who refers to himself in our gospel as the Son of Man, comes to us as the special flame of illumination. It's not that the light has not been here all along. It's that we have hidden it, and Jesus suddenly exposes our subterfuge. Look at Jesus, lifted up in crucifixion. Can we keep up the blinders that allow us to ignore or deny the unrighteousness our way of life tolerates? John's point is that when we see Jesus, when we really look at him lifted up, the blinders fall off and we see the light. The light is not new. The sight of the light is new when we see Jesus.

To what then are we called with the acknowledgment of the light? John says "eternal life." This is one of his main symbols for salvation. Throughout his Gospel he is careful never to parse that to mean "more life of the sort we have now without end, on and on." Nor does he ever say that death is the end, pure and simple. He says rather that the content of eternal life is loving other people and God. This is a hard project, not so much a matter of will but of learning and practice. It surely is not a matter of merely deciding on belief in the name of Jesus. See the Farewell Discourse in John 11–17 for the

Sickness

complicated story here. When Philip at the Last Supper asked how we know the Father, Jesus answered, have you been with me all this time and still do not get the point? To know the Father is to be a lover, of your neighbors, of Jesus, and of the Father. Such love is a tremendous achievement. Yet Jesus said that those with whom he had worked would not be lost. Becoming a lover is a possibility for us all.

What then does it mean to see Jesus lifted up as Moses lifted up the serpent in the wilderness, and to believe in Jesus? God did not send Jesus to condemn the world. God sent Jesus to be loved by the world, so that the world could return to the wholeness of love. Jesus was the consummate lover. His loving taught the disciples how to love, how to overcome the blinkers of selfishness, how to open hearts to the loveliness of people different from ourselves. But Jesus's lessons in love are not half so important as his own loveliness, the winsomeness of his unconditional acceptance of people he was supposed not to touch, his quick ability to fall in love with people, his refusal of the structures of injustice, most of all his refusal to deal when the authorities wanted him to play their games rather than simply to shine light. Jesus's light shows up the temporizing politics of Pilate, the defensiveness of the Jewish officials, the slinking fear of the disciples, and our own begrudging willingness to love Jesus only when he is the victor and on our side.

Lifted up on the cross, Jesus is only a man, a lover, a prism of the light we want to deflect from the shades of sin. If instead we can love him, then we can gain the wholeness that gives sex its divine centrality in our personal identity, that lets us struggle with our government to bend it toward more impartial justice, and that lets us live with the ambiguities of life that otherwise make us think that, if we do not look out for ourselves, no one else will. Wholeness, the original meaning of "salvation," is not total perfection but rather acceptance of the whole light, and subsequent action in accordance with that. When Jesus is lifted up, we can see that wholeness.

Let me close by saying that the healed life of wholeness has a double quality. On the one hand, it is already to be embraced within the eternal life of the loving God where we do not have to pretend, in our darkness, that things are not what they are. On the other hand, wholeness means that we live day by day, not in some perfect heaven, but in Boston, where our good deeds are mixed with evil consequences and our projects rarely reach conclusion. If we truly attempt to love Jesus, and to live the life of lovers, then this would be a little like sending our son, not to condemn the world, but to save it at the cost of his own life. Do we love enough to sacrifice love for love? If so, then our love has broken through the limits of finite love to ride God's infinite passion. All this makes sense when we realize that love in its wholeness cannot really die, but has eternal life. Amen.

27

Religions[1]

Jeremiah 31:31–34; Hebrews 5:1–10; John 12:21–23

As we move toward the end of Lent and into the Christian Holy Week, Christians become conscious of the peculiarity of our religion. In order to appreciate the peculiarity of our faith, we would do well to see how it relates to some other religions, and ask about the importance of religious difference. This is part of the Lenten discipline of coming to terms with who we are.

The passage from Jeremiah is the famous prediction of a new covenant, written on people's hearts and minds so that they do not have to learn it. Christians have long construed that text to refer to the New Covenant in Jesus Christ. That can't be quite right, however, because the Christian New Covenant still has to be learned; we preachers would be out of business if that were not so. Moreover, Jeremiah was not thinking about Christianity as a new religion at all, rather about a reform in the religion of the house of Israel, as he said. The New Covenant Jeremiah promises will be internal to people's hearts and minds, and their iniquities will be forgiven. This is a prophecy of great hope, something that Jeremiah did not deliver all that often. Should Christians accept this prophecy, respect it as applying to Judaism, not directly to Christianity, and allow it as somehow parallel to our own sense of Covenant? Good question.

---

1. Preached April 2, 2006, the fifth Sunday in Lent.

Nurture in Time and Eternity

The passage from Hebrews is even more startling when it comes to how Christianity relates to other religions. One of the main themes of the Letter to the Hebrews is that Jesus Christ is the one who leads us into the presence and glory of God. The background is the conception in ancient Israelite religion that human beings need to be pure and holy in order to approach God. When people break one of the Covenant strictures, becoming unclean or unholy, the priests can make sacrifices for them; the people provide the animal or grain to be sacrificed. Priests themselves need to be pure and holy in order to enter into God's presence in the tent or temple. The book of Hebrews understands Jesus Christ to be both the sacrificial animal and the sacrificing priest, a very non-Jewish recurrence to human sacrifice. His death on the cross was a sacrifice powerful enough to redeem the whole world. And his role as priest is to bring all his followers into God's presence. Hebrew's metaphor for Christ, the double role of priest and sacrifice, comes from the Jewish Levitical understanding of the role of sacrifice rituals. How astonishing it is, then, that Hebrews says that Jesus Christ is a priest in the order of Melchizedek. Melchizedek was a Canaanite priest and king of Salem, later called Jerusalem, who blessed Abraham in the name of the Canaanite "God Most High," who is maker of heaven and earth. Later Melchizedek's "God Most High" would be identified with Abraham's God Yahweh, but at the time, according to Genesis 14, Abraham accepted the Canaanite blessing. Now the author of Hebrews could have identified the priesthood of Jesus with that of Aaron, brother of Moses, or of Levi, the head of the house of Israelite priests. The point of identifying Jesus Christ with Melchizedek is that Jesus represents a priesthood more general than that of Israel, a priesthood inclusive of Gentiles, even the accursed Canaanites against whom the cult of Yahweh contended for centuries. Jesus is a priest of all people, even in recognition of the fact that people have different religions, for instance the Canaanite High God worship and the Abrahamic worship of Yahweh.

Our gospel from John begins with some Greeks wanting to meet Jesus. They go to Philip and Andrew, disciples with Greek names, who make the introduction. We have no reason to think that Philip and Andrew were not Jewish—they certainly went along with Jesus's talk about his relation to the worship of the God of Israel. But Philip and Andrew were open to the Greeks, and so was Jesus. In Palestine at that time Jews and Samaritans, Greeks, Romans, and many other people lived together, often with blurred ethnic and religious distinctions. Although Jesus himself focused mainly on addressing Jews and Jewish worship, he also healed the daughter of a Canaanite woman and the beloved slave boy of a Roman centurion, without requiring either to become Jewish. Earlier in the Gospel of John, Jesus's conversation with a Samaritan woman is recorded in which he tells her, respecting the Samaritan worship of God on a mountain versus the Jewish worship of God in Jerusalem, that "the hour is coming, and is now here, when the true worshipers will worship the Father in spirit and in truth, for the Father seeks such as these to worship him. God is spirit, and those who worship him must worship in spirit and in truth." Though he gives priority to Judaism, Jesus says in effect that true spiritual worship transcends the differences between religions.

So the question is, what is true spiritual worship? What is the true spiritual worship that transcends religions without annulling them? When the Greeks, representing non-Jewish religions, come to see him, Jesus tells them that now he himself will be glorified. He says his glorification means that he must die, by being lifted up on the cross. Crucifixion does not seem like glory to the eyes of the world. But to Christians, Jesus's crucifixion is indeed glory. How can this be?

Last week, our gospel was from the third chapter of John, in which he said that the metaphor of Jesus being lifted up in crucifixion is like Moses lifting up the snake in the wilderness so that the Israelites could be healed from the sickness of snakebites. In our text for today, the lifting up of Jesus heals all people, not only the descendents of Moses's people. Like Melchizedek, Jesus is a priest for all people who brings all to God. Like Jeremiah's New Covenant, Jesus's saving work accomplishes worship in spirit and in truth, not in external observance. What is that saving work? John is very clear about this: it is the establishment of loving communities of friends who love God and one another. Both of these things are accomplished in some way by loving Jesus, and accepting God's love in Jesus, and Jesus's own love. What could be lovelier than the man Jesus, accepting crucifixion for our sins?

What a silly question! Who could think of a crucifixion as lovely? Gruenewald's famous picture of the crucifixion is probably right about its gruesome gore. The actual crucifixion must have been horrible! John, of course, does not mean the crucifixion merely as an historical event but rather the interpreted crucifixion, the crucifixion by which God so loved the world that we have eternal life. In the interpreted crucifixion, Jesus is lifted up as the one the love for whom can cure our sinful blindness. In the interpreted crucifixion we learn the extent of divine love. In the interpreted crucifixion we see the teacher who brings us to love, which is the content of eternal life. In the interpreted crucifixion we see Jesus drawing all people to himself, regardless of their religion.

Interpreted in John's Gospel, Jesus saw himself as presenting the way of love of God and neighbor that redeems all humankind from the blindness that keeps us from realizing the full healing love of God. This was not a new religion for him, but rather a transcendent way of love that brings worship in spirit and in truth to any religion, first the religion of Israel and then all the others. But how could Jesus's way be passed on except by being made into yet another religion? How could the interpreted, meaningful life and crucifixion of Jesus be made effective beyond his immediate disciples without becoming yet another religious cult?

So now we have a paradox. On the one hand Christianity is a religion with all the cultic peculiarities we are going to celebrate as we move to Easter, including the Eucharist today. On the other hand Christianity is not exclusive of those other religions, but rather a way compatible with them that fosters the profound love of God and neighbor that Jesus taught. In this latter sense Christianity sees Jesus not as a Christian priest but as a universal priest, like Melchizedek. Of course, other religions might not see Jesus this way—not even all Christians do. And other religions might have many things of religious import to contribute that are not found in Christianity, from which we should learn.

Our faith lives with this paradox. We cannot say that Christianity should deconstruct and let the other religions do it, for they might miss Jesus's point about transreligious spirituality. We cannot say that Christianity is the only true religion, existing alongside others, because its own cultic activities can lose the very worship in spirit and in truth that Jesus taught. We must live with the tension, never condemning another religion, as Jesus never did, and never failing to be faithful to the peculiarities of Christianity in which Jesus is glorified as the Crucified One, lifted up to bring us all to God in love. Amen.

28

Politics[1]

Isaiah 50:1—9a; Philippians 2:1—11; Mark 11:1—11

The involvement of Christians in politics did not begin auspiciously, if we take Jesus's Palm Sunday entrance into Jerusalem as its beginning. Although Jesus hitherto had tried to downplay people's speculations that he was the messiah, the rightful king of Israel, when he came to Jerusalem on what turned out to be his last week he flaunted it. He rode into the city like a king, and the next thing he did according to the Synoptic Gospels was to go to the temple and assert his authority by releasing all the animals and upsetting the money changers. After that, the authorities could hardly ignore him. He taught publicly in the temple all week, was arrested Thursday evening, and executed the next day for being a danger to the peace. Neither the Roman nor Jewish authorities had much interest in his religious message, only in his pretence to be king of the Jews, which was a volatile assertion in an occupied country filled with Jewish pilgrims from all over the world assembled for the Passover. From the fact that the authorities did not arrest any of his followers, we know that his movement was not regarded as very dangerous. It was only his personage as a political trigger for rebellion during the festival that got him into trouble. In many respects, it seems that he was arrested and executed as something of an accident, a person caught at the wrong place at the wrong time in an inflammatory political situation. Pontius Pilate was trying to keep the lid on violent rebellion, the

1. Preached April 9, 2006, Palm Sunday.

temple authorities, associated with the Sadducees, were trying to defend the privilege of traditional temple worship under an occupying power; the Pharisees (like Jesus) were pressing for a purification of Jewish practice, which had been compromised by three centuries of foreign occupation; and Zealots and other revolutionary groups were calling for open rebellion against Rome. About thirty years later, the revolutionary forces did spark a major rebellion, the Romans brought in overwhelming force to destroy them, the temple was torn down, Levitical temple worship ended for good, and Judaism went in the direction of the Pharisees, who developed synagogue worship throughout the Diaspora. We have to sympathize with Pilate and the temple leaders, because they knew that peace, the Jewish nation, and traditional religion were at stake, all of which in fact were lost in the next generation when their successors failed to keep the lid on. Because we Americans are playing the role of Rome in Iraq today, which is a situation just as volatile with just as much at stake, we can empathize with the Jerusalem authorities when Jesus rode into town acting the part of yet one more pretender to the throne, or so it seemed to them. Of course, Jesus was not really pretending to be king—he spent the next days in the temple as a teacher; Pilate knew he was innocent of the insurrection charges, and knew that it was wrong to execute an innocent man. But when so much is at stake, what is a little collateral damage, as we say?

We Christians, of course, have reinterpreted Holy Week to have cosmic religious significance, not merely a successful, if compromised, peacemaking effort on the part of the Jerusalem authorities. We have depicted the Roman and Jewish leaders, not as harassed but successful politicians keeping the peace under trying circumstances, but as symbols of all the evil in the world that crucified Christ. One legacy of this rewriting of history, or perhaps we should say the invention of a Christian saga, is a shameful tradition of anti-Semitism based on the role of the temple authorities and their crowds in Jesus's condemnation. Another legacy for nearly three centuries was a kind of antiestablishment bias in the early Christian church where the establishment, as Saint Paul argued, was the source of justice and peacekeeping, and the early Christians often were disturbers of the social order. This second legacy was limited by the fact that Christianity itself became the establishment religion under Constantine in the fourth century, and ever after has been in something like Pilate's compromised position, sacrificing the purity of Christian ideals for trade-offs that are supposed to work.

Politics

Set aside these large-scale political ironies for the moment, however, and think with me about Jesus's intent regarding politics. The most important point to make is that he seemed to care very little about who was in charge, the Romans or the temple leaders or the puppet Jewish monarchy. When they tried to draw him out on this point a day or so after Palm Sunday, Jesus said to render to Caesar the things that are Caesar's and to God the things that are God's. We should note that during Jesus's own lifetime, the economy was doing rather well. The Romans were building a new city a few miles from Nazareth, and Jesus's family was in the building trades. The families of his friends, Simon and Andrew, and James and John, were in the victualing business with their fishing boats. This situation was radically changed after the Jewish revolt thirty years later when the Romans bore down painfully on the occupied populace. We should remember that the Gospels were written in this later, painful period, reflecting much tougher relations between Romans and Jews. Jesus himself got along well with the Jews, Romans, Greeks, Samaritans, Canaanites, and others who coexisted in his area. So Jesus had no special reason to oppose the Romans, and he did not. He did have special reason to oppose the puppet Jewish monarchy of Herod, who had assassinated his cousin, John the Baptist. But he did not express any significant opposition against the monarchy. As for the temple, Jesus worshiped and taught there regularly, as did his disciples for a generation after him. He did not attack the temple leaders in any political way even during his trial. So Jesus was not political in the usual sense, which makes his almost accidental arrest and execution all the more ironic.

What then was Jesus's complaint? To judge by what he taught during that last week when he was courting trouble, his complaint was about the hypocrisy and corruption of just about all the leadership factions, which will bring about judgment on the whole. The Gospels record many bitter parables in his teachings of this week, but Matthew catches the drift with Jesus's diatribe of woes, of which I shall quote part:

> The greatest among you will be your servant. All who exalt themselves will be humbled, and all who humble themselves will be exalted. But woe to you, scribes and Pharisees, hypocrites! For you lock people out of the kingdom of heaven. For you do not go in yourselves, and when others are going in, you stop them. Woe to you, scribes and Pharisees, hypocrites! For you cross sea and land to make a single convert, and you make the new convert twice as

much a child of hell as yourselves. Woe to you, blind guides, who say, "Whoever swears by the sanctuary is bound by nothing, but whoever swears by the gold of the sanctuary is bound by the oath." For which is greater, the gold or the sanctuary that has made the gold sacred? ... Woe to you, scribes and Pharisees, hypocrites! For you tithe mint, dill, and cumin, and have neglected the weightier matters of the law: justice and mercy and faith ... You blind guides! You strain out a gnat but swallow a camel! Woe to you, scribes and Pharisees, hypocrites! For you clean the outside of the cup and plate, but inside they are full of greed and self-indulgence... . Woe to you, scribes and Pharisees, hypocrites! For you are like whitewashed tombs, which on the outside look beautiful, but inside they are full of the bones of the dead and all kinds of filth. You snakes, you brood of vipers!

Preaching like that did not make Jesus many friends among the leadership community. Yet Nicodemus and Joseph of Arimathea, members of that community, knew he spoke the truth. When Jesus entered Jerusalem on Palm Sunday, he rode a donkey, the symbol of the king of Israel entering the peaceful city in the humblest way. Had Jesus intended to assert real political authority, he would have ridden in with an army behind him! Riding the donkey, he asserted what true kingship, true messiahship, is about: the honest administration of justice, peacekeeping, care for the poor and oppressed, and healing for the suffering, all in truth and without hypocrisy. Just as he shamed Pilate's compromises by his acceptance of judgment, so he shamed all of Jerusalem with the donkey bearing a teacher of justice, peace, charity, and healing.

What moral should we draw from this for Christian life today? That we should not care about who is in charge? Not quite, although the politics of winning should never be a matter of ultimate concern itself. We should exercise due prudence with regard to which political parties will do the best, with regard to whether to force democracies on nondemocratic nations, whether we should support sheiks of oil countries who are friendly to Americans, or whether this or that tax plan best helps the poor. These are all secondary and instrumental questions to the basic ones of how best to bring about justice, peace, help for the poor, oppressed, and weak, and healing to those who are suffering; what can we do to value God's creation? Jesus detailed these and other basic values throughout his teachings. His ultimate goal was to bring about communities of love in every place. And what stands in the way, Jesus taught, is not that these values are not widely accepted; they are. What stands in the way is hypocrisy that allows us and our leaders to think we are promoting them when in fact we are corrupting them with greed, arrogance, power madness, and love of being honored. Woe! Woe!

So as we contemplate Jesus' attack on Jerusalem mounted on a donkey, let us ask ourselves some hard political questions. When we say we favor justice, do we add in the secret recesses of our heart that we do not favor any change that would diminish our own advantage? When we say we are peacemakers, do we add in secret that we do not favor taking any risk in that venture? When we say we are charitable, do we add in secret that this cannot put a limit on our own greed for more wealth? When we say we favor liberation, do we add in secret that others' freedom should not limit our own? When we say we favor healing the suffering, do we add in secret that no resources should be spent for this that might be needed for our own healing? When we say we are not greedy, how can we countenance a foreign policy that justifies any coercion in the name of national interest? When we say we are not arrogant, do we countenance a patriotism that says, America right or wrong? When we say we do not lust for ever more power, how can we increase spending for arms and decrease spending for education and welfare? When we say we do not need to be honored, why is it so hard to be humble?

My friends, a Christian approach to politics is not about winning or losing, nor about any particular policy, although these are important in secular ways. No, a Christian approach to politics asks whether our promotion of the values we largely share and that Jesus so eloquently described is honest. For, the religious dimension of politics is how we behave politically before God. Is our heart clean and honest? Or are we hypocrites, deceiving ourselves and attempting to deceive others? Political issues never have only one side, and all political actions are ambiguous in their results. We should never let the infinite passion of religious commitment become attached to a political program, no matter how important and right it is. No, the infinite passion of religious commitment belongs to the task of presenting our heart honestly to the God who loves us even in our hypocrisy, but who says, Woe! Amen.

29

Into Your Hands I Commit My Spirit[1]

How could a man writhing against the nails of a cross, who cries, "My God! My God! Why have you forsaken me?" die with the words, "Into your hands I commit my spirit"? To understand this is to understand what makes Jesus the Christ.

Of course, we have no way of knowing Jesus's exact thought processes. But from other things the Bible says and from what we know of his culture, he might well have held out hope that God would send angels to rescue him at the last minute, as his taunters opined. As he neared the end, however, he gave up that hope, and realized that God had abandoned him. Even if we say, as some scholars do, that Jesus was only reciting psalms, and that this line is the beginning of the twenty-second Psalm, his choice of that psalm makes the point. He despaired of rescue by the God he thought would do so.

Most of us will not be crucified. But many of us will suffer wasting illness, be disabled by accidents, lose lovers to death or betrayal, or fall into a situation of war, poverty, or chaos. Each of us will die, and for most of us death will seem too early, like Jesus's. Jesus's crucifixion, whatever else it means, symbolizes for us the gift of life which includes devastating suffering as well as triumphant joys. The lesson of Jesus is that we must accept that gift. We can hope for success and rescue, for healing and companionship. We can rail about the unfairness of life all we want, and should struggle with all our strength to make life fair. But true faith means that in

---

1. Preached April 14, 2006, Good Friday.

the end, when we see that nothing will keep us from loss, we accept the life God gives. We accept the mixture of pain and pleasure, and the inevitable entropic loss of life itself. If we are honest, we know that it is the Lord who slays us. Jesus shows us how to submit to the God who gives and takes away.

When Jesus said "into your hands I commit my spirit," he refused alienation from the God who abandoned him. He did not say God is well-intentioned but weak. He did not say God was malevolent. He did not say that God is indifferent. He had expected God to succor him, and from that expectation his death seemed like abandonment. We too often look to God to fix things for us, and yet God's cosmic process washes over us like a blind force. We too feel abandoned. In spite of all this, Jesus committed his spirit to the creator who dashed his hope and sent him to an early death. He loved the master whose love includes cruelty among its blessings.

Now the blessing of crucifixion is that it sets us free. If we love the God who gives us our lives with the hurts as well as joys, we cannot be in bondage to our expectations. We cannot be in bondage to our images of God as one who is on our side against our foes. We cannot be in bondage to any expectation. However we might be disappointed by this or that turn of events, we cannot be disappointed by God, because, understanding Jesus's crucifixion, we expect from God only what God gives, and takes away.

By committing his spirit to God, Jesus mastered the art of loving the God who is unlovable in the ordinary sense. Jesus taught us to learn to love this God by saying that we should love our neighbors, an unlovely bunch! He taught us to learn to love this God by saying we should love our enemies, because God so often seems to be our enemy. He taught us to love this God by accepting crucifixion himself and refusing to let this separate his spirit from God. The old kind of being, the kind most of us have been, would turn from God in anger. The new being, which Jesus was and teaches us to be, can love the Creator despite everything and, in so doing, conquer sin and death. Because Jesus committed his spirit to God, nothing whatsoever could keep him from God, even in death. Because we too can commit our spirits to God, the wiles of Satan and the terrors of death present no obstacle. Blessing the Lord who gives and takes away, we have nothing left to lose and the freedom to live with the abundance of God's grace. Oh, what a happy death took place on Good Friday. Amen.

30

Fear[1]

Mark 16:1–8

The day after Jesus died, which began at sundown on Good Friday and continued until sundown Holy Saturday, was a death day. By belief and habit, the principals of our story, all Jews save Pilate, observed the Sabbath, a particularly important Sabbath because of its inclusion in Passover. The Jews had rushed the Romans to finish the crucifixions quickly before the Sabbath began, and Jesus's family and friends rushed him into a temporary grave in order to wait until the Sabbath was over to embalm him properly. The ancient meaning of Sabbath was to celebrate the days of work by resting. The sudden new meaning of Sabbath for Jesus's followers was numbing grief at the ruination of a life and work. Perhaps they would have been better off if they could have rushed around with funeral arrangements. But they had to stop everything and sit with their grief.

The Gospel of John does not dwell on grief. In John's account, Nicodemus and Joseph of Arimathea had procured the spices for burial and taken care of the embalming before the late afternoon of Good Friday turned into Sorrowful Saturday. Matthew's Gospel says nothing about the women carrying spices when they went to the tomb early Sunday, only that they found the tomb empty. Luke agrees with Mark that the women went early Sunday with spices to complete the embalming. Given what we know now about the failure of communication between men and women, both accounts

---

1. Preached April 15, 2006, the Easter Vigil.

Fear

might be right. Perhaps the men did in fact embalm Jesus and didn't tell the women, who fretted all through Saturday about how to get that organized and then went at first light on Sunday with spices of their own.

The remarkable thing about Mark's Gospel, the very first of the Gospels to be written, is that it simply ends with the three women struck dumb with terror, amazement, and fear. They had worried about how they would roll the stone away from the tomb entrance, but found it moved when they arrived. Inside was a young man in a white robe, who might have been an angel, the traditional account. Matthew also reports an angel, and Luke and John report two angels. Or Mark might have meant the young man in the white robe with Jesus in Gethsemane who fled naked when the police tried to grab him, obviously a close secret disciple of Jesus. At any rate, the young man instructed them not to be alarmed, the kind of instruction that hardly ever works, especially if you think the instructor is an angel. Then he said that Jesus had been raised after being laid in the tomb, and that the women should tell Peter that Jesus was going on to Galilee where they should meet him. But instead of telling Peter, Mark says that "they said nothing to anyone, for they were afraid." That is the last line of Mark's Gospel.

Now this was obviously an unsatisfying ending for the early Christian community, especially in light of the endings of the other gospels. Although they differ among themselves concerning who went to the tomb, the number of angels, whether the tomb was opened before or after the women arrived, and what happened at the tomb, the other gospels all record appearances of the resurrected Jesus. Mark has only a secondhand report about the resurrection, and leaves the women simply numbed by fear. Later manuscripts of Mark's Gospel than the earliest ones attach other endings, written in a different style from Mark, that borrow from the other gospels' resurrection account. But we know that these were later additions. Mark's Gospel ends with dumb fear.

The profound truth in Mark's authentic ending is seen from Saturday's perspective. After Jesus's bloody crucifixion, his family and friends were broken with grief. Their hopes in Jesus's messianic message were shattered. Their confidence in the power of his teaching was ruined. Their faith that he was the instrument of God, the Son of Man, the Son of God, the Anointed, was destroyed by Jesus's overwhelming defeat. Those close to him had given up much to follow him, and all that was ruined. They must have been fearful that the temple police or the Romans might come after them too. And all day Saturday, the Sabbath, they could do nothing but sit with their devastation. When the dull and unclean routine of burial rites brought them to the tomb Sunday morning, and they found it empty, save for the youth in white, how else could they act but in dumbstruck fear? Something wholly unexpected had happened. Nothing in their previous life with Jesus prepared them for this. Nothing in their Saturday despair prepared them for this. The young man did not explain things: his message was the problem. Something new, and inexplicable, whose consequences were wholly unknown, had happened to their broken Jesus, and to them, and they simply shut down in fear.

We too live with this fear. I don't mean the small rational fears we all have, fears of illness or accidents or disappointments in our careers. I mean the deep fear that our lives have no real meaning despite our projects. Jesus's devoted followers had found the meaning of their lives in following him and buying in to his vision of the new age. When that was shattered, they had nothing to fall back on except the Sabbath rituals of their inherited religion, rituals that Jesus had taught were not enough. Every one of us, too, harbors a deep fear that our lives are meaningless in the ultimate sense. Of course, we have our projects that give meaning to our lives. We nurture our family and friends, we work at academic programs, we engage in specific ministries, and each of these projects has a meaning, significance, and value. We can measure relative success in life by how well we do with projects such as these. But they have only the meanings they have, small finite gains in significance, or loss when they fail. Neither by themselves nor cumulatively do they give ultimate meaning to our lives. Beneath the surface of our activities, rich as they are, we fear the sulfur smell of ultimate vanity. Vanity of vanities, all is vanity.

Of course, we cannot admit often to this fear, and most of us bury it deep in our unconscious lives. Moreover, we cover over the fear with many forms of whistling in the dark, religious tunes, I must say. Very much of our religion has to do with assuring ourselves that everything is all right, that our lives do have meaning before God. Think of all the brave texts and stirring hymns we have sung tonight. We all know, however, that God did not really help the Israelites rip off the Egyptians and urge genocide on the inhabitants of Canaan; that was just the story the Israelites told themselves to make sense of their migration from Egypt to Canaan and to legitimate their claim to the land. We all know that God did not really guarantee that a descendent of David would sit upon the throne of Israel for ever; his dynasty barely lasted two generations. We all know that the defeat of Israel at the hands of the Assyrians and Babylonians was not in punishment for Israel's sins but an accidental conflagration in the politics of empire. We all know that Jesus as messiah had none of the major marks of the messiah: he did not bring in a reign of peace and justice. We all know that the second coming Paul expected within his lifetime did not happen, and has not happened since, and that the arguments for indefinite postponement are wearing thin. We all know that if we take the prophetic judgments and promises at face value, they either have been just plain falsified or else made so distant and unfalsifiable as to have no immediate impact on our lives. If we know all this and still keep our faith, we are to be congratulated. Our catechumens and soon-to-be baptized members will put on the Christian way, including the Christian story, with a faith that we welcome. But if we are honest, we acknowledge both the cognitive and emotional dissonance of that story with what we know to be true.

Yet we rehearse these stories throughout the year, and on this night of despair and fear, we put them all together in a great symphony of whistling in the dark. I suggest that we stop this for a moment and confront the traumatic fear of the absence of ultimate meaning. With Mary Magdalene, Mary the mother of James, and Salome, let us simply accept and own what our conscience tells us, that the grand Christian saga we had thought to give us meaning is false at face value. You can deny this with a flurry of affirmative convictions and slogans about God's promises. But that evasion is not appropriate for Holy Saturday. It would be a blasphemous denial of the cruel fact of the crucifixion. With the death of Jesus, the religion of promises dies, and with it hope based on those promises. If we cannot confront this awful and honest truth, then we cannot accept the life God has given us in this time when we understand how people invent fictions to give their lives meaning and justification. God did not give us life in a mythopoeic age when people simply told those stories and lived in them as if they were true. God gave us this sadly enlightened life, here, in the basement of a university church.

Lest we move from despair to cynicism, however, remember that after Saturday comes Sunday morning. Jesus is not in the tomb but is waiting for us up north somewhere in Galilee. Of course this news should strike us dumb with fear. We cannot go back to the innocence of the Christian story as before. Those who do, live in denial, and in that denial many are tempted to outrageous power plays of doctrine and morals in the name of religion. The resurrected Jesus did not regroup his followers and lead them on another teaching mission after Passover, like the ones before, nor did he raise an army to establish a worldly kingdom. He did not reaffirm the old story at face value.

Nor can we go on to a known new history, to a confident participation in a historical situation described as the reign of Christ. We cannot even say, with many theologians, that we are already in the early stages of the new age. We must admit that, despite our best efforts, things still might go from bad to worse. Neither of those scenarios would be terrifying: returning to the old story at face value or believing a new story of divine success. However, those would be false moves, knowing what we do on Holy Saturday. What is terrifying is that the claim about the risen Christ is wholly new. If we are not terrified by the risen Christ, then we probably have not admitted the full weight of the knowledge of the deaths of the old story and the magical fix-it hope gained on Holy Saturday.

For you to find out what I think about the wholly new reality of the risen Christ, you will have to come back tomorrow morning at eleven. Tonight I can tell you, however, that in the new reality it is still possible to inhabit the Christian story, but not at face value. We should know that other religions have their own stories, and they also can be inhabited, but not at face value. We ought not try to live without stories of salvation. It is still possible to enact the rites of the church, to welcome new members, and to celebrate our union with Christ through the Eucharist, but only with studied innocence, the innocence that knows how fictions and symbolic actions are true in ways other than what they seem. We should acknowledge the practices of the other religions in the same way, with studied innocence. We ought not try to live without practices that shape our lives toward ultimate reality, but religious practices are not safe without the studied innocence.

Tonight I can tell you that the spirit of Easter morning is one of ecstatic joy. Transformative as it is, that joy cannot and ought not be allowed to extinguish the awesome fear of the new reality in Christ. The resurrection of Jesus Christ can never be an "I told you so!" experience. The experience is, "Oh my God!" Mark's ending is an essential and true version of the gospel. Until we come to accept deep in our hearts, with appropriate anguish and fear, the death of our human projects as providing ultimate meaning, including the death of our religion, we cannot begin to accept the power and the majesty, the surprise and shock, the beauty and holiness, of the empty tomb and the young man's command to go somewhere to meet Jesus.

31

Do Not Hold Me[1]

Acts 10:31–43; 1 Corinthians 15:1–11; John 20:1–18

Welcome to this Easter celebration of the resurrection of Jesus Christ! Easter is a festival that has many layers of meaning, all of them valid in their contexts. The most obvious comes from its name. The term "Easter" comes from the name of the Saxon goddess Eostre, who presides over the spring equinox. Christianity gave new meaning to her name but retained the old meaning of the celebration of spring, the emergence of crops, new life, renewal, and the return of the Red Sox. If Easter means nothing more to you than a rite of spring, that is still a powerful meaning and worth much celebration, especially in Boston's climate.

Another level of Easter's meaning is that the events around the crucifixion and resurrection of Christ changed history. Christianity has become an astonishingly powerful force in history, now affecting all cultures and lands.

The cycle of seasons and the course of history relate to the passage of time in a horizontal direction, so to speak. A vertical dimension of the resurrection of Christ is also important, and surely more important from the standpoint of salvation. In our gospel text from John this morning, Jesus appeared to Mary Magdalene when she visited the tomb. She thought at first that he was a gardener in the cemetery. When he called her name, however, she recognized him, exclaimed a familiar title, "Rabbouni," and

---

1. Preached April 16, 2006, Easter Day.

reached to embrace his feet. But Jesus said, "Do not hold on to me." Titian has a powerful painting of kneeling Mary stretching out toward Jesus who is bending away out of reach.

Jesus said, "Do not hold on to me, because I have not yet ascended to the Father. But go to the brothers and say to them, 'I am ascending to my Father and your Father, to my God and your God.'" For John's Gospel, the resurrection was only the first step on the way to Jesus's union with God in the ascension. Whereas Luke said that Jesus's ascension took place forty days after the resurrection, John rushed things. John said that Jesus commissioned the disciples and breathed the Pentecost breath into them on the evening of the very day of resurrection. For John, the issue was less what would happen next, the horizontal dimension, but what was happening now to bring Jesus to God, the vertical dimension.

The salvific significance of Jesus's ascension is that he takes us with him. Remember, earlier in John's Gospel he had told the disciples that he was going to the Father where he would make a place for them. This point is accentuated in our text for today in which Jesus says he is ascending "to my Father *and your Father*, to my God *and your God*." Jesus's ascension, of which the resurrection is the first step, establishes a connection with God that we all can share.

Now, the ascension language, going *up* to God in heaven, is more problematic for us today than it was for Jesus's audience, who believed that God really did reside very high in the sky in or beyond the highest heaven. Most people in the ancient Mediterranean world believed that there was a stack of heavens or planes of existence above the earth, as well as a stack of hells beneath. Each heavenly level has its own natural properties, according to that belief, with those closest to the earth being rather physical like our plane and the higher ones more ethereal or spiritual. When a being traverses from one heaven to another, it changes physical properties to fit the new heavenly layer. Paul, for instance, said that Jesus left the highest heaven with God and descended to earth where he took on the fully human form of a slave, and then returned to God; Paul also said that in our resurrection we shall go to a high enough heaven that our mortal bodies will be immortal. Probably in John's idea of Jesus's resurrection, his body was already being changed so that it could not be handled easily, and he could pass through closed doors. We don't share this worldview about levels of heavens.

What then can the ascension mean to us? It means that we must supplement our account of temporal life with an account of eternity. The

Do Not Hold Me

vertical dimension is eternity, which intersects with time at every moment on the horizontal dimension. Ordinarily we forget about the eternal dimension and concentrate on the hopes and fears of the temporal. The temporal dimension of life is fully complicated enough to occupy our whole attention. All the problems of living manifest themselves in things we should appropriate or put aside, in things to enjoy or loathe, in projects to strive to accomplish or evils to deconstruct. Taking care of family and friends, working out careers, caring for the earth, making peace, pursuing justice, keeping our health, passing on culture, and preparing new generations are all meaningful projects. And yet by themselves, even taken all together, they do not give ultimate meaning to life. Our projects are nearly always somewhat incomplete, and ambiguous in their consequences. If we are only our projects, we are worth only what they are worth, and they pass away, most soon to be inconsequential. The religiously motivated effort to find ultimate meaning in worldly success usually turns sour, and we secretly harbor resentment that life in the long run, as Thomas Hobbes said, is "solitary, poor, nasty, brutish, and short." Even the most successful of us fears that successes do not add up to ultimate meaning. Fear and resentment lead to alienation from the eternal God who creates our world this way. Even our religion, which employs the symbols of temporal action and success, shows itself to be a fiction if interpreted in merely temporal terms: God has not made a perfectly just world despite promises, nor brought us into a satisfying glorious history.

So, the human problem of time and eternity is that we look to time to do what only eternity can do. Then, frustrated by that failure, we alienate ourselves from eternity, blinding ourselves even to its reality. Jesus calls us back to the eternity within our midst, our eternal relation with God. He teaches that within time, we need to learn the eternal lesson to love one another, with all the social and political justice and peacemaking elements required for that love. In the dimension of eternity, which is in every time, we need to learn to love the God who gives us this ambiguous and fragmented temporal life. God is our Father, the creator of all of us together. We come to love God by appreciating how God's love both creates us and gives us the resources to love God and one another, even when resources for other things in time are short. Most particularly, we come to love God by seeing how precious Jesus is, how lovely. He is lovely in loving us and in loving God. He is lovely in his teachings and in his ministries. He is lovely in his acceptance of the evils and frustrations of the world, accepting even crucifixion as somehow a gift of God. When Jesus was lifted up on the cross, we were in agony at the destruction of his loveliness. When he was buried we were in despair at the extinction of his beauty. When word comes of his resurrection and ascent to the Father, we look for Jesus and see the eternal God in whom we live and move and have our being. The astonishing new reality symbolized by Jesus's resurrection and ascension to God in heaven is that we are offered the opportunity to live openly in the eternal dimension of life as well as the temporal.

Look again at the logic of Jesus ascending. It means first of all that he is leaving the temporal world. After a few appearances at the merely resurrected plane of things, Jesus will leave forever. So Jesus told Mary Magdalene not to hold on to him. She could no longer be dependent on him as she had been before. And we too do not have Jesus personally with us as our temporal guide. Like Mary, we have to continue our temporal lives with all their projects, successes, failures, and ambiguities. For this, Jesus told the disciples that he would send the Holy Spirit to be our guide. The Spirit on the one hand helps us to understand Jesus's love as the guide for our love of neighbor and God, and on the other hand helps us to keep in touch with divine eternity when historical things go bad, as Jesus said they would. See John's Gospel, chapters 11–17, where these points are spelled out. (That's an assignment: this is a university church, you know!) The point is that we are responsible for our own lives within both time and eternity, guided by the Holy Spirit but responsible for identifying that Spirit among all the evil ones. We are no longer under tutelage to Jesus as slaves of the master: Jesus now calls us friends.

Our eternal lives to which Jesus leads us are lived in the infinite fecundity of God's eternal life. We each have our moments from birth to death, and each of these is an intimate part of God's creation. We do not need more moments, or different moments, because each of them is part of the infinite worth and glory of God. When we see that each and every one of our moments, with all we do and suffer, is part of the infinite glory of God, we have an ultimate meaning that cannot be compromised by anything the world can do to us, even crucify us. We will die, of course, but that does not matter in light of the eternal life we have in God, no matter how short that life is in time.

The astonishing result of this new realization of eternal life is that we can return to the projects of our temporal life with perfect freedom and absolutely full commitment. Our ultimate reality in God has nothing to lose by risking itself in the dangerous causes of justice and peace, in the struggles for excellence and creativity, or in the fragile commitments of love and friendship. With abandon we can embrace our lives and the issues peculiar to our watch in history, because our ultimate salvation and meaning is in the eternity of God's life, not in our success or failure in history. Because Jesus, raised and ascended, has brought us to the eternal Father in love, and because we abide with him now and always in that divine eternity, we fly through time on eagles' wings. Alleluia! Christ Is Risen! Amen!

32

Touch and Light[1]

Acts 4:31–35; 1 John 1:1–2:2; John 20:11–31

Last Sunday, Easter, the gospel reading was the first half of the twentieth chapter of John, and today's gospel is the second half. I mentioned last week, in describing John's interest in the vertical dimension of eternity rather than the horizontal dimension of time in history, that John telescoped the events Luke spread out from Easter to Pentecost into a much shorter time. We read this morning, for instance, about how Jesus breathed on the disciples, giving them the Holy Spirit, and then commissioned them to forgive sins or retain them, on the very evening of Easter Sunday. The Holy Breath is John's version of Pentecost, and his version of the Great Commission has nothing to do with baptizing people in all nations, as Matthew said, though it agrees with Luke's version, which is also about repentance and forgiveness.

Today I want us to slow down, to back away from meditating on the ascension and eternal life, and linger on the details of Jesus's resurrection appearances, from John's point of view. We have not only the gospel reading but the reading from the letter of 1 John which, if not written by the same person, was written by someone in his school. The First Letter of John opens with resonant drama: "We declare to you what was from the beginning . . ." The Gospel of John opens, "In the beginning was the Word . . . ," which in turn refers back to the first line of Genesis: "In the beginning when God

---

1. Preached April 23, 2006, the second Sunday of Easter.

Touch and Light

created the heavens and the earth . . ." So the author of the First Letter of John was not talking about the beginning of Christian understanding but the very beginning of the world. This is serious metaphysics, from which John's tradition does not shy away.

But listen to what comes next: "We declare to you what was from the beginning, what we have heard, what we have seen with our eyes, what we have looked at and touched with our hands, concerning the word of life . . ." What we have heard, seen, looked at, and touched! The deep, metaphysical Word, the Logos, had become palpable. John meant, of course, that the Word was incarnate in Jesus, but that sounds too bland. What he really meant is that the person, Jesus, whom they had heard, seen, looked at and touched with their own hands, was in fact the very Word of God fitted into human form. The author of 1 John was writing in opposition to some members of the Johannine community who emphasized the divinity of Jesus at the expense of his humanity. The author's point was that it is the man they had touched who is the real Word.

Touch is also at stake in our gospel reading, is it not? Thomas had missed Jesus's first visit to the disciples on the evening of Easter Sunday and, when told about it, had said, "Unless I see the mark of the nails in his hands, and put my finger in the mark of the nails and my hand in his side, I will not believe." Thomas did not want someone else mistaken for Jesus, nor some kind of unhuman ghost or angel. He wanted touchable Jesus. When Jesus suddenly appeared a week later where Thomas was with the others, he invited Thomas to touch. In point of fact, Thomas did not touch him. Seeing Jesus was enough, and Thomas exclaimed, "My Lord and my God." That confession of Thomas's, "My Lord and my God," is the dramatic high point of John's Gospel.

What were the disciples touching when they did touch Jesus? According to the First Letter of John, they were touching the word of life—"this life was revealed, and we have seen it and testify to it, and declare to you the eternal life that was with the Father and was revealed to us." As I said last week, eternal life, for John's tradition, is the vertical connection with God that is there all along, that we usually miss, and that Jesus revealed to us. Jesus said many things about how to live in this life: admonitions about justice and peace, forgiveness and mercy. John's stress is on the eternal divine dimension that accompanies all our moments and projects in which we pursue the Christian Way. What is that eternal divine dimension? Listen to how the author of 1 John concludes his amazing opening sentence: "we declare to you what we have seen and heard so that you also may have fellowship with us; and truly our fellowship is with the Father and with his Son Jesus Christ." Then the author adds, "We are writing these things so that our joy may be complete."

If you did the assignment I gave you last week, namely, to read the thirteenth through seventeenth chapters of the Gospel of John, you recognize immediately what this fellowship is, involving the disciples, Jesus, and God. Jesus told the disciples that he was giving them a new commandment, to love one another as he had loved them. Then he explained that this loving fellowship of friends was bound together not only because he loved them and taught them how to love. It was bound because God loved them and had commissioned Jesus to love and teach them. So, their fellowship of loving one another included being loved by God and loving God in turn. No matter what their lives would involve, and Jesus predicted trouble and pain, their loving fellowship with one another, with Jesus, and with the Father was an eternal life that would keep them safe in the bosom of God. The first lesson to draw from this is that we have many Christian projects to do in the world, concerning peace, justice, care for the poor and sick, and relief of suffering. The second lesson is that, regardless of how we succeed or fail in these projects, our eternal life is that we are living with God in fellowship with one another. As the author of 1 John says, this makes our joy complete, even when we suffer in all the worldly ways.

Living in loving fellowship with God is no simple matter, however. In this respect, the author of 1 John said "God is light and in him there is no darkness at all. If we say we have fellowship with him while we are walking in darkness, we lie and do not have what is true." You remember that the Prologue to the Gospel of John says that the word of life in Jesus "was the light of all people. The light shines in the darkness, and the darkness did not overcome it." The divine light is present all the time, but our darkness prevents us from seeing it. What is our darkness? According to the author of 1 John, it is our deceptive claim that we have no sin: "If we say we have no sin, we deceive ourselves, and the truth is not in us. If we confess our sins, he who is faithful and just will forgive us our sins and cleanse us from all unrighteousness." Notice that the author assumes that we sin. There is the hope that we do not sin, but also the plain recognition that we do sin. The light of life in Jesus is not sinlessness but sins confessed and forgiven. Human darkness is the pretence that we do not sin.

Here is how I understand this point. Our life within time inevitably leads to sin, and in many ways. Hardly anything we can do is only good, even in the great projects of peace and justice. Nearly every action is morally ambiguous: good in some ways, bad in others; good for some people, hurtful to others. The best we can do is to optimize the good-to-bad ratio. Then we need to acknowledge and confess the bad sides. As human social beings, we are surrounded and defined by conflicting obligations. We can never do enough for our families, never enough for our jobs, never enough for charity, never enough for community service, never enough for worship, never enough to improve our characters, never enough to help those who suffer, never enough on and on. At best we try to balance things so as to fail our obligations the least. But we know in our heart that we have failed in all sorts of directions. And some of us have folks reminding us of that with depressing regularity. We need to acknowledge and confess our sins of omission. You can list your own sins of commission! Confess them too.

This inevitably sinful condition is just the nature of life. We do not have to be perfect. Jesus told the rich young ruler, with some annoyance, that only God is good in the sense of being perfect. But we do have to be realistic and live in the light of judgment, confessing our sins. The confession of sins is absolutely essential to our fellowship with one another, with Christ Jesus, and with God. It is not enough to say liturgical confession, although that is a good reminder. The requirement is to seek out the light that reveals us in brutal clarity, to give up our attempts at self-deception, and to admit the judgment upon us openly in our fellowship with one another, God, and Jesus. Of course you know how hard this is. So much of spiritual life is picking the scabs off denial! Even harder sometimes is hearing and accepting someone else's confession. I would much prefer that you keep your sins to yourself, and for two reasons. If you confess yours, I have to own up to mine, which are probably altogether too much like yours. Moreover, if you confess your sins, I have to forgive you, as Jesus commissioned his disciples to do. Forgiving is even harder than confessing, is it not?

Now you see something of the texture of the fellowship of love to which Jesus calls us as our eternal life. Being buddies, delighting in one another, building a culture together, engaging in worship and in the disciplines of the Christian life together, are all helpful but not enough. Perhaps they are not even essential. We are called to love those we would not want to spend time with, those who are our enemies, those from alien and competing cultures, those whose worship sensibilities are different, those whose interpretations of the Christian life are opposed to ours. The fellowship of love to which Jesus calls us as eternal life is a fellowship based on the divine light of confession and forgiveness.

Oh, what a task this is! Can white Americans truly confess the racist sins of our ancestors who enslaved Africans, and continued to segregate them after slavery was outlawed? Can white Americans confess the privilege we enjoy because of the consequences of that multigenerational racism? Can we confess the racism in our stereotypes today? I doubt it, if we mean confession to be deeper than political correctness. But if we did, could African Americans forgive their confessing racist oppressors? I doubt it, if we mean forgiveness by everyone. Yet there is hope for walking in the divine light of confession and forgiveness.

That hope comes to us in the resurrected Jesus, who shows us that confession first and forgiveness second is backward. Jesus is the one who taught his disciples and died for them. They abandoned and betrayed him, and he forgave them before they confessed. In fact, only because they understood his dying undying love and its forgiveness were they able to confess. The author of 1 John said, "But if anyone does sin, we have an advocate with the Father, Jesus Christ the righteous; and he is the atoning sacrifice for our sins, and not for ours only but also for the sins of the whole world." You see, those other people, those non-Christians, do not have to confess. They are already forgiven. If they can accept that forgiveness, perhaps they then will have the power to confess. If they confess, they can move into the divine light, and enter the fellowship of love in which consists eternal life. Brothers and sisters, the same is true for us. We do not have to begin with confession. We begin by accepting forgiveness. "For God so loved the world that he gave his only Son, so that everyone who believes in him may not perish but may have eternal life." The saving belief is belief in forgiveness, which makes it possible for us to accept ourselves enough to confess. If we both confess and forgive, then we live in fellowship with one another, with the Father, and with Jesus Christ, who overcame the world in his forgiveness.

Do we ever touch Jesus? Of course we do. Every time we meet someone who forgives an unconfessed sin, particularly our own, we touch the resurrected Christ. Every time we forgive someone without demanding or even expecting that he or she might in turn confess, we are in Christ and our touch is that of Jesus. We still are sinners and are surrounded by sinners. But we are also surrounded and filled by the grace of forgiveness. Because of this we can move into the light of confession. With that, we enter into the fellowship of love that is the content of eternal life. The crucifixion did not kill the forgiving grace of God in Jesus. On the contrary, the crucifixion made it overwhelmingly real, for the risen Christ is to be touched in every hand that blesses sinners. Amen.

33

Beginnings and Endings, Wisdom and Choice[1]

Deuteronomy 30:19; Ecclesiastes 7:1–14; James 3:13

Our text from Deuteronomy says that beginnings are important because they are determined by what we choose. The Israelites had just about completed their forty years of wandering and were poised to cross the River Jordan to begin life in the promised land. Moses told them that they had a life-and-death decision. They could choose faithfulness to God and live, or forget God and die. Alas, like us in most of our decisions, the Israelites did a little of both and never again lived in the laser-light of unambiguous life or death. How does this bear upon our inauguration of President Brown? In the first place, he already has crossed the river to what someone told him is the promised land.[2] That was a decisive choice, and we will not ask him about whether he has any regrets. In the second place, he already has forced some decisive choices on us at the University. He has demanded that the University study itself and devise a strategic plan, when we were all prepared to study Bob Brown and divine his plans. So he has set before us our own version of the choice between life and death, in this, a new beginning for us all. Thank you, President Brown.

---

1. Preached April 27, 2006, at the Thanksgiving Service for the inauguration of Robert Brown as President of Boston University. The Brown family chose the texts.

2. President Brown had been Provost at MIT, across the Charles River from Boston University.

Beginnings and Endings, Wisdom and Choice

Our text from Ecclesiastes, however, says that "Better is the end of a thing than its beginning." Dramatic opening moves are fine, filled with large choices. But life is lived in the living, not the starting, and we do not know how to assess it until the end. Ecclesiastes is an extremely sobering book. "In the day of prosperity be joyful, and in the day of adversity consider; God has made the one as well as the other, so that mortals may not find out anything that will come after them." Surely good times are coming for higher education, but also bad times. Most likely, the good and bad times will be mixed, so that too much joy for abundance will seem vulgar to those sections of the University in disrepair. Moreover, the mixtures will change so that the first will be last and the last first, and then around again. The success of the presidency of Robert Brown will be measured in large part by his management of prosperity and adversity as dual gifts of God. His watch will have both. Presidents Silber, Westling, and Chobanian have delivered up to him a University of great energy and ambition, with a vigorous mixture of prosperity and adversity.

Our third text, from the Epistle of James, says that wisdom is what counts, and we in the University count on that from our leader. It wouldn't hurt if the rest of us also exercise some wisdom. James says, "Show by your good life that your works are done with gentleness born of wisdom." Gentleness is the key point, and it applies to leadership in the University. With gentle leadership, all the people and their work will flourish. With ungentle leadership, people feel bruised, even if made to do good things. Gentleness does not mean weakness, or waiting for others to take the lead, or failure to exercise judgment, or tolerance of foolishness, or lack of a temper when anger is the honest response. Gentleness in leading means nurturing those who are led so that they develop strength, courage, confidence, and direction born of wisdom, to do their jobs ever better.

James's qualification of gentleness is that it needs to be born of wisdom. Of course it is possible to be gentle, nurturing everyone, without much integrating direction, with the result that everyone gets better and better at pursuing their agenda at the expense of others. We do not need chaos of that sort. Wisdom is understanding how things work, with the art of putting first things first. No university can be hospitable to every worthy intellectual ambition, and choices will need to be made constantly for the definition of the large, tolerant, but still singular identity of Boston University. The shape of the University does not come only from decisions at the top, however wise and gentle. It comes from thousands of decision points throughout the institution and its social environment. Wise leadership guides the complex process of decision-making so that the decisions are made in the right places in the right order, with appropriate modification of directions as we learn from the results of actions taken. Moreover, we look to the president to model sagacity for the rest of us. If it seems as if I am saying that the president needs to be wise like a philosopher, that surely could not be because my own training is in philosophy!

No, it is in the Bible, in passages such as those we've read. God has given us a world with abundance and prosperity, plus intelligence, creativity, and skilled excellence, mixed with adversity and poverty, plus stupid unwillingness to learn, dogged repetition of the past, and strong convictions that nothing is better than anything else. We enjoy the bounties of life, leave a legacy, and suffer and die. The fragile habitat for civilized human life floats among the vast impersonal forces of the cosmos. These are the conditions God has given us in which we are to live, to create, and in the end to render an account of how we handle these conditions on our watch. Each one of us is in this human situation. The president of a university is a kind of epitome of human accountability in general. Each one of us lives amidst an ever-changing confusion of prosperity and adversity, making the daily choices that add up to the lives for which we must give an account. President Brown does with all the University what each of us does with the environments of our lives. By this service of Thanksgiving, we at Boston University give thanks for the leadership of Robert Brown and his wife, Beverly, whose promise of strong wisdom already shows fruit. At the same time, I dare say that President Brown gives thanks to have Boston University as the environment for his watch, with our peculiar tumble of prosperity and adversity. Because his work is so significant for all of us together, such thanksgiving on both sides should take the form of a very long prayer. Amen.

34

Homily for Simon Parker's Funeral[1]

Psalm 110:1; 1 Corinthians 15:21–58

For a sophisticated and sincere Christian who loved the Hebrew Scriptures as much as Simon Parker did, the obvious place to find the gospel for his life is in the New Testament use of the Hebrew Bible. Contrary to what you might expect, the most cited text in the New Testament is not from the prophets or from Genesis 1 or from the passages about Noah, Abraham, Moses, or David—all of which do figure prominently. It is the first line of the 110th Psalm: "The LORD says to my lord: 'Sit at my right hand, till I make your enemies your footstool.'" In the Hebrew Bible that is likely a coronation hymn, and the line means something like, God says to the new king, take your place under divine protection while I establish your reign in power. But the Christians took the passage to refer to the Messiah: God says to the Messiah, Jesus, reign at my side until the battle against evil, especially death, has been won. Matthew, Mark, and Luke cite Jesus quoting the passage to prove that the Messiah cannot only be a son of David. The assumption ascribed to the Pharisees with whom Jesus was speaking was that David himself wrote the hymn to say that God says to one of David's sons who will be the Messiah, sit at my right hand, etc., and Jesus said that David would never have referred to his own son as "my lord." Peter cited the passage in his first sermon recorded in Acts to prove that God had made

---

1. Simon Parker was a much-beloved professor of Hebrew Bible at the Boston University School of Theology. This funeral sermon for him was preached May 5, 2006.

Jesus both Lord and Messiah. The author of Ephesians uses the passage to describe Jesus's resurrection to God's right hand in heaven where he has dominion over all things. The author of Hebrews uses the passage to prove that Jesus is higher than angels. Paul, in 1 Corinthians 15, cited the passage to refer to the cosmic drama within which Jesus would conquer the forces of evil, even death, and hand the world back to God redeemed. In all these and other usages, the line from Psalm 110 stands for the victory of God as Christians understood that.

In our grief about Simon's sudden, untimely, and unfair death, we look for signs of victory. Taking Professor Parker's hermeneutic practice as a clue, we know to distinguish carefully between the historical meaning of a text in its original context and the uses made of the text later, and again between these and the spiritual meaning we might derive from the text in our own usage. Of course that 110th Psalm was not written about Jesus, and its author was not even David! Nevertheless, the Psalms took on new and important meanings for the Jewish religion when later they came to be regarded as David's writings. Moreover, when the first-century Christians referred the passage to Jesus, they were constructing a new meaning at the very heart of the nascent Christian gospel.

Saint Paul, for instance, in the 1 Corinthians passage citing Psalm 110, was addressing questions people had about resurrection. He made two points. First, in the cosmic geography commonly accepted in his time, the plane of Earth has physical bodies with various properties appropriate to our plane, including the fact that our bodies are mortal. Above the plane of Earth is a stack of heavenly planes, each with its own set of properties. For instance, Aristotle said that below the orbit of the moon, bodies naturally travel in straight lines, whereas from the moon's orbit and above, bodies naturally travel in circular motion; above the orbit of the sun, bodies naturally spin as well as circle. Paul said that in resurrection we shall be moved from a plane of mortality to a heavenly realm higher up where our bodies will take on the properties of celestial immortality. Also it was assumed that in that heavenly plane we will be able to associate with Jesus and God the Father, and with people who did not live in our own time, something impossible for the natural properties of the earthly plane, however natural for heaven. These observations of Paul addressed the "what's it like" question about resurrection.

Paul's other main point was that, when we are enthralled by the forces of evil in our age, the death characteristic of the earthly plane is the last word. But God in Christ Jesus has broken the power of these forces and in the course of history will eventually wholly subdue them so that the way to heavenly immortal resurrection will be open to us. Paul viewed this as a cosmic battle in which Jesus had won the way to heaven for himself, the "firstfruits," and lined things up for us, giving us freedom from the bondage of death. These observations addressed the question of the meaning of resurrection, and Paul's moral was that resurrection is more about God than about us. Paul was against what we now call "spiritual materialists," who promise a heavenly reward for doing something. Rather, resurrection is a gift from God that we receive because God has won victory over the forces of evil that would keep us in the thrall of death. When we wake up to this fact in faith, we participate in this cosmic victory.

Now Simon would be the first to point out that these reflections of Paul are set in the cultural context of the first century. We no longer believe that, going up, one passes through a stack of heavens with different natural properties. Moreover, we are suspicious of those who reduce cosmic history to a moral saga, especially one that fosters a vision of the world as divided between the righteous and the unrighteous, with an invitation to go to war against those you think are unrighteous. Paul, of course, never pushed the imagery of cosmic warfare that far, claiming to the contrary that everyone is a sinner and that governments in general are divine agents.

Yet to find our own signs of victory, we need to ask how these first-century texts deliver the gospel to us in our own historical situation, faced as we are with Simon Parker's death as a faithful disciple of Christ. The other side of Simon's hermeneutic, after the historical analysis, was to see through the texts as symbols opening onto the divine. What a lively literary imagination he had for seeing the point where others got stuck on the broken symbols!

The first thing we see through these symbols is that Simon, with the rest of us, now is fully present with the eternal God who created and sustained him all his days. Death in time cannot change the eternal God who eternally sustains Simon together with all those with whom he has been connected. Sitting together with God and Jesus, with footstools, is one good image of this, though I rather suspect Simon would prefer to imagine making music together. For sure, God the Father is a bass and Jesus a heldentenor; now they have an accompanist.

The second thing we see through these symbols is that because God our creator who holds all times together is eternal, Simon is eternally alive in God with all the moments of his life as present experience: his childhood and youth together with his mature life. Moreover, within the divine life he is connected to all those with whom he was connected at any time in his life. We who are limited to merely temporal experience live one day at a time, and the past seems lost while the future is not yet. The veil of temporality gives us a merely abstract vision of life within God's eternity. Simon gets eternal life face-to-face.

The third thing we see is that the enemy has been put down, the evil, the selfishness, that makes us believe that the veil of temporality is the whole truth, and that death is the last word. Jesus revealed and taught a way of love that overcomes both selfishness between people and resentment of God so that we can accept ourselves as eternally together in the divine economy. Simon was fully committed to this way of love of neighbors and God, and was free of sin's bondage. As Jesus's disciple, nothing can separate him from the love of God in Jesus Christ.

The fourth thing we see is that God's victory over the forces within creation that would blind us to the light of salvation embraces us as well as Simon. We all miss him deeply, in many different ways. For some, he was like a part of us, and that grief is very deep indeed. His wife, Sonia, now suddenly and unexpectedly, needs to plan a life without him: how can that be borne? It can be borne because God embraces all of us together with the grace that gives each of us a place in the divine economy. Within the veil of temporality, our community of love and support expresses that divine economy in a real, if abstract, way. The divine love by which the enemies of life are put down is in Sonia and in every one of us, as well as Simon. This is what is meant by the communion of saints. It is not something we have earned. This grace is something that we enjoy from God, which we know as we imagine sitting around with our feet propped up on the bondage of evil. Our own lives yet to come will have plenty of pains, evils, and occasions of selfishness; but those things do not define us. Because Jesus is on that throne, his feet on the enemies, we know his way is not susceptible to anything that might separate us from the divine glory, "neither death, nor life, nor angels, nor principalities, nor things present, nor things to come, nor powers, nor height, nor depth, nor anything else in all creation." "Death is swallowed up in victory. O death, where is thy victory? O death, where is thy sting? The sting of death is sin, and the power of sin is the law. But thanks be to God, who gives us the victory through our Lord Jesus Christ." Despite our shock and grief, we can be confident that in eternal life, Simon

Homily for Simon Parker's Funeral

Parker shares the footstool of Jesus, and we can hope to join that party some day. Amen.

35

The New Commandment: Love One Another[1]

Acts 10:41–48; 1 John 5:1–6; John 15:1–17

The authors of the Synoptic Gospels—that is, Matthew, Mark, and Luke—all record Jesus citing the Great Commandment, which is dual, to love God with all your heart, mind, soul, and strength, and to love your neighbor as yourself. The first part of the Great Commandment, about loving God, is a paraphrase of Deuteronomy 6:5, and the second part, about loving neighbors, paraphrases Leviticus 19:18. Jesus cited these texts in answer to the question, what is the greatest of the commandment? And his answer received approval from his questioners for identifying the very heart of the law of Moses.

The author of the Gospel of John does not record Jesus citing the Great Commandment in this form, but instead records Jesus's saying in our gospel for today: "This is my commandment, that you love one another as I have loved you." Our text embeds this saying in a very complicated context involving God the Father and the nature of love and friendship. In a moment I'll lift up some aspects of this context, but first I want to say some obvious things about the commandment to "love one another as I have loved you."

---

1. Preached May 21, 2006, the sixth Sunday of Easter.

The New Commandment: Love One Another

First, although love is a theme in all the gospels, and in all the other books of the New Testament, it is the dominant, controlling theme in John's Gospel and in the Letters of John, which reflect the same tradition, if not by the same author. What we call the "Johannine tradition" is defined by the emphasis on love, although it includes the other major Christian themes such as justice, righteousness, humility, peace, judgment, mercy, forgiveness, resurrection, and eternal life. John sets all of these other themes in the context of love.

Second, the controlling theme of love means that the Christian emphasis is on the quality of relationships, relations among people and with God: those relationships should be loving, and all faults come from some failure of love. This controlling theme stands in sharp contrast with another biblical way of organizing Christian thought, namely, the victory of God within history over the forces of evil, opposition, and disobedience. Whereas love emphasizes relationships, victory emphasizes roles in narrative. God's victory is the organizing theme in the writings of Paul, for instance, and the book of Revelation. Paul's picture of the human situation is complex, including all the other Christian themes—love, justice, righteousness, humility, peace, judgment, mercy, forgiveness, resurrection, and eternal life: indeed he writes about love even more beautifully than John does. Perhaps some of you remember Dean Hill's recitation of 1 Corinthians 13 in his sermon three weeks ago. But Paul organizes these themes against the narrative background of a war between God's divine forces of righteousness on the one hand and the forces of disobedience and unrighteousness on the other.

Third, the two organizing themes of love and victory have competed for Christian understanding since the days of the early church until now. Conservative American Christians read the same texts as the liberal Christians but organize them under the narrative theme of victory. For them, the distinction between the righteous and the unrighteous is very important, and they are responsive to political appeals that contrast our righteousness with the unrighteousness of other nations, perhaps other religions, justifying war against them. They think of life as a battle against those not in their in-group, a battle against evil empires and axes of evil nations. Of course, conservative theologians know that Paul also said that every person is a sinner and that our righteousness comes from God's grace, not our own achievements. Moreover, the credulity of conservative Christians is beginning to be strained when they are asked to support two wars against nations that did not attack us, wars justified by lies and deceptions, wars that stoke anger in the Islamic world against the West, wars that divert funds from the legitimate constituencies of government aid, wars that put the American economy in increasing debt to foreign nations. How long can conservative Christians let their commitment to the victory motif of Christianity make them vulnerable to appeals to a kind of patriotism that stands condemned by nearly all the other Christian themes of justice, righteousness, peace, humility, mercy, forgiveness, and love?

The weakness of liberals in this situation is that nothing in the preachment of Christianity organized around John's theme of love has the dramatic appeal of a call to arms in a battle against the unrighteous. The Christianity of love is soft and tender. Its hero is the Lamb of God who was crucified according to the ways of history, and is victorious only in the sense that love is far more important, ultimately important, than any victory in history.

The weakness of the conservative theme of victory is that it simply is falsified by history. Jesus did not come again within history to destroy the forces of evil, and the argument that he will come still later can be sustained only by extreme fantasy. The victory proclaimed over the Iraqis has turned out to be a devastating loss for American morality, respect, and economic standing; in real life there are very few true historical winners and losers—all sides are losers in most wars. Conservative Christians can say that Christ's victory two millennia ago was only the first step, and that history still will bring about a complete vindication. Yet that theology seems like a desperate strategy to shore up a fantasy that is not only false to history but a force for evil within history, for it breeds warmongering. John's Gospel is far more realistic about history when it cites Jesus saying that we will always have troubles and persecutions, and that love is the only way to survive in history.

I have contrasted the controlling theme of love with the controlling theme of victory in order to indicate what is at stake in Jesus's commandment to love one another. Now let us ponder that commandment directly. What did Jesus mean by love?

From the Gospels we know that love carries a range of meanings. At one end its bottom line is being kind. Kindness itself has many modalities, as in kindness to those we know versus kindness to individuals and groups we do not know, kindness to people mediated through taking care of institutions, kindness to the environment, and to the whole of God's creation. Yet all modes of kindness are characterized in two ways. Kindness is never cruel, and it is never neglectful. When we say we are Christians practicing a piety of love and yet are cruel or neglectful of those we might help, we know our love is hypocritical.

At the other end of the spectrum, love has something of an erotic dimension. This does not mean only sexuality, although there is much discussion now about the *Da Vinci Code*'s claim that Jesus and Mary Magdalene were sexually involved. This was suggested in some early writings that did not make it into the New Testament. The Gospel of John describes a physical intimacy between Jesus and the Beloved Disciple that seems to have been accepted without comment by the other disciples. Of course we have no solid historical evidence one way or another about Jesus's sexuality, and it will always be a matter of speculation in which people will see what they want to find. But erotic love does not have to mean sexual love. It means fascination with the beloved, a desire to reach out and touch, to be present and united with the beloved, a friendship that does not easily respect boundaries, that gives more than is deserved, that wants the welfare of the beloved more than one's own, and is willing to sacrifice to help. Love in its erotic dimension has little patience with reciprocity and Golden Rule–like measures of justice. Love does not love for a reason—its only reason is the delightfulness of the beloved. It overflows boundaries and is creative and self-giving. You can see why sexual love provides the metaphors for divine love in its erotic dimension.

Our gospel text this morning began by saying, "As the Father has loved me, so I have loved you." Here is the heart of the Johannine tradition: God loves us with kindness and erotic exuberance. God's relation to the world is not primarily that of a creator who demands justice, although it is that in secondary ways. The primary relation is that God is our lover who wildly creates us in the fecundity of the cosmos. God does not have a calculated reason for creating. God does not have intentions for creating. God simply creates things with value and thus becomes lover and creator together. Genesis says that God first creates, and then sees that it is good. Hosea says that even when we are wicked, God loves us like a husband impassioned for his whoring wife. John says God comes to be with us in Jesus, sacrificing his only begotten son that we might have eternal life and happiness. Where we are blind, because of our own selfish interests, God heals us gratuitously with the light of Christ. You recognize all of these images, do you not?

What does it mean, specifically, for God to love us? According to Jesus in John's Gospel, it means for God to create us in this fecund world full of grace and light, to become lovers ourselves, finite versions of the infinite God as lover. For God to love us is to make us into lovers. For us to be lovers in turn is for us to make our friends into lovers, and to love God the supreme lover. God's passion is to love lovers. God's mercy is to help us when we are faulty lovers. We have biological and social impulses to love, but also countervailing impulses. Selfishness and self-imposed blindness bind us to sin and frustrate our loving. Therefore we need to purify and cultivate our love in loving communities of the sort Jesus founded among his disciples. Jesus said that the Father loved him so much that he, Jesus, could love his disciples, an otherwise unlovely group (rather like us). The power of Jesus's love for his disciples was that it turned them into lovers, so that he called them his friends, no longer disciples in subordination to him but mutual lovers. His commandment for them to love one another was simply the commandment from God by which God completes his loving creation of creating lovers. Jesus had taken his loving friends out of the world of sin where victory is narrated by historical success and into the heavenly world of God where love is what counts: passionate, creative, overflowing love.

Now here is a puzzle for us to think about for the next several weeks. Is the community of friends that Jesus established an exclusive church? Does our baptism into the Christian life mean that we make all our relationships outside that community secondary to the Christian family? Is being a Christian the only thing that counts for love? John has been read that way. Or does Jesus's community of friends comprise all those who understand that God's love can make them lovers who work to perfect love in all their relationships? On this second reading the church is where we nourish ourselves with Jesus's teachings and the sacraments of his demonstration of God's love. But the specific loves we are to pursue are not primarily within the church: they are the various ones within our families, our groups of friends, our workplace, our cities, with people of other religions and cultures, with the institutions of civilization, and with the environment of God's whole creation. I am inclined to this second reading. If we look at the church as itself a community of mutual love, it is pretty much a failure. As much as I love you in the pews, I love my grandchildren more, and you would think me crazy if I did not. But if instead we look at the church as a community for the nurture of love in all its other dimensions, then it is a divine vehicle of God's love and it hosts God's presence in all those other relationships in which we should be loving. According to John, God is incarnate in the world, not just the church. Let us think about these things, and rejoice that we are friends of Jesus because we can love one another. Amen.

36

Jesus Leaving[1]

Acts 1:1–11; Ephesians 1:11–23; Luke 24:41–53

Jesus is no longer with us in person. This fact is celebrated in the church as the Feast of the Ascension, which is today. Luke tells the ascension story twice, once at the end of his Gospel and once at the beginning of his book, the Acts of the Apostles. These were written as connected narratives, and it is somewhat misleading that, in the customary order of our Bible, the Gospel of John is inserted between them. Our reading from Ephesians is about where Jesus has gone to, having departed from our history.

The symbolism of the ascension is rich and connects with nearly all Christian beliefs. Yet it must be admitted that the doctrine of the ascension serves a very practical purpose, namely, what to think of the resurrected Jesus. Christians can't quite say that Jesus was raised from the dead when a young man and lived more years to die an old man. Nor can we say that he aged and aged and aged and now has the body and mind of a two-hundred-year-old man. Some have thought that the resurrected Jesus would just stop aging and always be a thirty-something man, or a late-forties man if you take John's word for it; but then, Jesus would not be raised as a normal metabolizing human being. None of these possibilities for a raised but un-ascended Jesus is compatible with the Christian affirmation of resurrection to eternal life rather than just more life like Lazarus had.

---

1. Preached May 28, 2006, Ascension Sunday.

Jesus Leaving

The Christian symbolism of the ascension took advantage of the first-century common belief that there is a stack of different heavens above the earth, each with its own properties for what abides there. To move to a different level is to take on the properties of that plane. As Saint Paul suggested, when we go high enough our terrestrial bodies, which are mortal, become transformed to celestial bodies which do not decay. Jesus himself suggested that there are no gender differences or marriages in heaven. When Luke said that Jesus rose up into the sky to cloud level and beyond, he probably meant that rather literally.

Because we know that you find thin air and then outer space when you go up, not another layer of reality where bodies become immortal, we cannot take the ascension symbolism literally. But we do have to ask about the spiritual meanings of that symbolism. This morning I want to dwell on three important meanings of the ascension.

First, it means that Jesus is no longer with us in the flesh and that we are left to our own responsibility. Imagine what it would have been like to have known Jesus in the flesh. Although we have only the literary representations of Jesus in the Gospels, and reports of Jesus's effects on other people, we know that he must have been a truly charismatic teacher and leader. Would it not have been wonderful to listen to his words, to ask him our questions, to receive personally his corrections and comforting touch? What a great joy it would have been to dine and party with him! (Remember the wedding at Cana!) According to the gospel accounts, however, after a few postresurrection meals and conversations, Jesus left.

Then the disciples were thrown back on their own responsibility. They had to organize their movement, think through what it meant to be followers of Jesus, and to deal with the issues of their day. Christians have had that same responsibility down to our own time. What are our issues? First are the issues of social justice about which Christians need to speak a prophetic word and engage in committed action. Our world is bound by an economic system that is highly efficient for producing wealth and maximizing the freedom of those who have it, but that moves money from place to place in order to find the most efficient return and in doing so is mindlessly destructive of cultures and cruel to those it supports on Monday and abandons on Tuesday. How can capitalism be regulated to be fair and kind to all people? Our world's military situation is dominated by American and European oil interests that have led to two aggressive wars and occupations, unjustifiable by any just-war arguments, and disguised as the promotion of democracy. How can we get out of that? The organization of American society, economically, politically, and educationally, increases the disparity of wealth and opportunity between the rich and the poor, and exacerbates racist attitudes toward African Americans, Native Americans, and other minority groups. How can this be amended? A strong and sometimes vicious division exists between Americans who want a pluralistic society and those who want a society whose laws and mores reflect a particular exclusive culture. How can this be healed? These are among the main social justice issues of our watch, which are in addition to more local issues and to issues of our own personal righteousness.

Now if Jesus were around today to advise us, he would be an extraordinary authority. In Jesus's absence, however, we have no divine authority, only the fallible authorities of our teachers. The most important thing to remember about our finite experts and authorities is that we give them the authority, and therefore we are responsible for what they do. Our political leaders rule at our sufferance. Our religious leaders, even when they claim unusual institutional authority as the Roman Catholic pope does, are to be believed and followed only on our own responsibility for believing and following. In Jesus's absence, responsibility—even for our religious, moral, and political authorities—rests with us.

The second meaning of the ascension is that, although Jesus is personally absent, we have his memory. How we interpret our memories of Jesus is a matter of the Holy Spirit, in our Christian symbolism, and next Sunday we celebrate Pentecost, the coming of the Holy Spirit. I'll talk about discerning true interpretations then. But now I want to emphasize that we have a very rich and complicated memory of Jesus. We have the Scriptures, particularly the Gospels. Of course, the gospels don't always agree, but then our collective memories of what happened yesterday do not always agree. Some memories might be just mistaken. But usually, disagreements in memory come from people seeing the same thing from different angles. So the gospels each lift up somewhat different aspects of the memories of Jesus, and we are richer for the diversity. Moreover, we have memories augmented and sharpened through nearly two thousand years of theology about Jesus. These historical memories are especially rich because they come from such different angles of vision, from the rich and the poor, from the educated and the uneducated, from Jews, Greeks, Romans, Europeans of all sorts, Africans of all sorts, Asians of all sorts, and Americans from the South and

Jesus Leaving

North. All of these contribute to a vast, if somewhat confusing, tradition of memories that pick up on Jesus from millions of viewpoints.

For people who have never heard of Jesus, this rich tradition might seem wholly novel and startling, a dangerous memory indeed. For those raised in the Christian faith, however, Jesus works his way into our memories in earliest childhood, in songs, stories, and visual illustrations. My deepest memories of Jesus picture him as a very English sort of chap, wearing a brown choir robe, who likes me because I am a little child and the Bible says so. Now that preschool memory of Jesus has been significantly augmented by much that I've learned since, including the prophetic side of Jesus that is not so tolerant of "anything goes"; nevertheless, deep down I know that Jesus is my friend. Most of our church music, art, prayers, sermons, and religious literature fill in memories of Jesus, so that in this sense of memory, he is still very much with us while being absent in person.

Memory is lodged in our imagination. That we remember Jesus means not only that we can think about him but that our memory of him shapes how we imagine the world. In fact, this is how we know one another in present time. In our interactions, we develop imaginative pictures of one another. The physical stimuli of sight and sound are rarely if ever pure. They are always received in some imaginative frame. Our interactions serve to correct the imaginative pictures we have of one another as the expectations we imagine are either confirmed or contradicted. Another way of putting this is that we respond to one another in terms of the imaginative pictures we have in our own minds, and these are continually modified by our interactions. This is exactly the way Jesus's disciples responded to him—in terms of what they could imagine him to mean. Time and again he said they got him wrong, and corrected their ways of objectifying him in their mind's eye. The difference between Jesus's first-century contemporaries and us is that they could get very quick feedback, with Jesus anxious to correct them. We don't get feedback from a present living Jesus, but we do get feedback more slowly from the scriptural and traditional memories of Jesus. In this sense, just as the objective picture of Jesus lived in the imaginations of Peter, James, and John, with quick corrective feedback, so the objective picture of Jesus lives in us, however slower the feedback. One meaning of Jesus's continuing life with us is that we continue to objectify him in our imagination, wonder whether our imaginative objectifications are valid, and imagine how he would advise us, touch us, comfort us, in our own issues. So the ascension means that the Jesus with personal subjectivity has left us, but the Jesus who lives in the objectified imaginations of those who remember him and look to him as a present companion has remained with us. This Jesus is our friend.

The third meaning of the ascension is that the subjective Jesus has left historical-temporal life and entered into eternal life. Moreover, we shall do that too. Eternal life is hard to comprehend from the perspective of temporal life. It always seems like a phantom double of temporal life running alongside on a different plane. This is how we commonly imagine heaven, a place like this one, contemporary with ours, but without pain, decay, or conflict. Eternal life looks like that we because we try to translate it into the ideas of temporality. But eternal life itself is the far richer concrete reality. It is our portions of the eternal act of God's creation in which time and space themselves are created. Within time alone, each date of our lives starts as future, comes to be, and passes away. In eternity, all the dates of our lives, from birth to death, are eternally future. All those same dates are eternally in the past. And all those same dates are eternally happening as present. Future, present, and past are all together in God, not in time, of course, but as constituting time's flow. The temporal life we think we know is merely the abstract part of each moment being lived out as present, one after another. Our eternal identity is in God's creative act which embraces all times together. And because we are together with one another in that act, and with all the places we have been, our true concrete reality is to be connected portions of the eternal living God, not merely the abstract, merely temporal, rather isolated selves we think we are in time. From the standpoint of temporal life alone, entering into eternity just looks like death. From the standpoint of eternity, death leads to the ascension from merely temporal life to the fullness of God's eternity. Jesus's ascension leads us to look forward to that, while corporately in the church we remain committed to being his body that deals with the temporal issues of our day.

I invite you to celebrate the ascension, my friends, with three moods deep in the heart of Christian piety. Because Jesus has left, we are responsible for what we do as Christians, with no appeal to special authority. This mood is sober and serious, and it brings home to us just who we are, and how we relate to one another in particular loves of many kinds. Because Jesus is remembered, we can imagine him to be with us in advice, comfort, and touch, almost as if he is with us, although connected to us through books and centuries of traditions instead of direct sight and sound. This mood is the joy of mystical passion, of companionship with Jesus in the

Jesus Leaving

Spirit. More of this next week. Because Jesus ascended to prepare a place for us, we know that we have eternal life in God far richer than the present passing days. This mood is the hope for bliss and glory. The sober mood for personal responsibility reflects God's creation of us in our particular characters. The mystical joy of possessing Jesus Christ in this life reflects God's incarnation in the creation. The hope for eternal life in God reflects that, in the end, God is in all, and is all there is. May we give thanks for this infinite benefit we have received from God's hands. Amen.

37

Spirit Coming[1]

Acts 2:1–21; Romans 8:21–27; John 15:21–27; 16:4b–15

Our texts for this Pentecost Eucharist Sunday are all about the Holy Spirit, God who is with us in daily life. At the outset, let me personalize this by telling you that today is a poignant one for my wife and me, because it would be the fortieth birthday of our daughter, Gwendolyn, had she not died instead at the age of four months. Her younger sisters, Naomi and Leonora, have flourished in the meantime, and many of you here have met them and their children, our grandchildren, one of whom, by no accident, is named Gwendolyn. But as you might imagine, I have groaned, to use Paul's words, for forty years to understand and internalize the eternal connection between us now and that brief life in 1966 and her young parents who knew joy and devastation so closely entwined. This special anniversary is the subtext for my reading the Pentecost texts this year.

The famous passage from Acts is about the actual Pentecost event. Jesus had recently been crucified, had been seen afterward by some in a resurrected state, and had then been observed by some to have left again, ascended into heaven. Left behind bereft and confused, many of his followers were gathered in a house, ostensibly to celebrate the Jewish festival of the Law of Moses but more likely just to mope about, caught up in their loss. After miraculously returning to them, Jesus had left them again. Suddenly in the house they heard and felt a violent wind. Tongues of fire appeared

---

1. Preached June 4, 2006, Pentecost Sunday.

Spirit Coming

over the head of each of them. Then they began to speak in languages they had not previously known, but that were understood by the foreign visitors.

You recognize these symbols. The Greek and Hebrew words for "wind" also mean "spirit," so that the people were filled with the rush of a violent spirit, the divine Holy Spirit. The Holy Spirit is also symbolized by fire. Moreover, the Holy Spirit is symbolized by people saying things they did not know they could say. Interpretation of the gospel is always a form of translation, saying in other words, perhaps in other languages, what the gospel is supposed to mean. But how do we know what the correct interpretation or translation is? Which is the Holy Spirit's interpretation? Or to ask my personal question, how do I find the true gospel in my daughter's short life?

John's Gospel, in our reading for today, says that, when Jesus ascends to eternal life in God, God will send the Holy Spirit to guide the disciples. Specifically, because the disciples are to function as the body of Christ, the Holy Spirit interprets for them the mind of Christ. Of course we have many witnesses to the mind of Christ, especially the Scriptures and nearly two millennia of traditions of theological interpretation. And herein lies the trouble. How do we tell which of the many spirits that appeal to us is the Holy Spirit? The Holy Spirit lies at the inward heart of our imagination by means of which we engage God and interpret the significance of Jesus Christ. But then all those other spirits also work within our imagination. Think of the questions that haunted my wife and me: had we done something to deserve our daughter's death? Were our sins being punished? Was she blasted like the fig tree by an angry deity? These are all kinds of biblical questions.

Saint Paul, in our Romans text, points out how inward and fundamental the Holy Spirit is. He says that the Spirit teaches us to pray by "sighs too deep for words." Of course, he does not condemn ordinary praying in words. But real prayer, for him, is not like addressing another person, however much we usually think of it that way. Rather, real prayer is God in the form of the Holy Spirit praying within us. We do not so much pray to God as God prays us to life and strength with movements like sighs deep within our soul.

Now the problem of discerning the Holy Spirit is that all those other spirits also seem like movements from the depths of our souls. The spirit of greed and avarice, which so often disguises itself as the love of freedom, is a movement deep within the soul. The spirit of self-centeredness and narcissism, which also disguises itself as the love of freedom, is another movement deep within the soul. The spirit of fanaticism and excess, which disguises itself as ecstatic devotion to a cause, moves deep within the soul. The spirit of guilt and self-condemnation, which disguises itself as confession, moves deep within the soul. The fact we want something from the bottom of our heart does not necessarily mean that this passion is from the Holy Spirit. Yet all these false spirits, and others, have presented themselves as religiously compelling.

To say in principle how the Holy Spirit differs from all those other spirits is not difficult. The Holy Spirit is God working to complete the creation, which, as Paul says in our text, groans with the labor of coming to birth. The Holy Spirit works especially in human beings, Paul says, for whom the fullness of creation includes our redemption from the evil effects of sin. Therefore, the Holy Spirit works for a kind of wholeness of the individual self, a balance among the needs of people, and a harmony of people with the whole of creation. Those other spirits are serious matters because they all are legitimate fragments of the wholeness of life. Wanting things is the engine of life, but is a perverse spirit when it turns to avarice and greed. Tending to our own business is at the heart of responsibility, but becomes perverse when it leads to self-centeredness. Ecstatic experience, which shows us that ordinary life is a thin veneer covering over the wondrous and wild powers of God, can become the perversion that leads to the fanaticism that has made religion so often more evil than good. Guilt and self-condemnation are bottom-line requirements for confession, but become mistaken and off-target if not made sane and realistic by the blessings of forgiveness: our daughter did not die for our sins—a blasphemous idea—but from heart disease.

How do we tell which promptings of the Spirit lead to wholeness, balance, and harmony? In the long run, Paul says in Galatians 5, "the fruit of the Spirit is love, joy, peace, patience, kindness, generosity, faithfulness, gentleness, and self-control." This is a fairly decisive set of criteria for outcomes of Christian living, because we all know of allegedly Christian cultures and theologies that give rise instead to resentment, bitterness, agitation, impatience, criticism, selfishness, capitulation to false gods, arrogance, and alienation from God and neighbor. Waiting for the long-run fruits of the Spirit, however, is not always helpful in our need to discern the Holy Spirit in daily life. How would it help find the gospel in our daughter's short life?

Having lived with this question for forty years (the biblical number, by the way), I have three practical short-run suggestions.

First, in the short run it helps a very great deal to have a personal, imaginative relationship with Jesus. From what we know from Scripture and from the multitudes of traditions of interpretation of Jesus, we can imagine Jesus with us in our circumstances, understanding what is going on, knowing the depths of our soul, our foul passions as well as noble ones, accompanying us in the worst moments of despair, sharing with us in the peak experiences, companioning us in the ordinary round of work and living. The gospel pictures of Jesus correct our attempts to imagine him as approving our weaknesses or going along with our foolish biases. They shame both our false righteousness and our false self-condemnation. How could anyone imagine Jesus letting us think our daughter's death was our fault, or God's punishment for our sins?

Second, because the Holy Spirit is the animation of Christ the Logos throughout all creation, its marks are unity and harmony everywhere. In matters of personal relations, even our enemies are to be loved as our brothers and sisters, no matter how much they stand for what we disapprove of or hurts us. In matters of history, all things are together in eternity because of the Holy Spirit, which means that our daughter's brief life lives eternally in God, along with that of her young parents of forty years ago, as well as with all of us now, so much older and sadly wiser. Whereas we have only photo albums, God's eternity has all lives together. Nothing is lost in God's eternity.

Third, the Spirit sighing within us gives us a glimpse of God's perspective from which each part of creation is infinitely valuable and beautiful to the divine eye. This is an easy point when contemplating the glories of nature or the genius of art. To see the value in evil things, especially our own unrighteousness, is much harder—but that is what the whole drama of redemption is about. The sighs of the Holy Spirit taught me to see positively the infinite beauty in our daughter's four months of life, and to give up dismay at their brevity. That we lost her is just the way God's creation works. That we enjoyed her is the miracle of creation itself, and is why the Spirit has taught us to bless with infinite gratitude the Lord who gives and takes away. God prays us to life and strength with movements like sighs deep within our soul.

Nurture in Time and Eternity

I invite you now to the table of the Eucharist with a sense that the Holy Spirit has harmonized this ritual meal into a larger process of spiritualizing the world. Please join in reverent awe at the Holy Spirit who, like a violent wind transforming all things, keeps Jesus in our midst, the whole creation in harmony, and the bliss of God's glory in the corner of our eyes. Amen.

38

To Be Born Again[1]

Isaiah 6:1–8; Romans 8:11–17; John 3:1–17

Do Christians live in two worlds? It would seem that we do. As Paul put it in the Epistle to the Romans, we all live in the world of the "flesh," but Christians are adopted by God to live in that world according to the rules of the "spirit." The spiritual world is not separate from the world of actual life, but has different rules, as it were. Jesus had another metaphor for this point. He said we must be born again. Poor Nicodemus thought this was an OBGYN event, but Jesus meant that we had to be born again to live according to the Spirit. Jesus made the point repeatedly that the ordinary life we live is somewhat blind to its own reality. In reality, we live in the kingdom of God, but think we live merely in the kingdoms of this world. To be born again is to wake up to our true spiritual birthright.

One of the earliest Christian heresy fights was about gnosticism. Gnostics claimed that the spiritual world is indeed separate from the world of the flesh, and that salvation means getting out of this world into some higher one. Two moral consequences follow from gnosticism. One is that this actual world is irredeemably evil, and the other is that we do not have to do anything about that, just rise above it. What turned out to be the orthodox position in the struggle over gnosticism says that there is just one world, God's creation, and that it can be lived in either according to the blinkered, half-asleep ways of the world, or according to the spiritual ways

1. Preached June 11, 2006, Trinity Sunday.

in which the world is understood to be God's kingdom, despite how the majority look at it. The moral consequences of the orthodox view are that we should rejoice with gratitude for the goodness of the world, despite its pains and sinfulness, and that where the world is unjust, impious, faithless, and despairing, we should do something about that to the extent we can. The general meaning of the theme of incarnation in Christian history has been the commitment to redeeming the world with God's presence that we mediate.

What is the difference between living according to the ways of the flesh versus the ways of the Spirit? The Bible contains many ways of expressing the difference, and it has been a persistent creative theme in Christian theology to this day. It has often been preached about from this pulpit. This morning I want to take an evolutionary approach.

Some social psychologists—and I'm thinking particularly of the work of Jonathan Haidt—say that there are five general moral projects that had great survival value when our primitive ancestors were evolving human moral sensibilities in the jungles and savannahs of Africa. That was a time when people lived in small family or tribal units that competed with each other for resources of food and safety. The five moral projects in which people should be trained, encouraged, and rewarded were, first, care and nurture of one another; second, reciprocity and justice; third, articulation and defense of the boundaries of the in-group; fourth, articulation and defense of hierarchical authority; and, fifth, the inculcation of disgust at the breaking of purity rules in matters such as sex, marriage, food, and the like. The inculcation of disgust might not seem like a moral project, though it often is. Most Americans, for instance, would find a diet of insects and grubs viscerally disgusting, although that was the original human diet; some Americans find homosexual relations disgusting, and some gays have the reverse sense of yuckiness; the passage in Leviticus that calls male-male sex an abomination uses the same label for sex during menstruation and cursing one's parents. To repeat the list of evolutionarily helpful moral projects: care and nurture, reciprocity and justice, enforcement of in-group boundaries, hierarchical authority structures, and a sense of yuckiness about what the group takes to be "impure," for want of a better term.

You can see why these moral projects would be virtues with great survival value in primitive conditions. Groups in which members nurture and care for one another will be stronger than groups with no mutual reinforcement. Groups in which people are just and fair to one another are stronger than those with internal strife. Groups that know their boundaries are clear about who their enemies are and can take action. Groups with organized authority structures can fight enemies and prey more efficiently than those whose actions are not coordinated. Groups that internalize their culture's sense of purity so that deviations elicit a common, bonding, visceral disgust make the rightness of their taboos seem like perceptions rather than mere conventions. These five moral projects count as the ways of the world, with obvious worldly advantage in primitive conditions in which human moral sensibilities were developed.

Nevertheless, Christianity says that we should be born to a higher, spiritual realm than mere evolutionary advantage under primitive conditions. So there are new rules for the spiritual realm. The moral project of care and nurture becomes elevated to the cardinal virtue of love and compassion. Love is the great attribute of God who so loved the world that he gave his only begotten Son for the world's redemption. The moral project of justice and reciprocity becomes the condition for human moral identity before God. Not only Christianity, but all the other major world religions that have spread over more than one culture have elevated these moral projects to the center of how to live in ultimate perspective.

Christianity has minimized the importance of, if not directly opposed, the last three moral projects, however. Jesus's inclusive table fellowship directly contravened the taboos defining the boundaries of the in-group with which he was supposed to associate. He was kind and sociable to Gentiles. He said true worship would be in spirit and in truth, not in accord with religious boundaries. Christianity affirms that God creates and loves all people. Jesus commanded us to love even our enemies, those in the out-groups.

Jesus was also critical of hierarchical authority. He said the first would be last and the last first. He thought the religious leaders were hypocrites and that the political leaders led a religiously trivial kingdom. He undermined the extremely authoritarian social structures of the family in every way he could and created Christian communities as alternatives to families based on friendship and equality, where everyone washes everyone else's feet.

With regard to the taboos of purity, Jesus lived in a Jewish society with many strictly articulated purity laws governing Sabbath observances, food, and sex. When accused of not observing Sabbath and cleanliness rules, Jesus said that the Sabbath was made for man, not man for the Sabbath. He denounced the purity rules governing family identity by saying that only God was his Father and that all people are his brothers and sisters. He refused the obligatory role of a married man (despite what the *Da Vinci Code* suggests). In many instances, he subordinated the purity customs to pragmatic considerations of whether and how they serve love and justice.

To put the point more generally about being born again to a spiritual way of life, in contrast to the worldly, fleshly way, Jesus and the Christian movement he founded rejected the ancient view that morality ought to give competitive advantage to groups in hostile relation to other groups in a primitive evolutionary environment. Rather, morality ought to assume that all groups should be able to live in peace with one another. Thus the moral projects of love and justice should be applied with universal scope. On the other hand, the moral projects of protecting boundaries, establishing hierarchical authority, and internalizing impurity-disgust responses, actually foster hostile relations between groups that have to define themselves over against others. Therefore for Jesus the boundaries, the hierarchies, and the purity taboos need to be undermined. In-group boundaries, hierarchical authorities, and purity taboos, in fact, keep people in bondage. Their destruction, or the reorganization of society to do without them, is the source of nearly all the liberation movements in Christian history. The spiritual kingdom of God establishes people in freedom from these worldly kinds of bondage. With different histories and symbols, the other great religions such as Buddhism, Hinduism, and Islam, and to some extent Judaism, say much the same thing.

Christian history, however, has always been a mixture of the merely worldly and the spiritual realms, never wholly spiritual. Although the early church was very clear, according to Paul and Luke in Acts, that all people are welcome, Gentiles as well as Jews, rich and poor, women and men, the church in many quarters came to define itself as an in-group over against Jews, pagans, and, in our own time, Muslims. Under the Emperor Constantine, the church adopted an extremely hierarchical model for its own government. The Anabaptist wing of the Protestant Reformation and later, in our time, the feminist movement, have struggled against such authority. Our current fights over purity rules that narrowly define the roles of women; condemn homosexuals; insist on specific rules for abortion, euthanasia, and other such battlegrounds in the culture wars, show how resistant such purity-morality is to being subordinated to the dominant ideals of love and justice. Similar struggles take place within the other great religions.

To Be Born Again

Social psychologists such as Jonathan Haidt suggest that the differences between contemporary conservative and liberal Christians in America amount to something like this. For the conservatives, all five of the major moral projects are of roughly equal importance. Identifying with an in-group, supporting a line of authority, and cultivating visceral disgust at breaches in the in-group's purity codes are just as important as love and justice. Love and justice are part of the conservative gospel, but only as balanced against a need to define us against them, to have authority clear, and to "just know" in an intuitive way that one's purity rules are right. For liberal Christians, love and justice trump the other three moral projects, and in fact often make those moral projects look immoral. I think the New Testament gospel is that we do need to be born again, to abandon the morality that serves competitive advantage in an evolutionary situation of primitive hostility, and to adopt the morality that respects all peoples as God's children, all individuals as responsible for themselves, not to an authority, and all cultures as bearing humanity. The gospel is to live in the freedom of the Spirit.

As a somewhat slow, liberal Christian thinker I have come to understand my conservative sisters and brothers in a new way through the distinctions I have been drawing. I never could understand before how Christians could relish the notion that other nations were evil empires against whom it is good to war, how they could draw such sharp boundaries about what kinds of people should be respected and what others should not be; but now I see that it is the in-group morality at work. I could never understand why Christians would need fundamentalistic authority for reading Scriptures, or for deciding and enforcing religious and political dogmas; but now I see that it is the hierarchical-authority morality at work. I could never understand why Christians would say that homosexuality is intuitively wrong or unnatural, or that gay marriage somehow threatens straight marriage, a ridiculous claim; but now I see that it is the purity-disgust system of a particular culture at work. When people say that sexuality is "defined" as heterosexual, or that marriage is "defined" as between one man and one woman, they mean only that for them the alternatives cannot be imagined without a sense of disgust, an offense to their purity code. They are not claiming that sexuality and marriage *ought* to be defined in those ways according to moral considerations that transcend their particular purity code. Drop the culturally specific disgust reaction, drop the authority structure, and drop the boundaries of the in-group, and sexuality and marriage can be defined by whatever best serves love and justice.

Now the Christian gospel is that we need to be born again into the spiritual way of life defined by love and justice, and the virtues attendant upon them. We need to abandon the worldly way of life in which evolutionary advantage says that virtue consists in superior power at hostile competition. The message of this new birth has been at the center of the Christian gospel since the beginning. But the rebirth itself is still not complete. Is it not a sad irony that, whereas the great revolutions of the last century in America—for civil rights for minorities, the liberation of women, and gay rights—have been led largely by Christians, the chief obstacles to those advances in freedom and civilization have also been Christians?

I invite you, therefore, to be born again, fully and in all aspects of our lives, into God's kingdom in which all are loved for what they are. Please do not try to escape the struggles for freedom in this world by seeking a spiritual realm elsewhere. This is our watch, and these are our issues. Jesus calls us to see that what counts in God's kingdom is love and justice. If we lose our lives in their pursuit, we gain our newborn lives. Amen.

39

To Grow[1]

1 Samuel 15:31—16:13; 2 Corinthians 5:1–10 (11–13), 11–17;
Mark 4:21–34

Some Christians believe that growth in the Christian life is not essential, although they note with approval the growth in theological belief from childhood to adulthood. What is essential, in their view, is the justification of human beings in the mind of God, a justification accomplished by the death of Jesus Christ. If people have faith in this justification, then they will be saved in the sense that they belong to the in-group of believers who will be rewarded by God. The only human contribution to salvation is the faith that accepts it, on this theological view, and even that faith is a gift from God. This theology requires an anthropomorphic conception of God as one who accepts some people and rejects others and whose anger is bought off by Jesus's faithfulness unto death.

In contrast to this theology is the view common to the Eastern Orthodox, Roman Catholic, Anglican, Methodist, and related traditions that salvation has to do with real differences made in people's lives so that they grow in godliness. The growth itself arises from God's grace in many forms, but it is not a function of God's relenting of anger at the unjust human race that has made itself the enemy of God. Growth in the Christian spirit is profound. Saint Paul, in our 2 Corinthians text, called it becoming a New Being. Jesus likened it to a plant that mysteriously grows from stalk to head

1. Preached June 18, 2006, the second Sunday after Pentecost.

to full grain, and to a mustard bush that grows from a tiny seed to a huge plant. The gospel for today has to do with the character of this growth.

At the outset, two paths to growth need to be acknowledged, even if they converge toward the end. One is the path of chronological maturation from infancy to old age within the church. Many of us were brought up in the church from an early age and went through more or less expected stages of religious growth in childhood, adolescence, young adulthood, mortgage holding, family raising, empty nesting, and settling in to reflect on things. Of course, a great many people, contrary to the stereotypes, never get married or grow through the nuclear-family phase. Many people come from such dysfunctional families that the stereotype of growing up simply does not apply. Reflecting on this model of Christian growth, we need to keep in mind our gay brothers and lesbian sisters, and the transsexual men and women in our midst, for whom this stereotypical model of growing up is a violent assault on their identity. Fortunately, the churches are themselves growing up to the need to break stereotypes of what infancy to old age is supposed to mean. At the last General Conference of the United Methodist Church, fully a third of the delegates voted against the antihomosexual stereotypes of human identity now codified in church law.

The far more important path of growth in Christianity is that from religious novice to spiritual adept. The novice might be young, but then again the novice might begin in mid- or late life. The first step for a novice is enculturation into the patterns of the Christian life. Congregations provide the standard patterns for this, both for the raising of children and for welcoming new Christians at any age. The patterns have to do with church attendance, learning the meanings of the symbols, participating in the liturgical events of the church, adopting practices for home life such as grace and prayers, and also reading religious literature. These patterns can be sustained throughout life, however modified at various stages and situations of living. Most outsiders recognize Christians by their observance and exercise of these patterns, and many Christians conceive their identities to be defined by them.

My sincere hope is that Marsh Chapel articulates a clear and contemporary version of patterns of the Christian life. We emphasize the importance of understanding, since we are a University Chapel. But we also emphasize the liturgical calendar that takes us through all the major doctrinal center-points in the course of the year. I am a lectionary preacher and so have lifted up the main texts in the three-year cycle of the lectionary during my term here. No matter how many times we go through the liturgical calendar and the lectionary, each time gives deeper understanding and appreciation of the patterns of the Christian life. Although growth in the Christian life also means growing to appreciate the patterns of other religious cultures for living before God, at its center it means growth in the deepening of Christianity's own patterns.

I dare not mention growth in the integrity of Christianity's patterns without stopping to call attention to the chief of those patterns, living for the redemption of the world. In liberal circles this means first paying attention to issues of social justice. Growth is absolutely necessary with regard to the Christian approach to social justice. We all know that the bottom line is that we ought to be kind to people, to love them where that term does not degenerate into something sappy.

But our ordinary notions of Christian virtue, even of Christian love, are closely tied up with manifesting the virtues of our own particular culture. We want everyone in the world to be like the ideals we hold for ourselves (of course, noting that we do not often live up to those ideals). The first jolt of maturation in social conscience for Christians is when we realize that other people have other ideals, and that those ideals might be far more worthy than our own. At the very least, this jolt in maturity causes us to ask whether our own sense of justice can make a good case for itself when set in fair competition with other senses of justice. The mark of immaturity about serving the needs of the world is to think that all good people are in our in-group, and the bad people are in the out-groups. The mark of first maturity is the recognition that the difference between the in-group and out-group is a desperately wicked concept, however it might have had evolutionary staying power in primitive times, as I discussed last week. As Saint Paul put it so often, everyone is a sinner. No one is in a naturally pure in-group, not even the Jewish community to which he adhered. Christian maturation for Paul consists in how we cope with our sinful selves in the face of God's offer of forgiveness. Under no circumstances would mature Christians go to war against unrighteous people because they are unrighteous. For, we have met the unrighteous enemies and they are we. War is acceptable only in the extreme cases of defense of the defenseless. Mature Christian social justice aims at peacemaking and the removal of all the social conditions that lead to violent frustration. The maintenance of the in-group thinking that advocates the superimposition of Christian patterns on non-Christian peoples is an evil. So is the insistence that our form of Christianity should be imposed on other Christians. In every case, we need to judge competing patterns of religious life by their fruits: do they lead to love and justice?

Serious maturation in Christian inner spiritual life continues this relativizing of standard Christian patterns. Our complex Christian traditions are rich in resources for spiritual formation. To see so many people these days pay attention to these resources, going on retreats, becoming explicit about the cultivation of their spiritual lives, is extremely gratifying. Deep prayer, long meditation, practiced contemplation, comfort with long silences, monastic submission to daily hours, communion with God's wildness in nature—all are patterns of spiritual development, and all are to be understood and judged according to their ability to propel us to become more god-like, more in tune with the divine, more a part of God's own wild glory.

The primary metaphors of explicit Christian spirituality have to do with sin and its forgiveness. As Saint Paul put it in his Letter to the Romans, sin sets us in contradiction to ourselves: the good we would, we do not, and the evil we would not, that we do. Nothing makes us more individual, more singular, more alone by ourselves, than this self-contradiction in which we deliberately sin. By God's mercy in Christ, we are forgiven our sins and their individuating selfishness, and much of spiritual life consists in coming to terms with God's unconditional acceptance of us. To learn to accept God's forgiveness when we already condemn ourselves is not easy task.

Now the metaphors of sin and forgiveness, with their individuating force, lead us to imagine and hope for an individualized heaven in which we continue more or less as we are but with no pain, suffering, enemies, or garbage to be taken out. These, of course, are childlike images that are understandable in children, and even more understandable for people whose lives have been degraded by suffering from beginning to end—heaven is where things get made right. The Jewish images of the heavenly court, the Christian images of the heavenly banquet, and the Muslim images of the heavenly garden all provide metaphors for individual life in improved circumstances.

Of course, as we mature and come to understand the way symbols work, we realize that heaven is about eternity and not about an improvement on our temporal history. Eternity is hard to imagine, however, and we do so with non-eternal, temporal images whose limits we need to know. Roy Sasi, our faithful radio member in Rhode Island, asked me whether those who have passed on to heaven will be able to observe how well those whom they loved on earth are doing in the coming years. I say yes, because in eternity we are all together in the creative act of God, and all the moments of our youth, adulthood, and old age are together with all the moments of everyone else's youth, adulthood, and old age. The limit to this metaphor is that most of what we mean by consciousness and observation has to do with the passage of time, not eternity. Within time, we wonder about people, suggest answers to our questions about them, sort out the answers, act on them, and get feedback about whether we are right about the people. All this takes time, and supposes distance between us and those whom we observe. In eternity there is no merely stretched out time, and no distance of this sort. So I do not know how far the analogy of ordinary temporal consciousness can be extended in contemplating eternal life, if you want to think literally. You can think of heaven as a balcony in a theater in which the saints watch us act out our roles on the temporal stage below, but I don't quite know what watching would mean in the eternal instance. Spiritual growth includes coming to terms with the ambiguities and limits of our symbolic thinking about God and eternal things.

Another, more important, step in spiritual growth needs to be mentioned, however, namely, the recognition of the limits of the individualism in our primary metaphors of sin and forgiveness. As we become comfortable resting in the loving and forgiving arms of God, the salvation of our own soul becomes of interest. I think we are then open to seeing the suffering of others as it really is, and to developing true compassion. The primary metaphors of Buddhism are helpful here. Our very concerns with sin and our own salvation come to look like sinful selfishness. The reality is that our sinful selves are transient realities within the wild processes of God's glorious eternal life. The reality is that within these transient realities, life has so much suffering mixed with joy and satisfaction. The reality is that a clear view of all this suffering, both in others and ourselves, is the very meaning of compassion.

In our time and culture the group that has been forced to recognize this the most consists of gay men who came of age in the 1980s when AIDS killed so many. How many friends and acquaintances can you bury before the blind ubiquity of suffering overwhelms you? So many of the dying young men had been rejected by their parents because of religious bigotry about homosexual impurity. What deeper suffering could there be than to be disowned by one's family and by one's own body's immune system, dying in cold sweats, suffocation, and madness? In the face of this plague, the surviving gay men developed new forms of friendship to care for the dying and to support one another. Not only did they care for their lovers, they cared for those who had no lovers, for the strangers, for those imprisoned by the toxins of life. This new form of friendship had to go beyond kinship and affection-ties to something like compassion for the sake of suffering itself. Many gay men became Buddhists because Buddhism begins with the recognition of suffering as more important than the achievements and guilts of one's own ego.

But the life of deep compassion in the face of incomprehensible suffering is also a profound form of Christian spiritual life. In the practice of such compassion our individual differences cease to be important, and our unity with one another in God's wild nature becomes palpable. What counts most in life is not what we build and hold on to, although of course we do have our responsibilities. What counts most is our loving, moment by moment, with compassion for whoever comes our way—friend, foe, or stranger. The simple reason for this is that at the deepest level, there is only one reality, God's wild life that we see as blasts of cosmic gases, blind forces of nature, chance births at chance times in chance places with chance encounters that people our transient lives. Our ultimate individual significance is nothing more than being short-duration waves within this grand divine creative act, at one with all the other waves in the ocean of God's eternal and singular glory. Knowing this, the ultimate spiritual goal of our lives is nothing more than to live each moment with compassion, loving our neighbors because that love is part of the vast love of God embracing us all. May we grow into that realization. Amen.

40

To Face Life[1]

1 Samuel 17:31–49; 2 Corinthians 6:1–13; Mark 4:31–41

Most of you know that today is my last Sunday as your preacher. Since the conclusion of the academic year I have preached five sermons in a series of which this is the sixth and last, trying to sum up for you what I believe the gospel to be. The first sermon was on Jesus' New Commandment, to love one another as he had loved his disciples, bonding them together as friends. This Commandment is the root of our faith, the rock of our salvation, the foundation of all righteousness, and our hope of heaven. Love is our purpose within time and our reality within eternity. The second sermon, for Ascension Sunday, was about Jesus leaving our historical, temporal world for eternal life in God. This means that we are left with full responsibility for what we do here, and that Jesus lives in us only, but richly, in the imagination of our hearts. As Jesus ascended to eternal life, so may we as well. The third sermon, for Pentecost, was about God coming from eternity to us in time in the form of the Holy Spirit. Of course, many spirits tempt us besides the Holy One, and we need to discern the spirits by their fruits of love and justice. In the short run, to live by the Holy Spirit means hunting always for the harmony of all creation, and looking at all creation from God's eternal point of view in which each and every thing has its beauty and value. The fourth sermon was about being born again, in which new life in Christ means rejecting the natural religion that

---

1. Preached June 25, 2006, the third Sunday after Pentecost.

was formed by evolutionary pressures on our primitive ancestors. In that "worldly religion," as it were, although high value is placed on mutual care and nurture, justice and reciprocity, equal value is put on the defense of the in-group, hierarchical authority structures, and visceral disgust for what one's in-group believes is impure. By stark contrast, for Jesus's religion of God's kingdom, the so-called evolutionary virtues of in-group thinking, authoritarian behavior, and conventional purity taboos are the very vices that cause hostility. Instead, the new life for which Jesus said we need to be born again combines care and nurture into love, and justice and reciprocity into righteousness, both of which have eternal and temporal dimensions. Last Sunday's sermon, the fifth, was about growth in this new life, which requires maturation in social consciousness beyond the in-group thinking that would impose our Christian patterns on everyone else. Growth also requires maturation in spiritual powers to rise above preoccupations with individual guilt and forgiveness to compassion for the suffering found throughout the cosmos, a compassion in which our unity with one another and with God ground the beatific vision.

A recurring theme in these sermons, and in Christian preaching since the beginning, is the profound relation between time and eternity. I hold, as Jesus did, that the ordinary way we live within time is oblivious to the greater reality that the flow of time exists within the richer dynamic of eternity. Wake up!, he said, for the kingdom of heaven is at hand. If we understand time and historical events only on their own terms, life will seem like a fight for advantage. But if we understand time and history in terms of eternity, advantage in the worldly sense does not count: the first will be last and the last first, and death is swallowed up in the larger victory that is the divine life itself. Praise God!

To live with a consciousness of our eternal reality does not mean escaping from time and history, however. On the contrary, living with an eye to eternity gives us the courage and realism to face life directly. To face life is to engage the issues of our watch without denial. Most of the issues of our watch are personal ones, and we are like one another in many of them. Everyone has issues growing up, for instance. Some of us live long enough to worry about growing old. You know how easy denial is regarding the issues of life's stages. Most of us also have issues with careers, with friends and family, with finding economic security, and enough adventure to make life interesting. Christians with the faith of eternal life have the courage to address the real issues as they come to us, even when they are painful. We have the courage to accept failure and loss and still go on. From the standpoint of eternity, everything that comes is a gift of God. Even the deepest suffering can be borne if we have Christ's compassion.

Beyond the personal issues of our watch are social ones that affect our capacities to live in loving communities. Probably the deepest issue in our society is racism, a poisonous stain that mixes evil into the very best of our inventive history of democracy and our love of freedom. Within my own lifetime our society has made enormous strides in eradicating the visceral sense European Americans have had that African Americans are inferior and can contaminate you. When I was a child, my white playmates "just knew" that it would make you impure to drink out of a water fountain used by blacks. This has changed. Nevertheless, the effects of that culturally induced but wicked set of instincts about what is pure or impure remain in many individuals, and in the social stratification of our country, the distribution of educational opportunities, and the availability of career paths.

If racism is not our deepest problem, perhaps the treatment of women is. In nearly all cultures, women have been scripted into roles of inferiority, isolation, powerlessness, and domesticity. American society is less vicious than many others in this regard, and it has made great progress here too. Yet many Americans still have a visceral sense of woman's place that is shocked by the thought of women in roles that run contrary to the cultural script for male domination. In some churches it is unthinkable that women could be ministers, for instance.

Lamentably, slavery, racism, and male dominance are solidly grounded in the ancient culture reflected in the Bible, and the contrary ideals of antiracism and equality in gender matters have required a genuine revolution in Christianity to reject that culture in favor of a better one. The most acute issue of this sort for Christianity on our current watch, however, has to do with equal human rights for gay, lesbian, bisexual, and transgendered people. On a superficial level, this issue has to do with recognizing the evil in the deep-seated social roles that deny full equality to these people, much like the traditional social roles for women do. On a deeper level, the problem is with the internalized visceral sense of purity and impurity among many in our culture who view these brothers and sisters as being perverted, deviant, broken in their humanity, or "intrinsically disordered," as some Roman Catholics believe. In point of fact, gays, lesbians, bisexuals, and transgendered people simply have sexual orientations that are in the minority in the population, and perhaps not as small a minority as some people believe.

Nurture in Time and Eternity

Their orientations are harmless to others, except in the same ways straight sexual orientations can be harmful, and the sexual minorities can function in all other social roles like everyone else according to their talents and the accidents of opportunity. This includes marriage, as the Massachusetts Supreme Judicial Council has said. Those among us who "just know" that marriage is between one man and one woman, and who used to think that it had to be between people of the same race, those who find gays, lesbians, bisexuals, and transsexuals to be deviants from "natural" sexuality, simply are enslaved to a visceral cultural code that itself is evil. The Christian issue on our watch is to free them from that bondage, and to defend the equality of all people as God's children.

Or if racism and various forms of sexism are not our greatest social problems, the problems associated with poverty surely are. Whereas the Bible's culture—not its theology but its culture—supported slavery, racism, and many kinds of sexual bigotry, the Bible has always been clear about the injustice of poverty and the constant obligation to help the poor and weak. We have come to realize, as the ancient world did not, that it is possible to change social conditions. So for us charity is not merely giving alms to the poor. Charity is to create a more economically just society. The problem is not merely that we happen to have an economic order that is unjust. The problem is that we have this economic order because of the greed of those in power who profit from it. Even those of us without much power and who are not superrich are reluctant to change an economic order in ways that might threaten our security. How can we persuade ourselves to abandon our greed in order to improve the economic situation of the poorest? This is a crucial issue of our watch, and the Christian imperative to do something is clear.

Beyond the personal and social issues of our watch is the special issue of national moral character surrounding the war in Iraq. I understand that one of the two soldiers who recently were kidnapped, tortured, and killed in the course of doing their duty honorably, had told his family that he did not mind being in Iraq because he was defending his country. Who could have lied to him to make him think that? Iraq had not attacked the United States or even threatened to do so. Iraq had no connection with al-Qaeda before the war, though our government lied to persuade us it did. Iraq had no weapons of mass destruction, although our government spun the few intelligence reports that suggested it might to make it seem so. What responsible government would go to war without making sure of its justification? Only a government whose reasons for war are not justified, such as wanting to control oil, or to beat back resistance to American domination! That poor boy was lied to about his mission. He was not defending his country. He was invading another country without justification, and in his high sense of honor he thought he was being patriotic. Despite some scandals, our armed forces in Iraq have behaved honorably, efficiently, and with a desire to do the least harm in a very dangerous situation—all testifying to their strong sense of duty. But the duty that has been given them is wrong, evil, and contrary to the American heritage of fairness and support of the underdog.

Perhaps most devastating to our national character is the macho swagger that convinces people that it is worse to look weak than to change a wrongful course. Only fools or villains would argue that we have to "stay the course" when we know the course to be based on lies and mistakes! Only fools or villains could say that our war dead "will have died in vain" if we abandon a war that was vain in the first place! Because this is a democracy, *we* are our government, and *we* are those fools or villains unless we do something to the contrary.

America will have deep obligations in Iraq for generations. I do not advocate any quick pullout or short timetable for withdrawal, as if we can pretend the war had not happened. Moreover, the real problems of Iraq go far beyond the American invasion. Saddam Hussein was a villain whose legacy will cause trouble for years. The disputes between Sunnis and Shi'ites are centuries old. The issues of the Kurds transcend Islam. The anti-Semitism of so much of the Islamic world is a grievous fault. The American invasion only stoked these preexistent fires and removed the balances that had contained them somewhat. Any way forward in Iraq will have to work out these and other issues over and above the American presence that exacerbates them.

No way forward for America is possible, however, without public admission to the entire world that the war was a colossal mistake. The lies and self-deceptions need to be brought to light. Profound and prolonged apologies need to be made. Such confessions of deep moral wrong are difficult for governments to make. Even when they do change course, they like to pretend they intended the change all along. Yet the very issue is that collectively we have committed a deep moral wrong and given our responsible power over into the hands of greed and arrogance that embarrass even our allies. Our deeply flawed national character needs to be redeemed, just as the German nation had to be redeemed after the Third Reich. Christians know that confession and repentance are essential to any change. This must be our message to our nation at this point in our watch.

Christians also know, however, that confession and repentance are virtually impossible without the conviction that God loves the sinner. Our Christian message needs to include the assurance that national redemption is possible because of the overwhelming fecundity of God's grace. That redemption will require confession and repentance, and then generations of work to pay for our mistakes. The gospel message, however, is that God's love is sufficient to redeem the people no matter how far wrong we have been. Grace upon grace, when we admit to ourselves the depth of evil, we glimpse beneath it the infinite, creative love in which we have the eternal life to face life on our watch.

Facing life in our time, particularly our political life, will not be easy. People do not want to hear the Christian word about justice, and in fear and secret self-condemnation they are not easily persuaded that the admission of their own evil opens them to the bounties of God's healing. We are likely to be scoffed at when we face these issues, or even worse, persecuted. Even our friends and family can be offended by this gospel call to the honesty of confession and the hope of eternity. But let us remember the words of Paul, in a similar situation:

> See, now is the acceptable time; see, now is the day of salvation! ... [A]s servants of God we have commended ourselves in every way: through great endurance, in afflictions, hardships, calamities, beatings, imprisonments, riots, labors, sleepless nights, hunger; by purity, knowledge, patience, kindness, holiness of spirit, genuine love, truthful speech, and the power of God ... We are treated as imposters, and yet are true; as unknown, and yet are well known; as dying, and see—we are alive; as punished, and yet not killed; as sorrowful, yet always rejoicing; as poor, yet making many rich; as having nothing, and yet possessing everything.

Beloved sisters and brothers, do not be tame Christians! May you face life with all the wild energy of God our Creator, with all the wild love of Jesus Christ, and with all wild courage of the Holy Spirit. God bless you. Amen.

www.ingramcontent.com/pod-product-compliance
Lightning Source LLC
Chambersburg PA
CBHW022013220426
43663CB00007B/1068